Earth Is My Mother,
Sky Is My Father

Space, Time, and Astronomy in Navajo Sandpainting

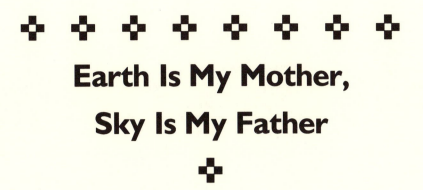

Earth Is My Mother, Sky Is My Father

✜

Space, Time, and Astronomy
in Navajo Sandpainting

TRUDY GRIFFIN-PIERCE

Foreword by N. Scott Momaday
Illustrations by Trudy Griffin-Pierce

University of New Mexico Press
Albuquerque

Library of Congress Cataloging–in–Publication Data

Griffin-Pierce. Trudy. 1949–
Earth is my mother, sky is my father:
space, time, and astronomy in Navajo sandpainting
Trudy Griffin-Pierce;
foreword by N. Scott Momaday;
illustrations by Trudy Griffin-Pierce.
1st ed. p. cm.
Includes bibliographical references and index.
ISBN 0–8263–1389–2 (cloth)
1. Navajo Indians—Religion and mythology.
2. Sandpaintings.
I. Title.
E99.N3G94   1992
299′.782—dc20
92–15470
CIP

Permissions information
appears on page 237.

Designed by Joanna V. Hill

To the Navajo chanters and consultants whose respect and concern for the preservation of this knowledge made this book possible, and especially to Shizhé'é and Shimá, hózhǫ́.

Contents

ILLUSTRATIONS

PLATES

Following page xxiv

Tables

Foreword

'Ahálááne

But instead of looking south in the direction in which he was going, he looked to the north, the country in which dwelt his people. Before him were the beautiful peaks of *Dibé Nitsaa,* with their forested slopes. The clouds hung over the mountain, the showers of rain fell down its sides, and all the country looked beautiful. And he said to the land, "*'Ahálááne!*" and a feeling of loneliness and homesickness came over him, and he wept and sang this song:

> That flowing water! That flowing water!
> My mind wanders across it.
> That broad water! That flowing water!
> My mind wanders across it.
> That old age water! That flowing water!
> My mind wanders across it.

'Ahálááne: Greeting! This translation from the Navajo by Washington Matthews gives us a young man who is taking leave of his beloved homeland. He has crossed the San Juan River and is looking back, and he is filled with longing.

In a real sense this intense longing, this love of the landscape of home, is at the center of the Navajo worldview. Diné bikéyah is for the Navajo the point in space from which all conceptions of the cosmos proceed.

Several years ago I had the opportunity to study the Navajo language intensively for a summer with Allen Wilson at the Gallup branch of the University of New Mexico. I had lived on the Navajo reservation—at Shiprock, at Tuba City, at Chinle—when I was a child, and so I had an ear for the sounds of Navajo speech. In touch with the language again, I recalled memories of that splendid country, and I felt something of the longing expressed in the song above. Allen encouraged me to talk to native speakers as often as I could. One day, while driving north of Gallup, I stopped for a hitchhiker, a young man who was on his way to the Four Corners. When I had exhausted my meager store of Navajo conversational expressions, I began to

point to features in the landscape and ask, "What is the name of that mountain (mesa, butte, wash)?" To my amazement there seemed to be a name for
virtually every object in sight. I had never encountered a more highly developed sense of place. I was left with the impression that this individual was
exactly where he belonged: he could never be lost, for he knew precisely
where he was in relation to this rock, that tree, the range of mountains in
the distance, the sun and moon and stars. He stood at the very center of
Creation.

Moreover, the landscape, apart from the beauty of its place names—
Na'nízhoozhí (Gallup), Lók'aahnteel (Ganado), Lók'a'ch'égai (Lukachukai),
'Ooljéé'tó (Oljeto)—is one of great physical beauty.

> Navajo country is a magnificent land of great variety: Canyon de Chelly with
> its weathered vermillion cliffs and winding canyons, the fantastic spires and
> pinnacles of Monument Valley, the dark fluted mass of Shiprock floating above
> the grassy sea, the broad cloud-dappled valley of the Little Colorado, the fra-
> grant high pine forests of the Chuska Mountains, the mountain grasslands of
> the Kaibab Plateau.

I quote this paragraph from the chapter 2 of the present text because it
establishes, early on, one of the principal powers of the book, a true sense
of the landscape of Diné bikéyah. Indeed the landscape, which incorporates
the concepts of Mother Earth and Father Sky, determines the worldview of
the Navajo people absolutely. There is no story of the *Diné,* or people, without the "magnificent land of great variety." The land, the earth, is the foundation of all belief, all wonder, all meaning in the story of human existence.
Navajo country is spectacular in its beauty and variety, from Canyon de
Chelly to Monument Valley, to Shiprock, to the valley of the Little Colorado,
the pine forests of the Chuska Mountains, and the mountain grasslands
of the Kaibab Plateau. Monument Valley is a window upon space unique
upon the earth. To behold the great monuments from the high rim of the
valley is to see into eternity. Canyon de Chelly and Canyon del Muerto are
calendars of geologic time. And time here is an extent too great to compre-
hend; we must enter into myth, so that story becomes our context. By means
of myth and story, humankind sees into the fourth dimension, beyond past,
present, and future, and into infinity.

The complexity of Navajo cosmology is very great. To understand the
structure of Navajo belief, one must see from the inside out, as it were. One
must become a Navajo, to the extent that that is possible. Such an assump-

tion requires a profound investment of time, study, and dedication, together with an aesthetic sense as acute as that which informs the Navajo perception of the universe. It is a lot to ask.

Trudy Griffin-Pierce is uniquely equal to this task. Through her Native American heritage, she has an ethnic appreciation of her subject, a natural identification, that is altogether fortunate to her purpose. Her aesthetic intelligence comes from the soil itself, and that intelligence is one of the great common denominators of the Native peoples. It constitutes a way of seeing that distinguishes the Native American people from others. In living with a Navajo family, she fitted herself closely into the Navajo way of life; and most important, she lived in the element of *Diné bizaad,* the Navajo language. The Navajos say of their language that it is endless, and indeed it seems so. It is at least indivisible with the cosmology, and it is an extraordinarily precise and accommodating instrument. Since she is an artist of singular ability and accomplishment, it is entirely appropriate that she should focus her attention upon the art of Navajo sandpainting. Her creative nature enables her to intuit the principles of symmetry, proportion, perspective, and design that are intrinsic to the sacred expression of that art. The artistic dimension of the Navajo world is intricate and profound. It is a dimension in which the artist realizes his whole purpose and being to the fullest extent.

The words *universe* and *universal* are critical here. The universe reflected in these pages is that of the cave painters, of Ptolemy, of Galileo and Einstein. People of all times have observed the same stars in the same heavens. But here is such an observation qualified by a cultural and religious experience peculiar and indigenous to North America and to a people who have inhabited this continent for many thousands of years. Indeed it is the Native aspect of the present book that gives it its special character and significance. We have known for many years that the Navajo system of belief is among the most inventive and imaginative in the history of the world, but it has been essentially inaccessible to us. Here, in this remarkable work, it is brought within our reach.

N. Scott Momaday
Tucson, Arizona
1991

Preface

Writing this book has been a journey of the spirit. I have felt like Toelken's Navajo weaver (whom you will meet in chapter 5), surrounded by time, by the forces of my shared history with Navajo friends and family. I have been inspired by the Navajo medicine men (or chanters, as many prefer to be called) I have met through my research, by my personal feelings about Navajo country, and by my own relationship to the earth, to that which ultimately sustains us all. I have based this work not only on present research conducted specifically for this purpose but also on memories of my first contact with the Navajos, over twenty years ago. I have reached even further into my past, to my childhood when, from the beginning, I did not want to learn *about* Navajo culture so much as I wanted to learn *from* Navajo culture.

I began this book with the goal of its completion, but it was only when my goal shifted from product to process, to gaining understanding for myself, that the writing began to flow. This is the way in which I have tried to portray the sandpaintings: not as static objects, but rather as dynamically sacred living entities whose meanings lie in the process of their creation and use.[1] It was only after I became aligned with the spirit of this book that the ideas and understanding began to coalesce into a whole.

Once I became attuned to what this book wanted to say, the thoughts and words began to move. For I have discovered in the process of writing that this knowledge wants to be shared. I will never forget the day I was writing about the omnipresence of the Navajo Holy People. I had just written about the Hail People when I looked outside my window to discover that, suddenly, the rain had turned to hail, quite an unusual occurrence for sunny Tucson. I felt then that the spirit of the Hail People was with me, saying, "Of course we exist; how could you ever doubt it? We're real; we're here; we're present in every moment all around you."

I share the Navajo belief that knowledge is alive and that it needs to be shared, to be kept alive and passed on. Knowledge is a living force to be used to enrich the lives of others. I also share the Navajo belief that while it is good to pass on knowledge, it is equally important to know which portions of one's knowledge are appropriate to withhold. The most sacred personal knowledge one must retain, passing it on only at the end of one's life. The implication is that by sharing all that one knows, by giving it all away, one completes one's life.

I believe that it is also true, as a Navajo friend told me, that by sharing everything one is stripped bare, degraded. This is one key to the natural dignity of the Navajo. In contrast to many Anglos who strive for immediate intimacy as they bare their souls with revelations, Navajos, even those whom one knows well, have a natural reserve in at least some areas in their lives. Although I want to share the knowledge that was imparted to me by my Navajo teachers, there are some things I do not feel that it is appropriate to tell, such as information my Navajo colleagues have told me for my understanding but have asked me not to reveal. Nor do I feel that it is necessary or appropriate to share the details of the Male Shootingway ceremonial that was given, in part, to bless me and to protect me in my work with the sandpaintings.

Because of the sacredness of sandpaintings, this book contains no photographs of actual sandpaintings, except for the sandpainting that includes Sky-Reaching Rock, which was done as a demonstration for the Wheelwright Museum. I have chosen, instead, to use my own black and white line drawings of sandpainting reproductions from museum collections. All figures and plates are my own artwork. During this study I have not photographed any completed sandpaintings. I have participated in ritual events, but I do not want to betray the trust of my Navajo friends by sharing ceremonial details. Nor do I feel that a detailed account of such ceremonies would further the purpose of this book.

In chapter 3 I include a brief account of a Navajo sandpainting ceremony so that readers will more fully understand that sandpaintings are not "art" in the Western sense of the word but rather are created for the purpose of reestablishing health and harmony in the life of the patient. Seeing how the sandpainting is used, one can then understand the destruction of the painting at the close of the ritual as part of the ceremonial process.

However, out of respect for the sacredness of sandpaintings and the ceremonial practices that surround them, I have purposely kept the account of the Holyway sandpainting ceremony as generalized and brief as possible. For this reason, my description contains no more information than is available in Kluckhohn and Wyman (1940).

The Navajos with whom I worked—my Navajo teachers—knew that the material they shared with me would be used in my dissertation, in various scholarly articles, and in this book. I have omitted their names—in one case, I have used a pseudonym—because opinions vary among the Navajo about sharing sacred knowledge. Half of the royalties resulting from the publication of this book are being donated to the Ned Hatathli Museum, Navajo Community College, Tsaile, Arizona, of which Harry Walters is the director.

My intent in writing this book is to make an understanding of the Navajo spiritual world[2]—a world that comes alive through the sandpaintings and the myths—accessible to a wider audience. I hope that such an understanding will enrich the lives of those who read this book so that they will take with them a greater respect not only for Navajo culture but also for the world we all share.

Acknowledgments

I would like to acknowledge the many individuals who have helped me in countless ways, beginning with Harry Walters and other Navajo consultants and chanters who must remain anonymous. I especially want to express my respect and appreciation for the chanter who recently died after a very long and full life during which his knowledge, concern for others, and wonderful sense of humor enriched the lives of all who knew him. Special thanks go to Harry Walters, Mary Willie, and Avery and Pat Denny for assistance with translations. I am also grateful to my Navajo family who introduced me to Navajo culture and to the chanter's family (who have become my second family) for their understanding, hospitality, concern, amd caring. The respect of these individuals for this knowledge and its preservation, as well as their patience and generosity, made this book possible.

I am very grateful to the individuals who contributed suggestions and support in the development of my ideas and who took the time to read the entire draft of the book: M. Jane Young, Richard Henderson, Von Del Chamberlain, the anonymous reviewer in the field of Navajo studies, and N. Scott Momaday, who also contributed his creative energy to the book by writing its foreword.

In particular, M. Jane Young, through the years, has provided valuable advice from her own research and much encouragement and friendship. In 1976, Von Del Chamberlain suggested that I document Navajo starlore. In 1980 two events stimulated my research: Mark Peterson generously shared transcribed interviews with Navajo chanters who had observed the stars in a planetarium setting, and Robert Clay shared his extensive sandpainting collection and gave me books on Navajo ritual. Although I was a stranger to them at the time, these individuals helped me because we had a mutual love and respect for this important knowledge and a strong desire that it be passed on. In 1981 Susan Philips provided the stimulus for exploring consensus and variation within the area of Navajo starlore.

My research was supported by a Comins Fellowship in 1983 and a Spicer Fellowship in 1987, both from the Department of Anthropology, University of Arizona, Tucson. Further research support came from the Graduate Student Development Fund, Graduate College, University of Arizona. My thanks go to Steve Rogers, Edson Way, and Susan McGreevey of the Wheelwright Museum of the American Indian; to Dorothy House at the library of the Museum of Northern Arizona; and to Jan Bell at the Arizona State Museum, for their assistance in archival research.

Interaction with other scholars in the field of Navajo studies has greatly facilitated the development of my ideas. Among these individuals are David Aberle, John Adair, Martha Austin, Mark Bauer, Chien Chiao, Bertha Dutton, John Farella, James Faris, Charlotte Frisbie, Sam Gill, Ed Garrison, Katherine Spencer Halpern, Ann Hedlund, Stephen Jett, Louise Lamphere, Jerrold Levy, Karl Luckert, David McAllester, James McNeley, Frank Morgan, Caroline Olin, Nancy Parezo, Rain Parrish, Rik Pinxten, Robert Roessel, Ruth Roessel, Mark Schoepfle, Barre Toelken, Oswald Werner, Anne Wright, and Leland Wyman.

Those who have shared other kinds of data and support are: Ellen Basso, Richard Diebold, Steve Feld, Jane Hill, Wesley Jernigan, Robert Murphy, Emory Sekaquaptewa, Peter Stromberg, Clara Lee Tanner, and Richard Thompson.

My special thanks go to John Carlson, Von Del Chamberlain, Claire Farrer, Ray Williamson, and M. Jane Young, my colleagues in the field of ethnoastronomy.

Jeff Grathwohl, my editor at the University of New Mexico Press, read the manuscript carefully. His skillful editing as well as his encouragement have added greatly to the quality of this book. Andrea Otañez eventually became my editor, contributing her considerable expertise and understanding of what I wanted to do. I also want to express my appreciation to L.A. Shore, my copy editor, and to Emmy Ezzell, production manager, for their painstaking attention to detail.

I am grateful to my mother for teaching me to love the Southwest and to respect and appreciate cultures other than my own, and to my father for his love of travel, which immersed us in many different cultures. My very special thanks go to Keith Pierce, who accompanied me to the reservation and whose support made it possible for me to write this book.

Pl. 1. "*Náiiłnii*: Prayers to the Dawn" (serigraph). A traditional Navajo says prayers at dawn and spreads pollen as a blessing; he holds his pollen bag in his hand.

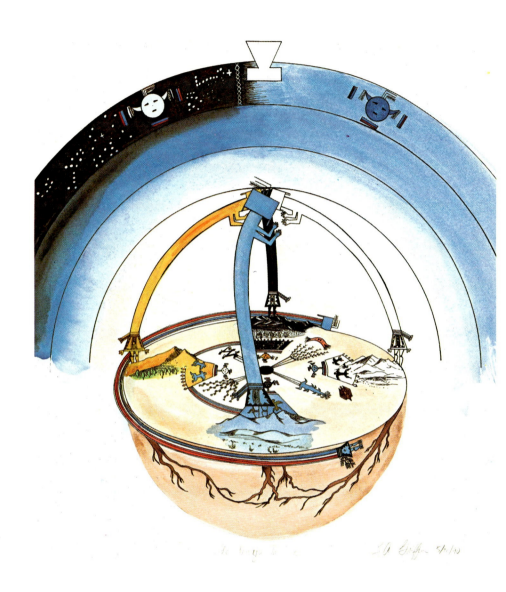

Pl. 2. "The Post-Emergence Navajo Universe" (watercolor). Some Navajos believe that we are in the Fifth World rather than the Fourth World.

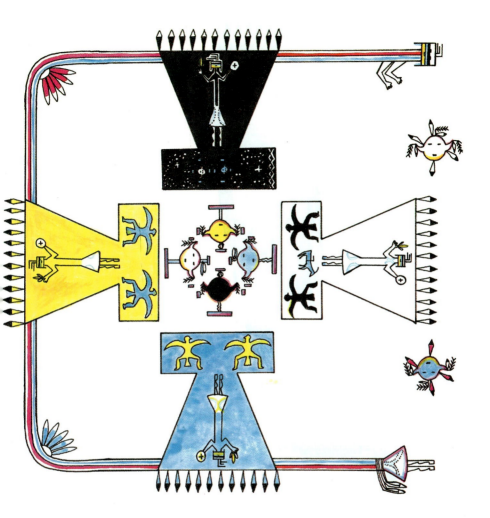

Pl. 3. "The Skies," Male Shootingway (watercolor). At the center are four storm figures surrounded by four keystone-cloud forms that symbolize the Sun's passage through the four divisions of the day and night. At the east is the white sky of dawn with hawks and antelope and Dawn Boy. At the south is the blue midday sky with two yellow hawks and Blue Sky Man. The yellow of evening light stands at the west with two blue hawks and Yellow Evening Light Girl. In the north is the black of darkness with the Sun, Moon, stars, and Darkness Girl. (Adapted from a painting by Newcomb; singer, Blue Eyes, before 1933. Courtesy Wheelwright Museum, P4#11.)

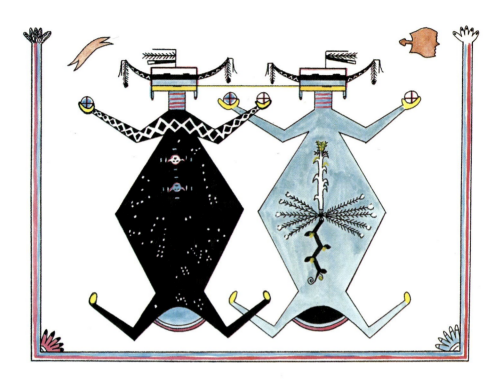

Pl. 4. "Mother Earth, Father Sky," Male Shootingway (watercolor). At the center of Mother Earth is the lake that filled the Place of Emergence. The four sacred plants—corn, beans, squash, and tobacco—emerge from this lake; the roots of these plants firmly connect them to the lake and to the Earth. The constellations fill the body of Father Sky, whose arms and legs lie over those of Mother Earth, just as the Sky lies above the Earth. (Adapted from a painting by Newcomb; singer, Lukai Yazzi, before 1930. Courtesy Wheelwright Museum, P4#4A.)

Pl. 5. Sky-Reaching Rock in the Double Sandpainting: Holy Man in Power of Thunders, Holy Boy in the Belly of the Fish, Male Shootingway. (Photograph courtesy Wheelwright Museum of the American Indian.)

Pl. 6. "*Déest'įį'įįł'íní*: Navajo Stargazer" (serigraph). A stargazer looks through his crystal at a star of the first magnitude to diagnose illness and to prescribe the appropriate ceremonial for healing. 'Átsé'etsoh and Gah heet'e'ii (which together compose Scorpius) and Hastiin Sik'ai'í (Corvus) appear in the sky.

Pl. 7. "Star Stories: Dilyéhé (the Pleiades)" (serigraph). A Navajo woman makes a string figure of Dilyéhé. Spider Woman taught the Navajo how to make these figures along with the allegorical stories that accompany them. "So we keep our thinking in order by these figures and we keep our lives in order with the stories. We have to relate our lives to the stars and the sun, the animals, and to all of nature or else we will go crazy, or get sick" (Navajo father in Toelken [1979:96]).

Pl. 8. "We Are All Related" (serigraph). A Navajo couple, sitting on a hill illuminated by the light of the stars, gaze up at Náhookǫs Biką'ii and Náhookǫs Ba'áadii, their celestial counterparts (the male one that revolves and the female one that revolves, respectively; the Big Dipper and Cassiopeia). A coyote, symbolizing all animals and evoking his role in the creation and placement of the stars, wanders by, unnoticed. As the couple listen to and follow the spiritual guidance from the stars, they contribute to harmony and right relationships among all parts of creation. The following poem is a translation of the title:

> Earth—growth of all different kinds
> Sky—and everything in the sky
> Earth People
> All are related to me.

> Nahasdzáán—Nanise ałtaas'éí
> Yádiłhił—Yótáhnaazléí
> Nohokáá' dine'é
> T'áa'ałtsoh shik'éí.

Introduction

We leave the small town at the foot of Black Mesa in the early afternoon under a January sun, a glowing disk set in a cloudy, opalescent haze of wintry salmon and gray. My husband, Keith, tries to avoid the rivers of oozing brown mud resulting from melted snow piled in crusty gray layers beside the washboard road. Guiding us is Zonnie, the youngest daughter in the chanter's family that befriended us several years before at Navajo Community College. She directs Keith to turn left just after we cross a small bridge that spans a sandy wash. "See, there's my brother's house." She points with her lips, Navajo fashion, as a sea of parked pickup trucks comes into view beside a freshly constructed ceremonial hogan.[1] Nearby stands her brother's well-kept concrete-block house; he and his family have been generous in hosting this nine-night Nightway (Yeibichai) ceremonial for his wife's stepbrother.

Parking our blue Honda beside a juniper bush, we make our way on foot between the pickup trucks to the hogan that has been built to house the large, complicated sandpaintings of this ceremonial. It was necessary to build a hogan because none existed in a large open area with room not only for the teams of dancers who will impersonate the Navajo gods known as Yé'ii but also for the cars and pickup trucks of the many people who will come from far and near to watch the ceremony of the final night and to partake of its benefits.

My first impression when we enter the semidarkness of the hogan is the shaft of sunlight floating with specks of dust that illumines a complex sandpainting lying on the hogan's earth floor. Hours of concerted effort have produced the graceful, elongated figures of Navajo Holy People painted in the rich ochers of Arizona sandstone offset by crisp black and white. In the suffused light of the smokehole, the mixture of white sand and charcoal appears to be a soft gray blue. Two of the four men who have been kneeling

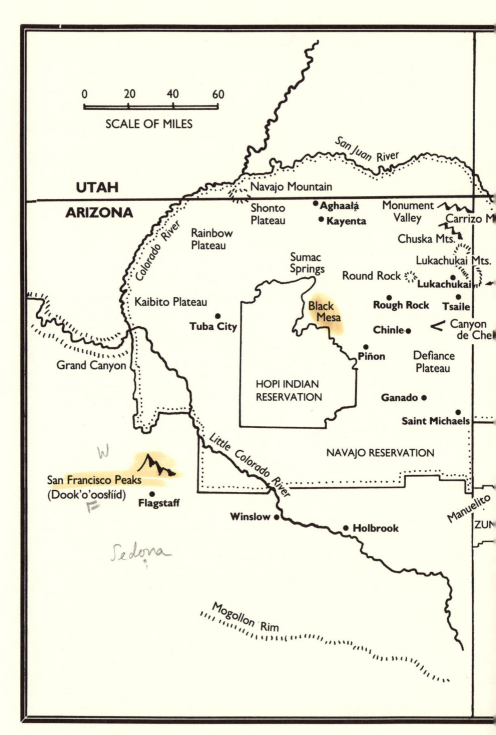

Fig. 1.1. Map of Diné Bikéyah, Navajo country.

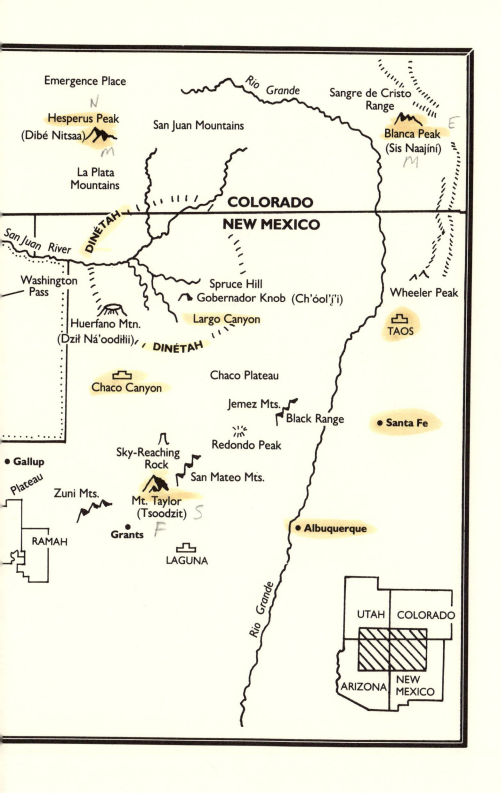

over the sacred painted images glance up to see who has entered; their eyes have the dazed look of those who have just refocused their powers of intense visual concentration. When they recognize us, they return to the task at hand, the completion of the precise forms of the eighth-day sandpainting called "The Four Directions."

The painting has been laid out with great precision, beginning with its central locality symbol, which situates the sandpainting by establishing its locale and characters: this is the lake where the Visionary, the hero of the Nightway myth, learned this sandpainting and the site where the story took place. Emerging from the central lake are the four sacred plants: an upward-thrusting corn stalk, a five-stalked bean plant, an angled squash stem topped by a delicately coiled tendril, and a five-stemmed tobacco plant, each oriented to the intercardinal directions. The roots of the plants are nourished in the central body of water, symbolizing an increase in power and intensity of purpose. The plants separate four directionally aligned sets of four *hashch'ééh,* or Yé'ii—two Fringed Mouths, wearing pointed red hats, are paired with other Yé'ii—whose heads lie in each of the four directions. Two Talking Gods alternate with two Humpbacks to guard the outer boundary as they lie lengthwise above the other Yé'ii. In its finished form, the painting is roughly sixteen feet in diameter.

As I watch the painting unfold with painstaking precision over the course of the next few hours, I reflect on the chain of events that has brought me to this hogan and to this family. I came to the reservation almost seventeen years before to live with another Navajo family, in response to a letter I had written to Raymond Nakai, who was then the Navajo tribal chairman. My letter simply asked if he could find a traditional Navajo family with whom I could live and assume the role of a daughter. I was willing to reimburse them for my food and to do my share of the work.

From my earliest childhood I had known that I would someday live with the Navajo. I was delighted once my mother taught me to read so that I could gain access to books about Native American culture. My parents soon accepted my consuming interest, which became the one constant in my rootless Air Force upbringing. I spent entire days as a Kwakiutl fisherman from Vancouver Island, a Chiricahua Apache warrior making forays from the Cochise Stronghold, an Iroquois statesman making eloquent speeches as I represented my longhouse.

I will always remember the night that my father brought home three Russian correspondents in his efforts to show American hospitality. They were consumed with curiosity about American teenagers crazed with rock-and-roll. Their faces registered utter amazement to find me sitting cross-legged on the floor of my bedroom dressed as a Lakota in authentically beaded buckskin, intently poring over my bead loom as I wove an intricately beaded belt.

Yet the Navajo always held the most special place in my heart. When we lived in Hawaii I had my Chinese friends join me in herding imaginary Navajo sheep, producing fine silver jewelry, and making sandpaintings for ceremonies of our own creation.

Perhaps it was the nomadic nature of my own childhood that made me feel a special kinship with the Navajo and turn to them when my mother died, rather than to the Catawba Indians of South Carolina to whom I am distantly related. Unconsciously, I sensed that with such a large land base, the traditions of the Navajo might be more intact than those of other groups. Yet ultimately it was my emotional bond with the Navajo and with their ingrained need for moving about the vast expanses of their dramatic and beloved landscape that drew me to them.

Only years later, when I saw the John Adair footage in the poignant film, "A Weave of Time," did I realize the extent to which I had bonded with my first Navajo family. A wave of memory swept over me, filling my eyes with tears, when I saw the Navajo woman gathering the ripe ears of corn in her fields. I could feel the sun hot upon my face as the shiny green corn leaves glistened in the sunlight; I remembered laughing with my Navajo cousins about the similarity in color and texture between the cornsilk and my own hair as we shucked the ears of corn in the shade of a ramada; I thought of the time when my inability to speak Navajo kept me from explaining that I was tired of grinding corn with the meat grinder, so that my Navajo family playfully kept me at the task. Seeing Adair's film, I could once more taste the sweet, delicate flavor and feel the soft, moist texture of the freshly baked kneel-down bread as it crumbled in my mouth.

Yet the memories penetrated even more deeply than these fleeting impressions, for what came flooding back was the tenderness and profound concern for my well-being that my Navajo mother had shown me. She had never had a daughter of her own, and I had recently lost my mother; although these losses remained unspoken, we helped to fill the voids in each other's lives. The language barrier made our only line of communication one of human warmth; yet, in many ways, our communication was even more eloquent because of its silence. I will always remember the day when I was about to set off in the family buckboard for the ten-mile trip to the trading post, and how she dashed back into the hogan for my hat. As she handed it to me, I could see concern clearly evident in her lined face; I did not need to understand Navajo to know that she was saying, "You're not used to the sun here, and the day is long. The sun is already high in the sky, and I worry that the sun might make you sick."

We came to know each other very well as we rose with the sun each morning to chop firewood and prepare breakfast before we left for the day's herding with the sheep and goats. The sheepdogs would quickly scatter the flock before us as we made our way into the valleys and washes that lay over the nearest ridge. While the animals grazed we sat in the shade of a lone juniper, spinning wool with the Navajo spindle and laughing at my unsuccessful efforts to replicate her evenly spun strands. As we wandered through washes I collected chunks of brightly colored sandstone I could not resist sharing. I handed them to her, saying, "*Nizhóní* [beautiful]," and she always replied quietly, "'*Aoo', nizhóní* [Yes, it is beautiful]."

It was this family and my bond with the Navajo that drew me to Arizona after I completed my undergraduate degree in art at Florida State University. And, when I decided to pursue my Ph.D. in anthropology ten years later, I knew that I could only work with the sacred sandpaintings. In the beginning it was their visual magnificence that spoke to me as an artist, as well as the astronomical content of some paintings that appealed to me as an astronomy-museum curator. But as I came to appreciate and to understand these ceremonial paintings, it was their rich context of belief and meaning, their very sacredness, that held me. After I completed my doctorate, I continued to attend ceremonials, and my understanding of the sandpaintings deepened. Out of this understanding came this book.

Navajo sacred sandpaintings have the ability to heal the one-sung-over through their indwelling power as sacred, living entities. They summon their power through the ability of their ritual symbols to help the patient focus inwardly as he or she is surrounded by the coexistent forces of the mythic past and the everyday present, which interpenetrate through the ritual. As the one-sung-over experiences firsthand the mythic chantway odyssey undertaken by the hero of the myth, the patient also experiences the same restoration to a state of harmony and health. Basic to an understanding of how the sandpainting heals is the concept of time as cyclic and circular, a principle fundamental to Navajo thought; this embracing, surrounding quality of time leads to an emphasis on dynamic process over static product.

Furthermore, everyday and spiritual realities are fused: the spiritual world informs not only ceremonial experience but also everyday experience.

Emory Sekaquaptewa, the Hopi scholar (personal communication 1990), uses a beautiful phrase to express the sense of inclusive multidimensional truth with which many Native Americans view the world—"mythic reality." In place of the exclusivity of the Western[2] notion of science-as-truth, this more inclusive perspective embraces the coexistence of a mythic, spiritual world alongside the physical, quantifiable world. This viewpoint also expresses a circular concept of time as opposed to Western linear temporal notions, a perspective founded on the coexistence of past and present, which is at the basis of the integral, reciprocal relationship Native Americans have with the spiritual world, the environment, and their immediate and extended families and clans.

To understand the sacred, living nature of the sandpainting and its power to heal, it is essential to suspend the Western notion that equates the "real" with the measurable. Only by accepting the possibility that time and space can have richer dimensions than the Newtonian ones can we even begin to grasp the depth of the Navajo sacred sandpainting. Although the sandpainting is visually appealing, the painting is far more fascinating when it is understood in its full magnificence, in its mythopoetic context of layered time, space, and meaning. Furthermore, if we can accept that the Western view of the world is but one possible conception of reality, then we not only open ourselves up to a deeper understanding of the sandpainting but also give ourselves the opportunity possibly to learn something new about the way the world really operates.

Anthropologist Paul Reisman (in Noel 1976:53) speaks to this idea when he says,

> Our social sciences generally treat the culture and knowledge of other peoples as forms and structures necessary for human life that those people have developed and imposed upon a reality which we know—or at least our scientists know—better than they do. We can therefore study those forms in relation to 'reality' and measure how well or ill they are adapted to it. In their studies of the cultures of other people, even those anthropologists who sincerely love the other people they study almost never think that they are learning something about the way the world really is. Rather they conceive of themselves as finding out what other people's *conceptions* of the world are.

Too often, anthropologists have made this mistake.[3] Under the guise of scientific objectivity, they have unwittingly judged other worldviews in terms of their own worldview. Morris Berman (1981:85) points out that "the price paid, however, is that what we actually learn about them [other cultures] is severely limited before the inquiry even begins. Nonparticipating consciousness cannot 'see' participating consciousness any more than Cartesian analysis can 'see' artistic beauty."

Many excellent books have been published about Navajo ritual, but most have been written from the analytical, science-as-truth standpoint described above. Culture can be seen in many different ways and from many different angles: given the richness of Navajo culture and the relatively narrow focus of each account, every new interpretation expands the depth of our insight into an infinitely complex subject. The purpose of this book is not to "fix one truth" but to present a somewhat different perspective of Navajo ritual, a perspective that steps outside the narrow band of quantifiable experience into a wider, more qualitative interpretation.

In a world that is characterized by profound disenchantment on the part of young and old, as humankind exploits the last of our natural resources from a perspective that seeks to dominate and conquer nature, we have much to learn from a culture whose ideals are based on harmony with the environment. Navajo spirituality affirms humanity's place within nature, as Navajo ceremonies restore and celebrate the interconnectedness of all life. The Navajo recognize our profound connectedness with the natural world and believe that illness—disharmony—results from failure to maintain our reciprocal responsibilities with the environment, as well as from infringement of ceremonial rules and from transgressions against our own minds and bodies.

The Western approach to nature has traditionally been one of dominance. As Joseph Campbell (1988:32) says, modern Americans have inherited "the biblical condemnation of nature . . . from their own religion [which they] . . . brought with them, mainly from England. [They believe that] God is separate from nature, and nature is condemned of God. It's right there in Genesis: we are to be masters of the world."[4]

The prevailing values of non-Native American culture have led to a country whose oceans and streams are polluted, and where the air is often too choked to breathe. The modern Euro-American lifestyle is too often emotionally overtaxing, highly pressured, materially oriented, and spiritually depleted.[5] We have come to expect immediate gratification and to be entertained through the media rather than learning to draw on our own powers of imagination and insight. It is not surprising that many young Americans turn to drugs as they seek escape, communion, and solace from the fast-paced, media-blitzed world.

The ultimate purpose of this book is the sharing of a more humane, more connected view of the world, a view that has a great deal to contribute in terms of reestablishing humanity's correct alignment with the universe. The Navajo worldview is based upon the recognition and honoring of our reciprocal responsibilities to the universe that sustains us. At a time when short-term economic goals usually take precedence over the long-range future of the environment, it is vitally important that we listen to another philosophy, another moral order based on the sacredness of the Earth. Put simply, our future on this planet depends upon our ability to live in a way that honors our mother the Earth and our father the Sky.

To this end, chapter 2 provides an introduction to Navajo ethnography, history, and worldview, focusing on the features that are most relevant to understanding Navajo religion. Chapter 3 explores the spiritual world and ceremonial practices of the Navajo, with particular attention to the sandpaintings. Chapter 4 discusses how cosmological order—Navajo conceptions of time and space as well as perceptions of solar, lunar, and stellar motions—serves as a model for Navajo philosophy, which in turn is reflected in the sandpaintings. Chapter 5 creates a composite view of the heavens as they are verbally described and visually depicted in Navajo chantway myths and their accompanying sandpainting images. The stars and constellations themselves are the subject of chapter 6, which brings together a body of oral narratives that for the most part lies outside the corpus of Navajo chantway narratives. Finally, chapter 7 centers on the best-known of Navajo sandpaintings, "Mother Earth, Father Sky," to show how one particular sandpainting is endowed with presence and animated with power and life to become a sacred, living entity. By focusing on this particular sandpainting, which brings together the entirety of creation, it is possible to achieve a greater understanding of the Navajo concept of reciprocity: the order that must be reestablished in the spiritual, mental, physical, and social realms of the patient's life reflects the order, balance, health, and harmony inherent in the timeless, continuous, repetitive motions of the cosmos. As the patient reconnects with this eternal balance of nature, health is restored.

✦ 2 ✦
The Roots
of Navajo Culture

August 1988

We turn off the New Mexico state highway onto a dirt road, plumes of dust billowing out from under our tires. Beneath the startling clarity of a southwestern sky stand the rugged mesas of the Colorado Plateau. These mesas are cut with deep canyons whose walls vary from steep yellow sandstone cliffs to naturally terraced rock outcroppings covered with stands of piñon and juniper.

The first stop on our Navajo Community College tour of Dinétah is Largo Canyon. This area in northwestern New Mexico is the Holy Country of Navajo mythology, and the rock art on the canyon walls depicts sacred images from the myths.

We follow the winding dirt road beside the dry streambed, going deeper into the canyon. Our guide, Harry Walters, director of the Ned Hatathli Museum at Navajo Community College, stops the four-wheel-drive vehicle and leads us on foot through a dry wash to a rocky overhang where a line of Yé'ii have been painted. The white forms have been outlined in red, which contrasts with the paler orange sandstone cliff on which they are drawn; time has given them a smudged, ethereal appearance appropriate for supernatural beings.

I recognize familiar sandpainting images. The Humpback, a personified mountain sheep, wears horns, and carries the traditional planting staff; his feathered hump contains mist and seeds. I recognize him from Nightway sandpaintings as well as the figure to his right, a Fringed Mouth, whose body is half red and who wears the characteristic pointed red hat. On the other side of the Fringed Mouth stand two Yé'ii wearing the trailing feathered headdress typical of Coyoteway and Mountainway sandpaintings. (See figure 2.1 for a comparison of these pictographs and the related sandpainting figures.)

Later we see petroglyphs of the Sacred Twins: the bow of Monster Slayer

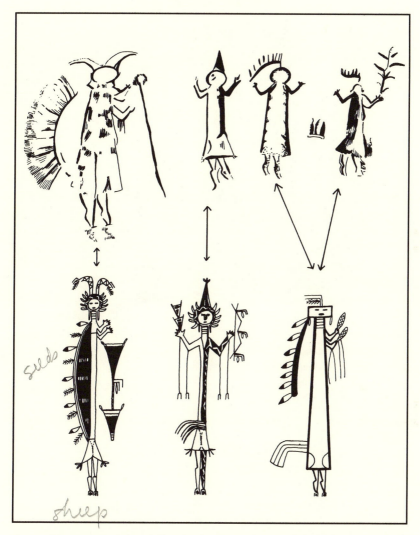

Fig. 2.1. Navajo pictographs (top row) and their corresponding sandpainting images (bottom row), left to right: Humpback, Fringed Mouth, and Yé'ii.

is repeated seven times over a band of six linked hourglass symbols, the scalp locks of Born-for-Water (fig. 2.2.).[1] The thought occurs to me, How appropriate that we are seeing depictions of beings from the Nightway when some chanters say that this is where the story of the Nightway begins (Van Valkenburgh 1941:155–56).[2]

Fig. 2.2. Petroglyphs of Monster Slayer's bow and Born-for-Water's scalp lock. (Crow Canyon, Gobernador Region, New Mexico.)

Dinétah was home to the early Navajos who settled here in the sixteenth and seventeenth centuries. After the second Pueblo Revolt (of 1696), the Navajos were joined by Pueblos who fled the Rio Grande area. In some sites, a traditional Navajo forked-stick hogan can be found within the wall of a Pueblo masonry compound. Many sites are fortified, built for protection against marauding bands of Utes and Comanches.

As would be expected, this was a period of intense Pueblo-Navajo acculturation. The Navajos had already acquired agricultural skills and rituals during their contact with Pueblos in the Rio Grande area. During the Gobernador phase (A.D. 1696–1775) the Navajos borrowed religious philosophy, as well as ceremonial procedures and paraphernalia (Schaafsma 1966:9). Archaeologists have found Pueblo and Navajo ritual paraphernalia together in excavated caches, lending credence to the hypothesis that much of Navajo ceremonialism is derived from Pueblo contact (Hester 1962:60). However, it is important to remember that this borrowing was mutual: while the Navajos were probably inspired by the Pueblo tradition of portraying sacred subjects in graphic form (on walls and altars and in sandpaintings), there was a noticeable absence of Pueblo-style kivas in the Gobernador region, signifying that a predominantly Navajo religious pattern prevailed at this time (Schaafsma 1966:9–10).

Unfortunately, little or nothing is known about the Athabascan Navajo art or ritual practices the Navajos brought with them into the Southwest. Navajo ritual practices and depictions were probably inspired by the Pueblos; Elsie Clews Parsons (1939:1036–56) cited more than 160 parallels between Pueblo and Navajo ceremonial practices, such as the use of masks, sandpaintings, prayer sticks, and color symbolism.

The Pueblos expressed their concept of the sacred through many forms—kiva wall murals, elaborate altars, mobile-like displays designed to hang from the kiva ceiling, fetishes, prayer sticks, masks, rock art, and costumes. The Navajos adopted the more portable aspects of Pueblo ceremonial equipment, those that fit in with their more nomadic way of life. Although the Navajos probably borrowed the concept of sandpainting, they soon elaborated the relatively simple Pueblo ceremonial designs into a vast system of complex images. The early Navajo rock art of the Dinétah bridges the stylistic gap between the initial period of borrowing and the first sandpaintings that were recorded (in 1880).

DINÉ BIKÉYAH

The Largo and Gobernador canyons of northwestern New Mexico also hold the earliest remains of Navajo habitation in the Southwest: twisted juniper beams of a forked-stick hogan, sherds of cooking pottery, and the ashes of old firepits (Schaafsma 1966:1). Although scholars disagree about the migration routes of the Navajos southward from the main center of Athabascan language in western Canada, they agree that the Navajos were probably among the last of the American Indians to have migrated out of Asia to North America and that the Navajos and other Apachean tribes were late to arrive in the Southwest. The Athabascan ancestors of the Apacheans probably entered the Southwest from five hundred to a thousand years ago, migrating in small groups from their homeland in western Canada and Alaska.

According to Navajo tradition, they settled within the area bounded by the four Sacred Mountains, spreading out from the Gobernador region into the what is now the Four Corners area—the Colorado Plateau country where

Arizona, New Mexico, Utah, and Colorado intersect (fig. 1.1.). Standing well above the lower basins of Nevada, southern Arizona, southwestern New Mexico, and the Rio Grande Valley of Albuquerque, the Colorado Plateau on which Navajo land is located has tolerable summers but much colder winters than these surrounding basins. The considerable range in elevation—Navajo Mountain is more than 10,000 feet high while the Painted Desert, the Chinle Valley, and the San Juan Basin are below 6,000 feet—is a major factor in the variety of climatic conditions on the reservation.

The Navajo view of Diné Bikéyah, Navajo country, is well documented in a book called *Between Sacred Mountains* (1982), from which much of the following discussion is derived. Much of the vegetation is characteristic of high country forest: pine, spruce, fir, and aspen. From east to west, the mountains of Navajo country include, first, Dził Łizhinii, the Jemez Mountains, which rise just west of the Rio Grande and were once a huge volcano that left obsidian used to make fine arrowheads. The San Mateo Mountains run northeast from Tsoodził, Mount Taylor, and were once home to the Canyoncito Navajo who still live just to the east. Navajos once raided the towns along the Rio Grande from hideouts in the Jemez and San Mateo Mountains. The Ramah Navajos once lived in the Zuni Mountains, which rise southwest of Mount Taylor; today this group of Navajos holds land farther south. A high mesa northeast of Gallup called Mesa de los Lobos has a wide valley with lakes and springs and contains a holy place at its highest point, Ak'iih Nást'ání, Hosta Butte, said to be the home of Hadahoniye' Ashkii and Hadahoniye' At'ééd, Mirage Stone Boy and Girl. The Chuska and Lukachukai Mountains follow the New Mexico–Arizona state line and contain the most luxuriant forests and grasses, and the best water supply on the reservation. To the north of the Chuskas rise Dził Náhooziłii, the Carrizo Mountains, the last home (on the reservation) of grizzly bears and bighorn sheep. Dziłijiin, Black Mesa, known for its coal deposits, is visible across the Chinle Valley from the Chuska Mountains; its southwestern slope sends water from summer showers and winter snows down lush green valleys to the Little Colorado. Naatsis'áán, Navajo Mountain, rises 10,388 feet and is the highest peak on the Navajo reservation.

As we will see, for the Navajo, most aspects of the natural world are divided into male and female beings; underlying this conceptual division is the idea that only through pairing can any entity be complete. Thus, it is not surprising to find a male and a female figure represented in groupings of these mountains, with each responsible for separate realms of existence: the male figure rules all plants and wildlife while the female being is in charge of water and water creatures. The late chanter, Frank Mitchell, said that the male figure lies along the Chuska and Carrizo mountains, which are often spoken of as a single person. His legs are located at the Carrizos, his neck at Béésh Łichíi'ii Bigiizh (Red Flint or Washington Pass) and his head at Chuska Peak. He is paired with a female figure who lies across the valley with her feet resting at Balakai Mesa, her body at Black Mesa, her arms in Shonto Wash, and her head at Navajo Mountain. Aghaałá, a tall black rock near Kayenta, is her cane.

Below the peaks on the reservation are the plateau regions where pine and fir are replaced by piñon, juniper, and sagebrush. From east to west the plateaus are the Chaco, the Manuelito, the Defiance, the Shonto, the Rainbow, and the Kaibito. In the deep canyons that cut through the piñon and juniper country, Navajos have traditionally found protection from their enemies and water for their crops. The best known canyons of Navajo country are Largo Canyon in the Dinétah, Chaco Canyon in Chaco Mesa, Canyon de Chelly and Canyon del Muerto in the Defiance Plateau, Tsegi Canyon in the Shonto Plateau, and Navajo Canyon and Paiute Canyon in the Rainbow Plateau.

Below the piñon and juniper country lies the Navajo steppe, covered with sage, greasewood, yucca, and grass. Only two areas in Navajo country are true deserts, so dry that few plants grow and most of the animals are small. The dramatic red sandstone buttes and towers of Monument Valley (Tsé Bii' Nidzisgai, or Plain in the Rocks) lie between Black Mesa and the San Juan River, while the bright banded clays of the Painted Desert border the reservation along the Colorado and Little Colorado rivers.

Navajo country is a varied land of magnificent vistas: Canyon de Chelly with its weathered vermilion cliffs and winding canyons, the fantastic spires and pinnacles of Monument Valley, the dark fluted mass of Shiprock floating above a grassy sea, the broad cloud-dappled valley of the Little Colorado, the fragrant high pine forests of the Chuska Mountains, the mountain grasslands of the Kaibab Plateau.

THE HISTORIC PERIOD

The people of Diné Bikéyah have had to meet enormous challenges to survive on this land. Many Navajos say that the four Sacred Mountains are the posts of a great hogan and that for a long time the Navajos, Hopis, Zunis, and other tribes lived together inside that hogan, fighting, trading, suffering drought, oblivious to the world that lay outside the boundaries. "A day came, however, when Spaniards from across the oceans pulled the blanket from the hogan door, and winds from the four corners of the world blew inside" (*Between Sacred Mountains* 1982:99).

When the Spaniard Coronado arrived in 1540, the Navajos were, in a sense, the most fortunate of these Indian groups because their relative isolation and dispersed settlement pattern made it impossible for the Spaniards to dominate them; these conditions also protected them from the epidemics of measles, flu, and smallpox that killed thousands of Pueblos. Furthermore, the Navajos easily captured Spanish horses, livestock, and steel weapons without fear of reprisals.

The acquisition of the horse had a profound effect upon Navajo culture. Not only did increased mobility enlarge the range and frequency of contact with non-Navajos, but also it altered the character of social relations within the tribe. It was now possible to visit more frequently and to attend ceremonial events from much greater distances. Thus, the audiences at ceremonials became larger, and this in turn may have led to the elaboration of the ceremonies themselves.

Sheep and goats also had a major impact upon the Navajos and their way of life. The Navajo had begun to take sheep and goats during their raids on Spanish settlements in the early seventeenth century, but it was probably not until the end of this century that they began to herd these animals after intense contact with the Pueblos, who understood Spanish animal husbandry (Bailey and Bailey 1986:14). In the late 1700s and early 1800s the Navajo population began increasing because these animals furnished such a dependable food supply. Sheep and goats and their products also provided a medium of exchange for European-produced goods. Navajos learned the art of weaving from the many Pueblos who lived among them following the 1680 Pueblo Revolt. Weaving quickly became a part of Navajo culture. By 1795, Navajo weaving had become so highly prized that one writer of that time described their weaving as "finer than that of the Spaniards" (Underhill 1953:110).

This prosperity, however, did not last. In 1846 the United States took control of the southwestern territories, promising settlers protection from Indians. The next fifteen years were marked by military operations, Navajo raids, and unsuccessful attempts at negotiation.

A major difficulty arose from the fact that the Anglos totally misunder-

stood Navajo social organization. U.S. authorities claimed that the tribe bla-
tantly disregarded treaty agreements signed by what they judged to be tribal
"chiefs." In reality, these men were *naat'áanii,* local headmen who led only
small groups of Navajos. Although *naat'áanii* were respected for their wise
counsel, which was usually heeded, these headmen had no coercive power
to command others to follow because the Navajo placed a high value upon
individualism.

In 1863, under government orders, Kit Carson and his soldiers began
burning Navajo crops and homes. Ute, Pueblo, and New Mexican volunteers
also took revenge for Navajo raiding by taking Navajo sheep and horses, and
capturing women and children for slaves. A brutal winter, combined with
the destruction of their resources, brought defeat to the Navajo.

The Navajo now faced the horror of the Long Walk—an arduous trek of
300 miles—to Fort Sumner, New Mexico, where they would be interned.
The period from 1864 to 1868 was the most tragic of their history. They
were a proud, independent people accustomed to moving freely across the
great spaces of their beloved homeland with its Sacred Mountains: they were
forced to become captives confined within a limited area, dependent upon
the government. They had to leave behind the land with which they had a
spiritual connection, land sanctified by the Holy People. In addition to the
emotional and spiritual anguish of exile there was unparalleled suffering and
death because of insufficient food, recurring crop failure, and disease.

Navajo spiritual beliefs and practices sustained them during this period.
The Navajos held specific ceremonies to help them to return home, such as
the Mą́'ii Bizéé' naast'ą́ (Put a Bead in Coyote's Mouth) ceremony (Roessel
1973). Barboncito, a Navajo leader, approached a female coyote, who was
facing east in the center of a circle of Navajos. "Barboncito caught the animal
and put a piece of white shell, tapered at both ends, with a hole in the center,
into its mouth. As he let the coyote go free, she turned clockwise and
walked . . . toward the west, [and] Barboncito remarked: 'There it is, we will
be set free'" (Mose Denejolie, in Roessel [1973:244]). And, indeed, the
Navajo were allowed to return to their homeland in 1868. Congress, realiz-
ing the economic infeasibility of continued detention, decided to make a
treaty with the Navajo; the terms of this treaty allowed them to go back to
their native land. The Navajos' continued faith in the Holy People and their
adherence to their ceremonials had brought them home.

Upon their return, they held a ceremonial chant for four days, which is
"why our population has increased rapidly up to these days. If it had not

been for the ceremony it wouldn't have been like this" (Francis Toledo, in Roessel [1973 : 147]).

The recovery of the subsistence economy was slow. After the return from Fort Sumner, the Navajos' dependence upon the hunting of game animals and the gathering of wild food plants virtually eliminated the country's wild game resources; by the late 1870s hunting no longer contributed significantly to Navajo subsistence (Bailey and Bailey 1986 : 50). With the development of trading posts and the expansion of herds beyond the subsistence level, farming also decreased as a means of subsistence, although families continued to plant small fields. Trade networks—trading posts, and intertribal and Spanish-American networks—supplied foodstuffs, manufactured goods, and items of Indian manufacture in return for Navajo livestock and the by-products of herding.

Unfortunately, drought, overstocking of Navajo rangelands, and lowered livestock and wool prices because of the collapse of the national economy combined to cause a severe economic depression for the Navajos in the late 1800s. In the early twentieth century, the Navajo economy reoriented itself, with increasing emphasis on wage labor as a regular seasonal activity. Subsistence-oriented herding gave way to commercial herding; weaving and silversmithing became even more market-oriented. As Navajos became less self-sufficient and more integrated into the national economy, the trading post became increasingly important to Navajo life by providing the items they could no longer provide for themselves.

By the time of the Depression, the Navajo population had outgrown the resource base. Severe overgrazing destroyed groundcover and led to wind and water erosion. To the Navajo, the federal government's program to control soil erosion seemed "presumptuous" because it meant interfering with the workings of nature (Kluckhohn and Leighton 1962 : 308–9).

In the 1930s, as a response to overgrazing, the U.S. government implemented the Stock Reduction Program. The Navajos remember stock reduction with the same sadness as Fort Sumner. Once acquired, sheep had quickly become a measure of wealth and status as well as a marker of cultural identity. Now the government was trying to take away the very basis of Navajo life. The emotional connection between the Navajos and their sheep is evident in this speech made by a Navajo at the tribal council (Kluckhohn and Leighton 1962 : 83): "Give us our sheep, give us our mutton, let us have herds as our fathers and our grandfathers had. If you take away our sheep, you take away our food, and we will have nothing. What then will become of our children? . . . You must let us keep our sheep or we die." Charlie Yellow, a medicine man of the Many Goats Clan from Kayenta, explained that many Navajos did die because sheep are life to the Navajo (in *Between Sacred Mountains* [1982:173]): "When they reduced the stock, many men, women, boys and girls died. They died of what we call *ch'ééná*, which is sadness for something that will never come back. Because of Stock Reduction, many people passed away."

When stock reduction brought about the collapse of the commercialized herding industry, more of the Navajo work force turned to wage labor. However, because few jobs were available on or near the reservation, unemployment was, and still is, widespread. Today, agriculture, sheep and goat husbandry, the sale of traditional crafts, and wage work provide income for many Navajos, but others are supported by welfare. Of those employed on the reservation, two-thirds work in public services: health, education, and government services (Goodman 1982:73). Other Navajos operate hotels, restaurants, service stations, irrigation projects, tribal parks, and a tribal museum.

Overpopulation for the existing resources has become an even more serious problem today. The inaccessibility of many family camps, which may be located miles from the nearest road, as well as the fact that many older Navajos do not speak English, makes it difficult for census workers to assess accurately the exact population of the Navajo tribe. In 1980 the population was estimated at 146,000; the projected population for 1995 is more than 300,000 people (Goodman 1982:61).

CONTINUITY AND CHANGE

Navajo culture has proven to be particularly resilient because of several factors: the kind of cultural contact they experienced, the relatively unstructured nature of their cultural institutions, and their cultural response to outside influences. With regard to cultural contact, the Navajos' experience was unusual compared to that of other Native American groups; this had a profound effect on the continuity of their culture (Bailey and Bailey 1986:289).

Geographical isolation and their traditional dispersed settlement pattern kept the Navajos free from outside domination until their exile at Fort Sumner in the 1860s. After their return, their economic self-sufficiency meant that the U.S. government had less leverage in controlling their assimilation. An Indian agent, William Parsons, expressed the government's predicament:

"Their very independence and industry makes them [the Navajo] less susceptible than other tribes to 'civilizing' influences" (in Bailey and Bailey [1986:99]). Fortunately, the federal government kept the reservation from being allotted,[3] while Indian Service officials worked to expand it in the late nineteenth and early twentieth centuries—factors that also contributed toward a greater degree of cultural autonomy for the Navajos.

The relatively informal, unstructured nature of Navajo cultural institutions made them more adaptable to changing needs. In contrast, most of the eastern tribes experienced deculturation when their rigidly structured political, social, and religious institutions could no longer be maintained during periods of dramatic change (Bailey and Bailey 1986:292–93).

The informal nature of Navajo traditional leadership—through the *naat'áanii,* or headman—has already been mentioned. There was no "Navajo tribe" in the sense of an organized political entity until the federal government imposed a tribal government system in the 1920s after oil was discovered on the reservation (Goodman 1982:17). The basis of local government is the chapter, whose members elect representatives to the Navajo Tribal Council, the legislative branch of Navajo government. The concept of representative government was alien to the Navajo, who were used to settling issues through meetings of the individuals involved. Furthermore, the Navajo traditionally tended to think more in terms of responsibility to relatives and to their local group than in tribal terms (Kluckhohn and Leighton 1962:160). These factors have made it difficult for the Navajos to form a truly representative, politically effective tribal government.

Kinship is so important in Navajo culture that the worst thing that can be said of someone is, "He acts as if he didn't have any relatives." Conversely, it is common to hear *naat'áanii* admonish others, "Act as if everybody were related to you" (Kluckhohn and Leighton 1962:100). (As we will see, Navajo prayers establish a kin relationship with the Holy People; such familial closeness is an essential part of reestablishing conditions of health and harmony.)

Traditionally, the Navajo did not live in towns, but rather in isolated family groups. The basic economic and social unit in Navajo culture is the resident extended family, a self-sufficient group that provides for cultural transmission from the oldest and most conservative members to the youngest. The Navajo ideal is a matrilineal, matrilocal society structured in terms of (1) the nuclear family; (2) the matrilocal extended family; (3) the "outfit," which Kluckhohn and Leighton (1962:109) define as "a group of relatives (larger than the extended family) who regularly cooperate for certain purposes"; and (4) the matrilineal clan (Spencer and Jennings 1977:303).

The fluid, unstructured nature of Navajo social organization—the very quality that has helped Navajo culture to be so resilient through time—has also made it difficult to describe. The anthropological literature is rife with conflicting analyses of Navajo kinship and family patterns.[4] What becomes clear from these conflicting analyses is that Navajo social organization is indeed very loosely organized, with many alternative ways to meet the changing needs of families and individuals. Since many Navajo families are dispersed within and outside the reservation because of wage work, various residence groups grow and divide through time; despite this change, however, there remains a network of overlapping ties that link domestic groups throughout the community. Depending upon the circumstances, an individual may call upon several different groups for cooperation. At the same time, cultural traditions are passed on from one generation to the next through the resident extended family. Thus, change in the local cooperative group does not mean the disappearance of cultural tradition.

The adaptability of Navajo culture is also evident in how their settlement patterns have changed through time. Traditionally, the Navajo lived in scattered, small family groups. They gave up their nomadic way of life soon after they reached the Southwest; instead, each family traveled within a defined range and lived in a single, relatively permanent camp near their fields. This settlement pattern changed in the late 1700s and early 1800s when the Navajos became pastoralists: in addition to the family camp located near their cornfields, they established a separate winter hogan in an area with an adequate supply of wood for fuel. Both camps had to have sufficient forage and water for their stock.

Many Navajos live in frame houses today, but it is still common to see a hogan in association with a house or by itself. Two types of hogan exist: the nearly obsolete, conical forked-pole (male) hogan, which the Navajo brought with them into the Southwest, and its replacement, the larger and more substantial round-roofed (female) hogan, which may be circular, hexagonal, or octagonal in shape (Jett and Spencer 1981:211–27). Built to ritual specifications, the hogan faces the rising sun (the hogan as an image of the cosmos will be discussed in chapter 4). Many Navajos still have a summer camp near their cornfields and a more substantial winter camp, which they occupy after the harvest.

As wage work became more important, regional differences on the reservation became more evident, with a demarcation between the areas where jobs and housing were available and those areas where they were not. Although rural areas remain more traditional, Navajo culture will continue to survive as long as the resident extended family stays intact. However, if more nuclear families become economically independent because of permanent wage labor that takes them away from their multigenerational families for prolonged periods of time, change will accelerate and tradition will be threatened. As long as the residential extended family remains economically interdependent because of sporadic wage labor, the continuity of Navajo culture will be ensured. The effects of the larger American culture will be moderated by the stories told by Navajo elders to their grandchildren, as well as by the ceremonials that bond Navajos together in a spirit of cooperative participation.

The relative lack of structure in the Navajo ceremonial system (in comparison to the rituals of other Native American groups) has also ensured the survival of Navajo tradition. There is no ritual calendar that requires particular ceremonials to be held on specific dates. The clan is important in establishing social identity; Navajos state their clan affiliations as well as their name when meeting a Navajo stranger. It also plays a major role in the regulation of marriage and the rendering of assistance to defray the expenses of a large, costly ceremonial. But the clan is not a ritual unit that controls specific ceremonials or ritual paraphernalia. Thus, the disappearance of a clan does not mean the extinction of a ceremonial. Furthermore, the medicine man, or chanter, functions on an individual basis rather than as part of an organized priesthood. The chanter conducts a ceremonial that meets the specific needs of an individual patient at the patient's hogan. By focusing primarily on the healing of individuals rather than on the welfare of the community (although this is a secondary function of ceremonials), the loss or change of particular ceremonials through time has not endangered cultural survival. Furthermore, since ceremonials are held in the hogan, which has been temporarily sanctified for ritual purposes, there are no permanent religious centers whose destruction could mean the loss of Navajo identity or cohesion.

The ceremonials are still changing, although there is remarkable continuity in such major ceremonials as the Nightway, whose songs and prayers remain identical to those recorded by such early researchers as Washington Matthews (1902). Some ceremonials have been lost, but this has not endangered the survival of other ceremonials or the incorporation of traits from extinct rituals into surviving ceremonials. Although Hailway died out with the passing of Hastiin Tł'aii,[5] its "Night Sky" sandpainting has been used in other, surviving ceremonials (Harry Walters, personal communication, 1990).

The Native American Church (NAC), a nativistic peyote religion, has affected the traditional ceremonial system. Although the vision aspect of peyotism is not traditional with Navajos, many other teachings of this religion are not in conflict with Navajo values (see Aberle [1966, 1982:219–31]). Peyotism and traditional ceremonialism share the same goal, the restoration of *hózhǫ́* (healing), and use similar ceremonial equipment (Frisbie 1980: 199). Part of the church's appeal comes from its shorter ceremonies and lower costs. The increase of wage work has made it difficult to meet the demands of time and money required by traditional ceremonials. A nine-night ceremonial means that the patient's family must make a considerable outlay of resources to feed the chanter, his helpers, and others who attend. Furthermore, apprentices must invest a substantial amount of time and energy to study with an older chanter in order to master the many songs, prayers, sandpaintings, and procedures of the long nine-night ceremonials. The NAC is not an exclusive religion, and many of its members are active in traditional ceremonialism. Gary Witherspoon (in Wyman [1983b:536]) points out that by the 1970s the NAC was seen by many Navajos as "simply another chantway, *'azee'ji* or Medicine Way." Although many Navajo chanters have become NAC road men, others remain strongly opposed to the Native American Church.

The final major factor in the resilience of Navajo culture is their cultural response to outside influences. When the Navajos made their way southward from their ancestral Athabascan home, they were forced to contend with many different ecological and social environments, and they did so successfully. Clearly, these were a resilient and highly adaptive people. The Navajo people are known for their willingness to accept innovation. They possess a distinctive cultural ability to borrow only that which is useful and appropriate and to rework the borrowed trait into a form that is distinctly Navajo, without any loss of cultural integrity. As Spicer (1961:530) pointed out, even the adoption of a new subsistence pattern such as sheepherding, which appeared to be an extreme change, turned out instead to be a "reinforcement of the interest in hunting and the tendency for moving about which had been important elements in Navajo culture for a long time."

Through time, the Navajos have successfully incorporated not only skills, such as sheepherding, weaving, and silversmithing, but also important aspects of their ceremonial system. Vogt (1961:329) explained this latter process as follows: "layers of Pueblo ceremonialism, Anglo-American Christianity, and Ute peyotism have been (and still are being) incorporated and reworked in terms of the central emphasis upon bodily health and curing ceremonies performed over one or more individual patients rather than upon communal ceremonies linked to lineages, clans, communities, or congregations." This distinctive ability to distinguish between traits that have the potential to enhance and those that threaten the existing framework of Navajo culture, and the ability to rework these borrowed traits into forms that become distinctly Navajo are cultural strengths that have ensured the vitality and strength of Navajo culture. Navajo culture has proven to be one of the most resilient of Native American cultures because of this adaptive style of meeting change.

A UNIVERSE IN MOTION

The Navajos' emphasis on motion is the foundation of their view of the world. Even when they relinquished their nomadic heritage for a subsistence pattern based on sheepherding and farming, the Navajos chose not to live in villages but rather to divide their year between summer and winter residences owned by individual family units.

What Toelken (1979:253) calls "the metaphor of movement" permeates Navajo mythology, religion, language, and thought. Navajo origin myths are rich in images of heroes traveling for sacred knowledge and healing power. Hoijer (1964:146) explained, "Myths and legends reflect this emphasis [on movement] most markedly, for both gods and culture heroes move restlessly from one holy place to the next, seeking by their motion to perfect and repair the dynamic flux which is the universe." In healing ceremonials, motion plays a major role not only in the ritually directed movements of the patient, the chanter, and the God Impersonators, but also in the prayers that include the well-known phrase, *sạ'a nagháí bik'e hózhǫ,* which evokes balanced, beautiful conditions that surround the petitioners in every direction as they travel along.

The structure of the Navajo language clearly emphasizes movement. As Hoijer (1964:146) pointed out, in three broad speech patterns, illustrated by the conjugation of active verbs, the reporting of actions and events, and the framing of substantive concepts, Navajo emphasizes movement and specifies the nature, direction, and status of such movement in considerable detail. Even the neuter category is relatable to the dominant conception of a universe in motion; for, . . . the Navajo define position as a resultant of the withdrawal of motion.

Witherspoon (1977:53) called movement "the basis of life," saying that "life is exemplified by movement." Young and Morgan (1943:145) translate the verb stem, *nááł*, as "a stem which has to do with movement, life, and duration." Clearly, these concepts are closely related in the Navajo view of the world.

This conception of the universe as a place of motion and process means that no state of being is permanently fixed. Thus, beauty, balance, and orderliness are conditions that must be continuously recreated. As we will see, this emphasis on dynamic order and regeneration means that sacredness with regard to space, such as the physical boundaries of sacred space within and around a consecrated hogan, and sacredness with regard to ceremonial objects, such as the chanter's *jish* (medicine bundle) and Nightway masks, must also be continually renewed.

While outer, ritual actions can renew harmonious, balanced conditions, the individual can also bring about these desired qualities by thinking about them. Thought is creative and attractive in the sense that people create their world through their thoughts. Through *hózhǫ́ ntséskees,* right thinking, people draw desirable experiences to them. The quality of one's thoughts determines the quality of one's life. Because life is an ongoing process, one must continue to practice *hózhǫ́ ntséskees* in order to live a life characterized by balance and harmony. The Navajo recognize that thought is a vital aspect of any creative act. The Holy People spent time thinking about and planning the Creation before they took action (Wyman 1970a:113–14).

The Navajo emphasis on active process rather than static product is evident in the films made by the Navajos themselves. In 1966 Sol Worth of the Annenburg School of Communication and John Adair of San Francisco State College taught Navajos how to use motion picture cameras so that Navajos could visually share, through film, their own perceptions of their world, including narrative style and their conceptions of time and space (Worth and Adair 1972). Susie Benally in her film on Navajo weaving devoted only about five minutes out of twenty to the woven product; instead, she chose to emphasize movement and creative process by using three-quarters of the film footage to show the weaver walking to gather vegetables for dye, walking to collect roots for soap, walking to shear the wool, and walking to and from the hogan between all activities (p. 144). The creative process began long before the physical act of weaving, with inspiration drawn from the natural environment. Thought is such a vital part of the creative act that Benally shot close-ups of the weaver's face to show that she was "thinking about the design" (p. 153). It was so important to portray the act of thinking that Benally overcame her discomfort at filming such close-ups, which would usually be considered a transgression of Navajo rules of privacy.

John Nelson's film, *A Navajo Silversmith,* showed a similar emphasis on movement across the landscape and on the role of creative thought: ten minutes of his fifteen-minute film showed the silversmith walking to the mine to find silver nuggets, walking back to the hogan to find sandstone for the mold, walking to his hogan again, and so on, while close-ups showed the silversmith with his eyes rolled slightly upward because "that's the way most people think" (p. 155).

In addition to an emphasis on movement and process, these films display another essential component of the Navajo view of the world: a powerful interaction with the land, which provides not only physical materials but also creative inspiration. Without such dynamic interaction, neither the act of weaving nor that of silversmithing would have been possible.

It is impossible to travel across the reservation without being touched by the immensity of the landscape, by a sense of the earth reaching off in every direction to meet the sky. A sense of continual movement and power is evident in the billowing mounds of swirling cumulus that move across the disk of the sun, casting racing shadows. Buttes and escarpments stand in momentary spotlights of illumination as the sun shines through holes in the clouds. The wind sweeps sand across the valley floor, creating *náás'ó'oołdísii*, huge rising dust devils, visible for miles. Every feature of the landscape, as well as the beings who live and travel upon its surface, is animated with movement, power, and life.

Navajo interactions with this powerful environment are characterized by a strong sense of connectedness to and respect for all living things, including the earth, which is personified as the beloved deity, Changing Woman. An important aspect of maintaining harmonious relations with the universe is the recognition of humankind's place in the web of life and the acceptance that nature is more powerful than humans. Kluckhohn and Leighton (1962:308) explained this fundamental premise of the Navajo worldview by contrasting it with the Anglo view:

Navajos accept nature and adapt themselves to her demands as best they can, but they are not utterly passive, not completely the pawns of nature. They do a great many things that are designed to control nature physically and to repair damage caused by the elements. But they do not even hope to master nature. For the most part, the People [i.e., the Navajo] try to influence her with songs and rituals, but they feel that the forces of nature, rather than anything that man does, determine success or failure. . . .

Many white people have the opposite view; namely, that nature is a malignant force with useful aspects that must be harnessed, and useless, harmful ones that must be shorn of their power. . . . Their premise is that nature will destroy them unless they prevent it; the Navajos' is that nature will take care of them if they behave as they should and do as she directs.

This passage explains the reciprocal quality of the Navajos' relationship with nature. On a human level, one of the most important premises of relations with one's relatives is just such an emphasis on reciprocity; the value placed upon taking good care of relatives must not be underestimated in Navajo culture. Earlier, I mentioned that the worst thing a Navajo can say of an individual is, "He acts as if he has no relatives" (paraphrase of Kluckhohn and Leighton 1962:100). The highest expression of maturity and responsibility is proper treatment of one's relatives. Because of the supreme importance placed upon kinship, aspects of nature are often personified as relatives. Thus, it is common to hear the earth referred to as "Mother Earth" and the sky as "Father Sky." Inherent in this use of kin terminology is a recognition of mutual responsibility: nature will take care of humankind if humankind fulfills its kinship responsibilities by taking care of and behaving responsibly towards nature.

In Navajo culture, as in all cultures, a kin relationship may be characterized by a high degree of respect as well as deep affection. The profound emotional and spiritual connection that Navajos have to their land is evident in this moving passage from the Mountain Chant:

But instead of looking south in the direction in which he was going he looked to the north, the country in which dwelt his people. Before him were the beautiful peaks of *Dibé Nitsaa* [Hesperus Peak], with their forested slopes. The clouds hung over the mountain, the showers of rain fell down its sides, and all the country looked beautiful. And he said to the land *"Aháláane!"* (Greeting!) [an exclamation of warm greeting between intimates who have not seen each other for a long time], and a feeling of loneliness and homesickness came over him, and he wept and sang this song:
"That flowing water! That flowing water!

My mind wanders across it.
That broad water! That flowing water!
My mind wanders across it.
That old age water! That flowing water!"
(Matthews 1887:393)

✦ 3 ✦

The Navajo
Spiritual World

Despite rapid acculturative changes in Navajo society and culture, many Navajos still follow their traditional philosophy and ceremonial system. The inseparability of spirituality from other aspects of life is reflected in the fact that there is no word for "religion" in Navajo; *nahaghá* (a ceremony is taking place) is the closest equivalent to this English word. Many Navajos reject the concept of "religion" not only because of its association with a way of life that was forced upon them in the 1800s, but also because the religions to which they were introduced were characterized by dogma, exclusivity, and an emphasis upon salvation in a spiritual world far removed from the earthly environment.

As a well-known Nightway chanter pointed out during the February 1986 Navajo Studies Conference, "Religion is a word from Europe." He objected to the use of the English words *religion, myth,* and *medicine man* in connection with Navajo ceremonialism because of their negative connotations. When asked about *diné binahagha',* which is usually translated as "Navajo religion," he replied, "That means 'moving about ceremonially'" (in Frisbie [1987:xxiii]).

In traditional Navajo thinking, spirituality, health, harmony, and beauty are inseparable. All the good things in life—health, prosperity, happiness, and peace—are a result of living life from a spiritual perspective that acknowledges all parts of the universe as alive and interdependent.

The Navajo perceive the universe as an all-inclusive whole in which everything has its own place and unique and beneficial relationship to all other living things. Humans, animals, plants, and mountains are harmonic components of the whole. An orderly balance based on the principle of reciprocity governs the actions and thoughts of all living things, from the smallest creature to the most complex, including human beings and the enduring land on which they live. It is the responsibility of humans to honor and maintain this balance.

Navajo artist and teacher, Carl Gorman (in Brown [1982:70]), explained
the Navajo relationship to the Creator and to nature in this way:

> It has been said by some researchers into Navajo religion, that we have no
> Supreme God, because He is not named. That is not so. The Supreme Being is
> not named because He is unknowable. He is simply the Unknown Power. We
> worship him through His Creation. We feel too insignificant to approach di-
> rectly in prayer that Great Power that is incomprehensible to man. Nature feeds
> our soul's inspiration and so we approach Him through that part of Him which
> is close to us and within the reach of human understanding. We believe that
> this great unknown power is everywhere in His creation. The various forms of
> creation have some of this spirit within them. . . . As every form has some of
> the intelligent spirit of the Creator, we cannot but reverence all parts of the
> creation.

THE *DIYIN DINE'É*

The universe contains two groups of beings: the Earth Surface People, who
are ordinary human beings, and the *diyin dine'é,* who possess supernatural
powers. *Diyin dine'é* is usually translated as "Holy People," although a more
appropriate translation would be "Supermen" or "Superbeings" because the
core of this concept is possessing special powers (Young in Aberle 1967:16).
(To avoid confusion, I will use the term *Holy People* because of its customary
use in works on Navajo ceremonialism.)

This class of beings includes such well-known Navajo deities as the Sun,
a great power; Changing Woman, the most beloved deity and one who represents the powers of renewal inherent in the earth; and their children, the
Hero Twins, Monster Slayer and Born-for-Water. Other Holy People—First
Man and First Woman, First Boy and First Girl, the trickster Coyote, and
Be'gochidi—played important roles in the Creation after the Emergence. Another group of Holy People, the Yé'ii, tried but failed to speak after their
creation and are called *hasch'ééh,* the Speechless Ones, because they are capable of uttering only calls, not words.

Each Navajo ceremonial is related to a particular group of Holy People
who are capable of assuming human form. Medicine man Mike Mitchell
described the many kinds of Holy People as well as the appropriate behavior
regarding them:

> Every creature, every aspect of nature has its holy people . . . even the stinkbug.
> Sometimes you can see them, if only for an instant. They are represented,

some of them, by colors: the blue sky, the evening dusk, the night—these are holy people and one prays to them. There are iron people, crystal people, then the other rocks "and such people." There are dawn people, twilight people, air, thunder, and cloud people.

One does not talk about such things in nature when they and their holy people are present. In winter, many will have left—bears, for example—so one can speak of bears in winter. The thunder people leave in winter. In winter, the snow people, the cold air people, are present—"like a day shift and a night shift."

White thunder is different. It comes in winter. Thunder in a snowstorm is startling. "Whoever is the leader of the thunder people sends white thunder back to their summer place to see what's going on. Navajos have summer and winter camps and they go check on them, just like the white thunder" (in Page [1989:87–88]).[1]

In Mike Mitchell's portrayal, as well as in the great body of Navajo oral literature, the Holy People are described as having human emotions—worry, jealousy, anger, fear, and joy—and are tied genealogically through the clan organization to the Earth Surface People (Reichard 1950:58–59). They have emotional, genealogical, and physical links to humans. Western religions tend to see a strong separation between gods and humans—quite different from the Navajo viewpoint. One of my Navajo friends explained why the Holy People are not perfect beings: "The Holy People are never described as being perfect because we aren't perfect either. They teach us to strive for perfection but to be compassionate and patient with ourselves if we fall short."

In a discussion about the glossing of *diyin dine'é* as "Holy People," Consultant A described the omnipresent nature of Navajo supernaturals: "They are Holy People but not in the sense that they're way up on high; Navajo Holy People aren't far away like the Christian God. Navajo Holy People hear you singing. They see you do all these things [in a ceremony]. You also see them when your day goes well." She explained that she meant this figuratively, since "they never make themselves visible but you interact with them on a daily basis, and they make your day go right." (For information about the individuals who served as consultants for this study, see the appendix.)

Navajo opinion varies concerning the visibility of the Holy People. When the Holy People left the Earth Surface People after the Creation, they remained nearby, although most Navajos agree that they cannot be seen in the form of gods. However, the Holy People can be seen indirectly, that is, they express themselves through sounds and sights in the natural world. Some Navajos see the Holy People as disembodied spiritual presences who appear at times of crisis to provide crucial guidance. One Navajo, who is studying to be a chanter, said that he sees the Holy People in the faces of individuals he meets during the course of his day. By this he means that he tries to see the holiness, the spirituality, in other people.

In his account of Blessingway, Chanter Slim Curley (in Wyman [1970a: 324–25]) explained that the Holy People told humans at the time of Creation:

> "This past day and this night alone you have again seen Holy People. From this day on until the end of days you shall not see them again [in person], that is final. . . . Although you apparently can see the wind [now], you will only hear its voice [in the future]. You will see a holy one when you see a white feather [of an eagle], when you see a bluebird, a yellowbird, a big blackbird. . . . And when white corn, yellow corn, blue corn, variegated corn, and plants move [grow?] this way, you will be seeing a holy one."

All Holy People are powerful—and thus dangerous. As chanter Mike Mitchell (in Page [1989:91]) explained, "The Holy People sometimes hurt us . . . the way we sometimes hurt little ants by accident."

Farella (1984:38) pointed out that one cannot make a list of Navajo Holy People from the least to the most powerful; instead, how dangerous they are depends upon the context: the same supernatural being who is relatively benign in a *hózhǫ́ǫ́jí* (Blessingway) context may be quite dangerous in the context of another ritual. This type of variation suggests far greater complexity than Reichard (1950:53) implied in her categorization of Navajo supernaturals as "persuadable deities," "unpersuadable deities," "undependable deities," and "beings between good and evil."

Although the Holy People are dangerous and often capricious beings who may inflict great harm and even death upon humans, they also want the Earth Surface People to survive and flourish; for this reason, "they naturally help in ceremonies" (Harry Walters, personal communication, 1989). Furthermore, they do not withhold themselves when their presence is sincerely desired and needed. The beneficent nature of the Holy People is implied in this comment made by a Navajo to writer Stephen Trimble (1986:91): "I can call Talking God, Father Sky, Mother Earth, First Man, First Woman, Monster Slayer, Child Born of Water. I can call them and they'll listen to me because the holy people have given me these songs, this language, these ceremonies."

Navajo prayers convey a sense of the respectful yet compassionate relationship that exists between the Holy People and humanity through the establishing of a kin relationship. The "Songs of the Earth's Inner Form" from Blessingway (Slim Curley's version is given in Wyman 1970a:123–31) show how such a symbiotic relationship is established. Prayers are addressed to the Earth, the Sky, and other supernaturals using kin terms, such as "my mother" or "my grandmother"; in turn, the prayers say that each of these Holy People "treats you as a mother [would treat her child], addressing you in endearing terms, 'my child, my grandchild,' in response to your pleas":

. . . As I stand along the surface of the Earth she [the Earth] she says child to me, she [the Earth] says grandchild to me.
Now as I stand along the surface of long life, now happiness[2] she [the Earth] says child to me, she [the Earth] says grandchild to me.
As I stand below the Sky she [the Earth] says child to me, she [the Earth] says grandchild to me.
Now as I stand below long life, now happiness she [the Earth] says child to me, she [the Earth] says grandchild to me . . .
(Wyman 1970a:123)

This view of the Holy People as compassionate and desirous of rendering aid to humans in a ceremonial context contrasts with Reichard's (1944b, 1950) view of Navajo prayers as "compulsive words," which must force supernaturals to respond favorably. She stated (1950:126), "The gods have . . . little choice about answering man's requests when properly formulated." I agree with McAllester (1980:231) that this view carries overtones of the nineteenth-century definitions of "magic" and "medicine man." Although a reciprocal relationship is established in the course of the ceremonial that, in a sense, obligates the Holy People to help, this relationship is patterned after that of a family wherein one wants to render aid to a family member. Reichard's interpretation dehumanizes this reciprocal exchange to a mechanistic transaction laden with magical overtones.

As McAllester (1980:232) pointed out, and as I have found in my own experience in Navajo culture, it is not mere formality when a Navajo addresses the deities as "my uncle" or "my grandfather" in song and prayer. The ceremonial procedures attempt to establish a kin relationship between the protagonist (with whom the patient is identified) and the supernaturals.

Inherent in such a relationship is the value placed upon cooperation and reciprocity. The language of the prayers expresses reciprocity rather than compulsion:

> Your offering I have made, for you I have made it,
> Today I am your child, today I am your grandchild . . .
> Whatever I say to you, you will do it,
> Whatever you say to me, I will do it.
> (Chanters DT, RM, RW, in McAllester [1980:232])

Gill (1974:537) agreed that, rather than expressing a quality of compulsion, each Navajo prayer is "an act of communication . . . an act of establishing relationships on the basis of reciprocity, and an act of re-establishing place, which implies the re-establishment of relationships." Chanter Denet Tsosie explained to McAllester (1980:232) that the prayer offering, which would accompany the Navajo text just given, establishes a kin relationship characterized by reciprocity: "The prayer offering is an exchange. It is an invitation to the Holy People and in return they restore the energy of the one-sung-over [the patient]."

The concept of reciprocity is not only the foundation for the relationship between mortals and Holy People, it is also the basis upon which ceremonials work to effect a cure. Kluckhohn and Leighton (1962:226) wrote that "the values which Navahos derive from ceremonials are . . . paid for. A fee is always paid to the singer, even if he is the patient's own father; otherwise the rite might not be effective." Aberle (1967:15–32) pointed out, however, that this "fee" is really much more of a prestation or offering, something that is characteristic of reciprocal relationships so prominent in Navajo life.

There is a morality of reciprocity that expresses the solidarity of interconnected individuals and groups. In Navajo ethics, it is vitally important to render aid—especially to relatives—when it is requested or when it appears to be needed. However, such expectations are not calculated: one does not give aid or gifts with the expectation of returned aid at a specific time in the future.[3]

Furthermore, an essential aspect of reciprocity is that in order to receive something of value, one must give something of value. One's offering is a direct measure of how much one appreciates the Holy People and the role they play in the healing of one's mind, body, and spirit. This "payment" is also a statement of faith, of belief in the power of the Holy People to heal. Thus, the "fee" given to the chanter can be seen as a gift to the universe for the healing that will follow. Harry Walters (personal communication, 1990) explained,

> The payment to the chanter is a measure of the patient's "good heart." It's a way of demonstrating to yourself that you are truly committed to your own healing. It's a way of actively participating in your own healing because it allows you to take an active role. These activities [the payment and the observation of ritual restrictions] return the responsibility for and control over your own health to you. It's also a way of reminding yourself that you are ultimately responsible—through your thoughts and actions—for the state of your own health.

The patient must actively *choose* to be well. The payment and adherence to ritual restrictions symbolize this choice.

This is very different from the misconception that the Navajo singer receives a "fee" in return for the services he renders. The effectiveness of the ceremonial depends upon the presentation of a gift to the chanter. If this gift is not made, the ceremonial is rendered ineffective. In the chantway myth, the hero both establishes a kin relationship with and gives a gift to the Holy People, who are then obliged to restore the hero to health and to teach him the chantway. The apprentice chanter gives an offering to his teacher in order to learn the ceremonial; when the apprentice chanter learns the ceremonial, he then possesses sacred knowledge which he has a moral responsibility to share. Patients show the proper respect and degree of commitment toward their own cure by giving a gift to the chanter, which in turn obliges the chanter to restore them with the help of the Holy People through the ceremonial. Thus, as Aberle (1967:27) succinctly explained, "an unbroken chain of reciprocity binds the supernatural figure, the hero, the singer and the patient together."

THE CAUSE AND TREATMENT OF ILLNESS

The all-inclusive nature of the universe means that all forces are integrated—good and evil, natural and supernatural, male and female—into a state of balance and harmony expressed by the word *hózhó*. People who become involved in an act that disrupts this balance may be made ill by the forces thereby unleashed.

The purpose of most Navajo ceremonials is the healing of one or more individuals. This healing is accomplished by restoring the patients to *hózhó*. Because healing is a by-product of the restoration to harmony, the root cause, rather than the recurring symptoms of an illness, is treated.

Illness can be caused by many factors: failure to display the proper respect for dangerous powers (*diyin dine'é*), such as lightning, winds, or thunder; improper contact with some species of animals, such as the bear; the mishandling of ceremonial paraphernalia at inappropriate times; or contact with the ghosts of Navajos, non-Navajos, or witches, including werewolves. Illness of the body and mind or other misfortune is the result of deliberately or unwittingly breaking the prescriptions of the Holy People. When such a transgression occurs, harmony and well-being can only be restored by invoking the power of the appropriate supernaturals on behalf of the patient in a ceremonial designed to deal with the particular factors that caused the illness.

To cure the patient, the practitioner must invoke the cause of illness and bring it under control, thereby transforming evil into good. The power to cure comes from the precise replication of ceremonial procedures that restore the patient to a state of orderliness and health. Harmony is restored simultaneously in the physical, spiritual, mental, and social domains of the patient's life.

As previously mentioned, patients also play an active role in their own healing. Once the family decides to consult a chanter, everyone's thoughts—especially the patient's—turn from illness toward the anticipated recovery. Beginning with the preparation period, the patient is actively engaged in constructive activities that instill not only the desire to get well but also the shared conviction that the individual will return to full health.

The patient and his family must find the money to pay the chanter as well as the food to feed the chanter and his helpers. While the patient devotes his energies to preparations for the forthcoming ceremonial, he is surrounded by friends and relatives whose presence conveys their concern and love. The chanter's prestige and authority, as well as the considerable financial contribution by the patient's kin, add to the conviction that the ceremonial will prove successful. Finally, the patient knows of other people who have been cured by the same ceremonial being conducted for him.

The ceremonial itself gradually transforms the patient's state of mind, through ritual actions that involve not only the healing touch of a respected, trusted chanter, one with many cures to his credit, but also the knowledge that the Holy People themselves are touching the patient with loving care through the chanter who serves as an instrument for their transcendent healing power. The patient also knows that the Holy People have given this specific ceremonial to the Earth Surface People for this kind of cure. The hero of the myth experienced difficulties far greater than those of the patient. The Holy People looked upon the hero as their beloved child and came to his aid; the same Holy People now look upon the patient with the same kind of approval and love and once more bring their powers to bear for another of their children.

With each successive day of the ceremonial, the patient passes from a state of hopefulness toward a state of mind in which he is assured of complete healing. At the midpoint of the ceremonial (for a nine-night ceremonial, this is the afternoon of the fourth day and the entire fifth night) the focus of the ceremonial shifts from purification and protection to invocation and blessing. By this time, the patient has begun to take control in his own mind over his illness as he is filled with a sense of inner peace.

The final night of the ceremonial summarizes the purification, protection, invocation, and blessing of the entire ceremonial. The patient concentrates on the songs and ritual acts; he is the center of attention for the audience, which has grown because of the many people who have come for this event. The darkness creates a dramatic setting: rather than being distracted by everyday sights, people focus on the spiritual meaning behind the supernatural events that unfold before them.

Finally, the patient demonstrates the strength of his commitment to healing through careful adherence to ritual restrictions, which last four days after the close of the ceremonial. The abstinence from specific activities and foods that the patient practices at this time is a concentrated act of thanksgiving to the Holy People, which ensures the desired healing. This liminal period also permits the patient to reflect on the events of the past days and to absorb mentally and emotionally the intensely powerful experience of the ceremonial.

THE *HATAAŁII,* OR CHANTER

As previously explained, Navajo ceremonials are conducted according to individual need rather than the dictates of a ceremonial calendar. In contrast to the institutionalized priesthoods and ceremonial societies of the Pueblos, a Navajo ceremonial is conducted by a highly trained practitioner called a *hataałii,* which means "singer" or "chanter," because singing is an indispensable component of Navajo ritual. The Navajo chanter possesses ritual knowledge that allows him to control dangerous things, cure witchcraft, exorcise ghosts, and establish immunity to illness from those same sources.

The Navajo chanter is a priest rather than a shaman; that is, instead of acquiring power through personal communion with a supernatural being, the chanter's power is derived from a body of codified ritual knowledge that he learns from older priests and passes on to his apprentices (see Lessa and Vogt [1958] for a discussion of these terms).[4] Although the chanter performs the ceremonial in a focused state of intense concentration, he is not in the trance state characteristic of a shaman.

Chanters specialize in only a few complete ceremonials because each ceremonial requires so many prayers, songs, medicines, sandpaintings, and ritual objects and procedures. Hundreds of songs and more than fifty sandpaintings belong to the Shooting Chant alone (Newcomb and Reichard 1975:10, 13). In order to perform a nine-night Nightway, the chanter must have memorized "scores of prayers, hundreds of songs, dozens of prayer sticks and other sacred paraphernalia, and several very complex sandpaintings"; he must also have assembled a Nightway *jish* (medicine bundle) that includes "the masks of God Impersonators made from sacred buckskin, perfect ears of corn for initiating women, and a host of other difficult to obtain items" (Faris 1990:79). Thus, the necessarily long period of apprenticeship to a knowledgeable chanter requires a very strong personal motivation.

A chanter gains prestige from having studied under a particularly respected chanter. Chanters often preface a ceremonial performance by saying, "This is the way Blue Eyes [or another respected chanter] taught me." James Faris (1990:19), in his recent book on the Nightway, diagrammed complicated Nightway apprenticeship genealogies. It is possible to detect such relationships through the way in which the myth is told and through the sandpaintings. I discovered in previous research (Griffin-Pierce 1987) that one reason for slight variations in sandpaintings is that different versions of the same sandpainting emphasize different episodes in the accompanying myth; thus, Blue Eyes's version (and thus, the version told by those chanters who learned from Blue Eyes) of the Nightway myth focuses on different episodes in the myth than those emphasized in the version passed on by Hastiin Nez. Karl Luckert (1982:190) explained, "Every telling of a chantway myth is an event which illuminates the institution of apprenticeship and the succession of singers."

A memory for exact detail is essential because the chanter is responsible for replicating his teacher's version of the ceremonial without errors. Furthermore, he must have the physical stamina to supervise all ceremonial details and lead the singing each day and during the final night. Chanters

must also have a generous, altruistic spirit. A chanter known for his successful ceremonials is seldom home with his family because of his almost constant ceremonial schedule. He may return home from the performance of
one nine-night ceremonial for a day's rest and then leave that evening to
begin another long ceremonial. In the rare times when he is at home, his
time is interrupted by the arrival of the relatives of potential patients who
come to discuss the scheduling of future ceremonials. The chanter must be
motivated by his concern for the welfare of others (see Frisbie [1987:77–
99] for a discussion of the reasons why an individual chooses to become a
chanter).

Some would-be chanters are discouraged by a fear for their personal
safety. For example, the Nightway is considered to be one of the most powerful, and therefore most dangerous, of all ceremonials. Chanter C, a respected Nightway chanter, related stories of personal misfortune that had
pursued the relatives of Hastiin Tł'aii as a result of his sharing ceremonial
knowledge—including the Nightway—with Mary Cabot Wheelwright. This
chanter also told me about the death of Washington Matthews, the Army
doctor whose meticulous recording of the Nightway remains a classic in
Navajo scholarship; the chanter felt that Matthews's death was a direct result
of his Nightway research.

Women chanters are few because of the risk of prenatal infection. This
means that unborn children can be harmed if their mothers attend a ceremonial during the period between their conception and birth. If a woman is
committed to becoming a chanter, she is more likely to do so after meno-
pause; at this point in her life, she will also have more free time to devote to
learning all aspects of the ceremonial. Post-menopausal women chanters are
not only freed from concern over prenatal infection but they also do not
have to worry about scheduling difficulties because of the taboos against
ceremonial attendance by menstruating women.

Women are more likely to be found among another kind of practitioner,
the diagnostician—the one who discovers the source of illness and pre-
scribes the appropriate ceremonial. In contrast to the chanter, the diagnostician is a shaman, that is, a person who has been born with or has acquired
personal power accessed through a trance state. Divination may take the
form of hand trembling, stargazing (which will be described in chapter 6),
or listening.

The hand trembler passes his or her trembling hand over the patient's
body as he or she says prayers to Gila Monster; the answer comes either

through the interpretation of the motions of the diagnostician's shaking hand, or as a direct revelation from the Gila Monster (Hill 1935:67-68). Stargazing may involve sandpaintings or fetishes; the dried and powdered lenses from the eyes of night birds with keen sight may be applied to the eyelids of the stargazer, the patient, and those who could assist in seeing something. The stargazer and his or her helpers then go outside to say prayers and, with the use of a quartz crystal, interpret flashes of light or images for information about the cause of illness and the proper ceremonial and chanter for treatment (Wyman 1936:244). Listening is similar to star-gazing but does not use sandpainting or fetishes, which may be used in stargazing. The dried and powdered eardrum of a badger may be placed in each ear; the listener then leaves the hogan to say prayers and then to interpret the cause of illness from something heard, such as the rattling of a rattlesnake or the roar of thunder (Wyman 1936:245). There is considerable variation in each of these techniques.

NAVAJO CEREMONIALS, OR CHANTWAYS

The Navajo system of ceremonials is highly complex. Haile (1938a:639, 1938b:10) distinguished *rites* (ceremonials in which a rattle is not used) from *chants* (ceremonials in which a rattle accompanies the singing).

Two major rites, Blessingway and Enemyway, stand apart from the chant-ways. (I use the term *chantway* as a synonym for *chant* because the suffix -*way* renders the terminal enclitic of Navajo names for the chants.) Unlike the chantways, which focus on curing, Blessingway is preventive in nature and invokes positive blessings. Thus, it protects from misfortune by ensuring prosperity, good luck, order, health, and all manner of positive blessings for the Earth Surface People and all that concerns them. The paintings of Bless-ingway rites (and the War Prophylactic rite) are more properly called dry-paintings rather than sandpaintings; instead of sand, ocher, and charcoal, the pigments are mostly, often entirely, of vegetable origin (see Reichard [1950:666–72]; Wyman [1970a:65]). These include corn and other plant pollens, cornmeal, powdered flower petals (especially the petals of blue flowers, called "blue pollen"), and charcoal.

The Enemyway, in contrast to Blessingway, is used to exorcise the ghosts of aliens, violence, and ugliness. It belonged to a group of ancient war cere-monials used to protect warriors from the ghosts of slain enemies.

The chantways can be performed according to one of three rituals, or patterns of behavior governing procedure: Holyway, Evilway, or Lifeway. Holyway ceremonials are concerned with restoring the patient to health by attracting good, Evilway ceremonials exorcise evil, and chants conducted according to Lifeway ritual treat injuries resulting from accidents. Chants may be conducted according to more than one ritual mode. Sandpainting ceremonies are a component of all, or nearly all, Holyway ceremonials and most, if not all, Evilway ceremonials (Wyman 1983a:50). Ceremonials conducted according to Lifeway ritual do not use sandpaintings.

Navajos name ceremonials according to the governing ritual (Holyway, Evilway, Lifeway), according to male or female branches (which deal with illnesses caused by different factors rather than the sex of the person for whom the ceremonial is sung), and sometimes for other reasons. Thus, Navajo informants may give forty or fifty names for song ceremonials (Wyman 1983a:21). Wyman (1983a:20) estimates that there were once twenty-four chantway complexes, of which only eleven are well known today, and only seven of these are frequently performed (Shootingway, Flintway, Mountainway, Nightway, Navajo and Chiricahua Windways, and Hand Tremblingway). Chants are grouped on the basis of association in the connected origin legends, symbolism, procedural similarities, ritual paraphernalia, and common etiological factors (Kluckhohn and Wyman 1940:8).

THE PROCEDURES OF A HOLYWAY CEREMONIAL

Since all (or nearly all) Holyway chants use sandpaintings, it will be helpful to describe the basic procedures that compose a Holyway ceremonial. A rich and complex body of oral literature describes the Lower Worlds, the Emergence into the present world, and the Creation. In addition to the story of the Origin, each chant, or ceremonial, has its own origin legend that explains how the Holy People gave the ceremonial to humanity.

Each ceremonial combines a number of discrete units, or ceremonies, which may be inserted or omitted depending upon the nature of the patient's illness. Each ceremony, which is a quasi-independent unit of acts and procedures, is clearly isolated by pauses in activity both preceding and following it. Some ceremonies are required and appear in every chant performance, others are supplementary. A typical Holyway chant usually contains at least ten distinct ceremonies; the characteristic combination of these ceremonies into a Holyway ceremonial is summarized in table 3.1. Each ceremony is

Table 3.1. Ceremonies of Holyway Chants

	Two-Night	Five-Night	Nine-Night	Time of Day
Consecrating the hogan	1	1	1	Sundown
Unraveling	1	1 2 3 4	1 2 3 4	Early evening
Short singing	1	1 2 3 4	5 6 7 8	Evening
Setting out of prayer sticks	1	1 2 3 4	5 6 7 8	Before dawn
Sweat and emetic	—	1 2 3 4	1 2 3 4	Dawn
Offering	1	1 2 3 4	1 2 3 4	Early forenoon
Bath	1	4	8	Forenoon
Sandpainting	1	1 2 3 4	5 6 7 8	Afternoon
Figure painting and token tying	1	4	8	During the sandpainting
All-night singing	2	5	9	Late evening onward
Dawn procedures	2	5	9	Dawn

Note: Numerals indicate the days on which the ceremonies occur according to Navajo reckoning (sundown to sundown). This is a partial listing of all ceremonies in Navaho chants but does cover those common to many Holyway chants. See also Kluckhohn and Wyman 1940.
Source: Adapted from Wyman (1983a:30).

held on one or more days of the chant; Navajo "days" are traditionally counted from sundown to sundown.

A Holyway ceremonial lasts from two to nine nights, and the two-, five-, and nine-night forms are divided into two main sections: purification and the dispelling of evil (ugliness), and the attraction of good. The purposes of the ceremonies or rites listed in table 3.1 are purification and/or invocation (the attraction of good). For example, the consecration of the hogan consists of blessing through singing, praying, purification, and pollen sprinkling both to purify and to attract good powers. The unraveling of bundles of herbs and feathers symbolizes purification from evil. Sandpaintings both dispel evil and attract good.

Different chants have different numbers of paintings. The chanter never uses the entire repertoire of paintings that belong to a chant on a single occasion; rather, he chooses the paintings he feels are best suited to the patient's illness.

Wyman (1970b:7, 1983a:50) estimated that Shootingway has around one hundred designs while, for some chants, scarcely more designs are known today than the four needed for a five-night or nine-night performance. Using his main theme criteria (see below), he (1983a:51) estimated that there are

153 main themes used to form 228 different designs, among 851 reproductions of Holyway sandpaintings in collections.

icon ?

THE PURPOSE OF SANDPAINTINGS

The Navajo term for sandpainting, *'iikááh,* suggests the place of entry where supernaturals "enter and go" (Franciscan Fathers 1910:398). Wyman (1983a:33) believed the description of the sandpainting as a holy altar is the most appropriate because "it is a place where there is sacerdotal equipment and on which ritual behavior is carried out."

A sandpainting assists in healing in four ways: (1) it attracts the supernaturals and their healing power; (2) the depiction of these supernaturals identifies the patient with their healing power; (3) it absorbs the sickness from, and imparts immunity to, the patient seated on it; and (4) the picture creates a ritual reality in which the patient and the supernatural dramatically interact.

The supernatural powers are thought to be irresistibly attracted by seeing their portraits painted in sand. Once they arrive, they actually become the sandpainted likenesses. As Haile (1947a:xiv) has said, the depictions are "identified with the supernaturals themselves . . . they enter the hogan in person."

The patient identifies with the supernaturals depicted in sand by sitting on the figures while the singer moistens his palms with herb medicine and presses them to various parts of the patient; the singer also presses parts of his own body to corresponding parts of the patient's body. At the same time he voices the sound symbolism associated with the chant. The singer is considered to be the surrogate of the supernaturals and is thought to be a *diyin dine'é* while he performs the ceremonial. Thus, the physical contact the patient receives from the singer reinforces the process of identification with the supernaturals, so the patient becomes strong and immune from further harm.

Through the establishment of this mutual pathway the evil, or illness, in the patient is replaced by the good, or healing power, of the powerful supernatural images depicted in the sandpainting. Gladys Reichard (1950:112) summarized this process of "spiritual osmosis": "The ritualistic process may be likened to a spiritual osmosis in which the evil in man and the good of deity penetrate the ceremonial membrane in both directions, the former being neutralized by the latter, but only if the exact conditions for the inter-penetration are fulfilled."

One reason that *'iikááh* have the power to heal is that the paintings and the rituals of which they are a part do not merely commemorate past events; rather, through the preparation and performance of the sandpainting ritual, these sacred events are created again in the present. It is the cyclical quality of Navajo time that makes the sandpainting ritual so powerful and so vivid (the cyclical nature of time will be discussed later). The forces of life are symbolically represented on the hogan floor, including locality symbols that serve to "place" the patient within this sacred setting; the patient then inter-acts with the *diyin dine'é* (supernaturals) within the ritual reality created by the paintings.

A HOLYWAY SANDPAINTING CEREMONY

Most of the sandpaintings discussed in this book belong to chants performed according to Holyway; sandpaintings from only two chants—Big Starway and Hand Tremblingway—are from the Evilway versions of these chants. As can be seen from table 3.1, sandpainting ceremonies are performed once during a two-night ceremonial and four times during a five-night or a nine-night ceremonial.[5] Sandpainting ceremonies usually take place during the day, with the construction of the painting beginning early in the forenoon. Depending upon how many helpers are working on the painting, completion of the image itself may take from three to five hours for one of the less elaborate paintings. Lunch may be served before the painting is completed. Shortly after noon, other preparations begin which may take up to an hour or an hour and a half, if the patient's body is to be painted. The use of the sandpainting, once it has been consecrated, usually takes less than an hour.

The process of sandpainting construction begins with clearing the cere-monial hogan of personal belongings and sweeping the floor. If the sand-painting is to be a large one made for a nine-night winter ceremonial, a larger ceremonial hogan may need to be constructed.

One or more assistants kneel or sit and begin the work under the chanter's direction. The assistants may be anyone, male or female, who knows how or who wishes to learn; however, they must have been sung over at least once or they may suffer ill effects from the power of the sandpainting. The size and complexity of the design determine the number of assistants and amount of time needed to complete the sandpainting; conversely, the number of assistants and amount of time available also help to determine the size and complexity of the design. One or two people may complete a small, simple painting, one or two feet in diameter, in an hour or two. It takes four to six people three to five hours to complete an average chantway sandpainting, which is usually six feet in diameter. The complex designs used for a nine-night winter ceremonial may take a dozen assistants nine hours or more to complete.

The chanter may participate in the painting process by laying out some preliminary guidelines, by beginning the picture with a particularly powerful symbol in the center, or sometimes by working along with the assistants. Usually he sits at the west side of the hogan, a little south of center (his accustomed place), to direct and criticize the work. He assumes full responsibility for any errors in the design. Mistakes are corrected by covering them with background sand and painting them over with the corrected design. When the figure wears special costumes or has figure painting, the sand is also superimposed in layers, with the slim, straight "naked" bodies of the figures painted first and the armor or kilts overlaid on them.[6]

The patient is present during this process only if he is learning the ceremonial or, in the rare case, if he himself is a chanter who knows the ceremonial. In such cases, he may even assist with the creation of the sandpainting or offer corrections about the form of the images.

For practical reasons, the sandpainting is generally begun in the center and then the creation of the design moves outward. The sand upon which the assistants have been sitting is smoothed with a weaving batten to serve as background for the painting. String is held taut between two points, snapped into the sand, and removed; the resulting indentations create a pattern whose outlines will be filled in with sand, ensuring the straightness of the long, slender bodies of sandpainting figures. String may also be used to make certain that figures are of uniform size. The designs are then drawn by allowing the sand to trickle onto the background between the thumb and the flexed forefinger.

Precise traditional rules dictate the form of all images. The assistants who have taken part in the creation of certain paintings know these rules, as does the chanter; all visual images are carried only in the minds of the chanter and his assistants. Only rarely, as in the depiction of the kilts and pouches suspended from the waists of anthropomorphized figures, is individual creativity allowed play.

As the design is created from the center outward, the spaces of the background are filled in with black (and often white) wavy lines. These lines are not shown in sandpainting reproductions because they detract from the entire design, but they are indispensable to paintings used in a ceremonial context because they add to the power of the painting, enhancing its capacity to heal.

The chanter studies the completed painting for any errors he might have overlooked. Then he goes outside to dismantle the mound of feathered prayer sticks and other ritual objects, which earlier was placed about six feet east of the hogan doorway to notify the supernaturals that their presence is requested for this ceremony. He brings the objects inside and places the bundle prayer sticks upright in points around the painting that have been designated in the myth; they represent the supernaturals connected with the chant standing around the sandpainting who will participate in the ceremony. A pollen ball, a small pill-like object, may be placed on the mouth of one supernatural in the sandpainting; if there are two patients, two pollen balls would be placed. Other articles, such as the chant lotion, infusion, and chant token, are placed in their proper positions. Pollen and cornmeal are applied to the painted figures to bless them.

The patient is summoned, and she enters to stand, facing the eastern edge of the sandpainting. She follows the directions of the chanter in strewing white cornmeal over the painting from east to west, from south to north, and around the guardian rainbow. The patient then takes her place at the northern side of the hogan, resting on many layers of cotton cloth that symbolize buckskin, a gift to the chanter.

If it is the final day of the ceremonial, the chanter may paint the patient's body to identify the patient with the supernaturals and their healing power. The patient's moccasins are sanctified when the chanter places pinches of meal and sand from the feet of the sandpainting figures into the moccasins. A token may then be tied to the patient's hair for four days after the ceremony as a gift from the supernaturals to the patient so that she may be recognized as kindred to these deities and gain their protection. The one-sung-over (the patient) then takes her place upon the sandpainting, where consecrated sand from the painting is applied to her body. Other ritual procedures may follow, such as the pressing of the wide boards (four paddle-shaped objects about ten inches long and about two and a half inches wide) to the patient's body. Used in conjunction with special songs, the wide boards further identify the patient with the supernaturals and help to withdraw illness and/or restore health. The patient then leaves the hogan to breathe in the sun four times. With these deep breaths, the spirit of the sun is invoked and its beneficent influence is taken into the patient's body (Kluckhohn and Wyman 1940:100).

While the patient is outside, the sandpainting is erased and the sand is disposed of; when the one-sung-over returns, she may sit upon a blanket that has been spread over the area where the painting had been and may be served cornmeal mush in a ceremonial basket to commemorate the food that was served in the long-ago times and to symbolize the childlike vulnerability of the patient (Kluckhohn and Wyman 1940:101).

THE NATURE OF SANDPAINTING DESIGNS

Wyman (1983a:61) classified the outstanding parts of a sandpainting as the main theme symbols and subsidiary symbols. He qualified this by saying that while such classification violates a fundamental Navajo principle—that all things in the universe have equal importance—it facilitates analytic convenience. Main theme symbols give the name and principal symbolic meaning to the picture and are the ones a Navajo would choose to state the nature of the picture. The subsidiary symbols (no less important to the Navajo) are smaller than the main theme symbols and are found in the quadrants of a radial design, or parallel to or above or below the main themes in a linear arrangement. As Wyman (1983a:61) stated, and as I have found from my own research, although studies differentiate sandpaintings by their linear, radial, or extended center composition, composition is not a significant criterion of differentiation for the Navajos. Thus, a painting with a radial composition and one with a linear composition that share the same main themes are considered by Navajos to be fundamentally the same.

The main theme symbols are representations of the human heroes of the origin legend belonging to the ceremonial, the supernatural beings encountered in the heroes' adventures, important etiological factors associated with the ceremonial, or other powers connected with the chant or rite through its myth or through Navajo belief. The anthropomorphized representations of animals, plants, natural phenomena, geophysical features, and material objects are depicted. Thus, Thunders, Wind, Hail, and Clouds may be depicted as "people." These forms are depicted as human to remind us that we share a kinship with these beings, a relationship that we must honor if the sandpainting ceremony is to be effective in restoring balance and harmony to the universe. As Harry Walters (personal communication, 1990) explained:

"Humans are made from the same elements as the mountains, plants, and stars. They were made before we were so we identify with them [instead of vice versa]. These beings [that is, the mountains, plants, and stars] are made in human form in the sandpainting to make them come alive so that we remember we are related to them."

The subsidiary theme symbols accompany the main theme symbols. In most instances, the subsidiary symbols are the four sacred plants: corn, beans, squash, and tobacco. Sometimes only one of the plants is used; one or more birds may be depicted as well. Medicine herbs, arrows, clouds, Cactus People, coiled snakes, and mountains are other subsidiary symbols (Wyman 1983a:63). Newcomb (in Newcomb, Fishler, and Wheelwright 1956:9) said that if a locality symbol is in the center of the painting, the figures which are placed in the semidirections (e.g., southeast) belong to that symbol; on the other hand, the figures oriented toward the cardinal points "represent the immortals or powerful forces expected to arrive at the ceremony coming from the four directions."

Table 3.2 shows the main theme symbols and designs found in the chantways, indicating the symbols peculiar to the ceremonial, those that are prominently featured but are shared by other ceremonials, and the minor symbols. References to illustrations and descriptions of the chantway and its sandpaintings are listed under the name of each chantway.

Guardian symbols protect the space covered by the design and bring it under control. They also provide for the exchange of evil and good with the outside world. The guardian is an encircling border with an opening to the east. Most frequently this is an anthropomorphized rainbow figure, an elongated ribbonlike form with skirt, legs, and feet at one end and hands, arms, and head at the other end. Next most frequently pictured is the garland, a similar ribbonlike figure with bunches of five feathers at each end. Less commonly seen guardians are the Mirage supernatural and the mirage or mist garland. All of these have spotted ribbonlike bodies with plain, white-bar, or black-cloud ends; these guardians are called rope of rain, sunray, or sunbeam. Sandpaintings of Thunders or the Slayer Twins have zigzag lightning arrows as guardians. Snake or Snake People sandpaintings have snakes as guardians. Uncommon guardians are the sunflower plants of Big Godway; Sunray or Dawn supernaturals; a rain rope; a black bar of darkness or black mirage; "rainbow ladders" or "mist" incorporated in a rainbow rope or "trail"; or lightning arrows with a rainbow bar to the west (Wyman 1983a:-67–69).

Table 3.2. Main Theme Symbols and Designs of Navajo Sandpaintings

Chantway (References) [a]	Symbols Unique to This Ceremonial	Prominent Symbols Shared with Other Ceremonials	Minor Symbols
Blessingway (Wheelwright 1942, 1949; Wyman 1970a)	Changing Woman, First Man Group (First Family); Follower Pair	Corn and Corn People; Pollen Boy and Ripener Girl; Emergence Place; Earth; Sky; Sacred Mountains	Miscellaneous People; Plants; Animals and Birds; Sun
Hailway (Wheelwright 1946a)	Night Sky	Rain (Storm); Thunder; Wind People; Cloud People; Sun and Moon (with Rays, with Mountains)	Big Fly; Thunders; Supernaturals' Houses
Waterway (Wheelwright 1946a; Haile 1979)	Night Sky with Stars Reflected in the Ocean	Rain (Water) People; Water Monsters	
Plumeway (Wyman 1983a; Wheelwright 1946b; Wyman 1952)	Big Game People; Hero of the Myth; Deer Raiser & His Daughter; Big Game Animals	Yé'ii; Sun; Moon; Thunders; Stars; Water Creatures; Ripeners; Corn; Domesticated Plants	Earth; Sky; Rainbow People; Birds
Coyoteway (Luckert 1979)	Coyote People; Coyotes; Day-Sky People; Houses		
Navajo Windway (Kluckhohn & Wyman 1940; Dutton 1941; Wyman 1962)	Wind People; Cyclone People	Snakes; Sun; Moon; Rainbow People; Cloud People; Cactus; Cactus People	Whirlwind People; Pollen People; Snake People; Thunders

Table 3.2. Continued

Chantway (References)[a]	Symbols Unique to This Ceremonial	Prominent Symbols Shared with Other Ceremonials	Minor Symbols
Mountainway (Matthews 1887; Wyman 1971, 1975)	Mountain Gods & Goddesses; Long Bodies; Bears; Porcupines; Great Plumed Arrows; Bear's den		Heroine of the Myth; Dancers; Whirling Rainbow People
Beautyway (Wyman 1957; Wyman & Newcomb 1962)	People of the Myth; Mountain People; Frogs	Snakes; Sun; Moon; Water Creatures; Corn	Dancers; Thunders; Rainbow People
Nightway (Stevenson 1891; Matthews 1902; Tozzer 1909; Faris 1990)		Yéʼii; Black God	Monster Slayer; Rainbow People; Corn
Big Godway (Wyman 1983a)	Big Gods; Sunflower People	Black God; Yéʼii	First Dancers
Eagleway (Kluckhohn 1941; Wyman 1971)	Eagle People; Eagle Catcher	Eagles; Hawks; Small Birds; Eagle's Nest	
Chiricahua Windway (Kluckhohn & Wyman 1940; Wyman 1962)		Sun & Moon; Whirlwind People	

Hand Tremblingway (Kluckhohn & Wyman 1940)	Gila Monsters	Big Stars; Big Flies	
Beadway (Reichard 1977)	Scavenger (the hero); Crooked Feathered (arrow); Snakes; Predatory (hunting) Animals	Eagles; Hawks; Houses	
Red Antway (Wyman 1973)	Ant People; Horned Toad People; Horned Toads & Anthills		Emergence Place; Corn; Corn People; Bows & Arrows
Big Starway (Wyman & Newcomb 1963; Wheelwright 1988)	Star People	Sacred Twins; Stars	Rain People; Earth; Sky; Cloud People; Thunders; Big Flies; Snakes; Mountains
Shootingway (Newcomb & Reichard 1975; Reichard 1977; Wyman 1972c)	The Skies; Cloud Houses; Sun, Moon, & Winds; Sun's House; Buffalo; Buffalo People; Kingbird People; Arrow People	Holy People (Holy Man, Woman, Boy, Girl); Sacred Twins; Thunders; Water Creatures; Snakes; Snake People; Corn People	Earth & Sky; Rainbow People
Shootingway Evilway (Wyman 1970b)		Sacred Twins	Snakes
Mountain Shootingway (Wyman 1970b)	People of the Myth; Sky People		Sacred Twins; Snakes

[a]References refer to illustrations of and information about the particular sandpaintings in the chantway.
Source: Adapted from Wyman (1983a:141–44).

At the eastern opening in the guardian of a sandpainting the control of the passage of good and evil is augmented by a pair of guardian figures. Usually, this may be supernaturals such as a pair of Big Flies, a pair of Bats, Sun and Moon, or Pollen Boy and Ripener Girl, but it may also be Bat and Sun's tobacco pouch (Wyman 1983a:71). Other guardians may echo the main themes of the sandpainting designs they guard (Wyman 1983a:72): pairs of snakes, buffalo, arrows, or beaver and otter. Sometimes they are associated only with the chant or its myth (Wyman 1983a:72): weasels for Mountainway and Beautyway; bears for Mountain Chant; stars for Big Starway; anthills for Red Antway; and eagles for Beadway. Additionally, there are other guardian symbols found only occasionally or uniquely.

Symbols of location are an essential element because they represent the place where the event commemorated in the sandpainting occurred. They may also symbolize the homes of the supernaturals depicted in the sandpainting or the place where the painting is carried out in the myth. Just as Navajo myths begin with a description of locale, so too do sandpaintings. As Reichard (1950:152–58) explained, place represents a power that must be brought under control. Thus, space is organized into a controllable unit inside the sandpainting guardian.

Locale is so significant to the sandpainting that nearly all of the three-dimensional features of the painting are related to the characterization of specific places. Mountains are made in relief by heaping up sand and covering it with colored pigments. The four Sacred Mountains may be made, as well as Spruce Hill (Gobernador Knob, New Mexico), the birthplace of Changing Woman, and Mountain-around-which-moving-was-done (Huerfano Mountain, New Mexico), the early home of Changing Woman. Sky-Reaching Rock (depicted in plate 5) is a supernatural rock that bridges the terrestrial and celestial realms. Significantly, instead of being made of sand, like other mountains in sandpaintings, Sky-Reaching Rock is a truncated clay cone measuring about a foot in height that is a permanent part of the Male Shootingway chanter's ceremonial equipment; thus, unlike other sandpainting features, it is not destroyed at the end of the ceremony.

In addition to mountains, bodies of water may also be represented three-dimensionally by burying shallow bowls, or even bottle caps, to their rims and filling them with water. The surface of the water is then covered with herbs to blacken it. The lake that filled the Place of Emergence is represented in this manner, as are the ponds on Black Mountain and on Mount Taylor and around the base of Sky-Reaching-Rock.[7]

Vegetation features may be represented three-dimensionally as well. Trees—the tops of evergreens measuring about twelve inches high—may be placed atop a mountain in a sandpainting; Black Mountain, where Holy Boy shot the mountain sheep with the grebe-feathered arrow in the story of the Male Shootingway, may be represented with two such trees with pine needles on the mountaintop under the trees. Mossy lichen may surround the base of Sky-Reaching Rock as well as each of the four lakes near its base. All of these features—mountains, bodies of water, and vegetation features—help to establish the locale of the sandpainting and thus to bring it under control for the purpose of restoring harmony and health to the patient.

Color is an outstanding aspect of Navajo ceremonialism and plays a significant role in sandpainting. Reichard (1950:187) said that color is never used consistently, nor does it have the same meaning in every setting. Every detail is calculated, however, and chance does not account for apparent exceptions to the rules. Thus, it can only be said that certain color combinations and sequences are *usually* found in certain relationships with sexual and directional symbolism.

Reichard (1950:187–203) described the significance of several colors. White (*łigai*) is the color of White Dawn in the east and apparently differentiates the naturally sacred from the profane (black or red). Blue (*dootł'izh*) signifies the bright Blue Sky of day and belongs to the south. Yellow (*łitso*) represents fructification because of its association with yellow pollen; belonging to the west, this color represents the Yellow Evening Light of sunset. Black (*łizhin*) is a sinister color; however, because it confers invisibility, black also protects. This color usually represents Night in the north. Red (*łichíí'*) is the color of danger, war, and sorcery and is often paired with black. Pink (*disos*) represents a reddish shimmering quality of light. Gray (*łibá*) is the color of evil, untrustworthiness, and despicability.

Directionality is significant in Navajo symbolism, and movements during a ceremonial must occur in the "sunwise circuit," or from east to south to west to north, except in Evilway ceremonials. There are two predominant directional sequences of colors for east, south, west, and north. Reichard (1950:164) noted the "Day-Sky" sequence, which consists of the subdivisions of the day associated with the directions (also known as the cardinal light phenomena, these are discussed in the next chapter): White Dawn with the east; Blue Day Sky with the south, Yellow Evening Light with the west, and Darkness of Night (black) with the north. Matthews (1897:216) notes a second sequence that consists of black-blue-yellow-white for the four directions, beginning with the east. Because it is used in connection with dangerous underground places, it is employed in Evilway chants, such as the Big Starway or Hand Tremblingway to protect against witches. Reichard (1950:221) termed this the "danger sequence" and says that black is placed in the quadrant from which danger is most imminent for the particular event depicted, because it confers protection.

Earlier, I noted the conceptual division of aspects of the natural world into male and female entities, citing the groupings of the mountains into male and female figures. This division embraces much more than mere sexual distinction: that which is male (*biką'*) also carries the connotation of coarser, rougher, and more violent, while that which is female (*ba'ááá*) is considered to be finer, weaker, and gentler. Reichard (1950:176) elaborated on Matthews's (1902:6) observation by saying that the concept of maleness also includes potency, mobility, bigness, energy, and dominance, while femaleness conveys generative capacity, passive power, endurance, smallness, and compliance. Again, it is essential to remember that neither is preferable or morally superior to the other but that both are necessary for completion, wholeness, and balance.

As would be expected, this conceptual division, so fundamental to the Navajo worldview, is reflected in sandpainting figures. Head shape symbolizes the male-female distinction: male figures tend to have round heads while females have square heads. In some cases this reflects a sexual distinction, but at other times, where both round and square heads are used indiscriminately for both genders, the round-headed figures represent deities with dominant power, a male characteristic (Reichard 1950:177–79). In still other sandpaintings, however, such as those of the Mountainway, the association of power and head shape does not hold.

Lightning marks, arrows, and snakes may also indicate gender. Crooked lightning on the legs, arms, and body of a figure indicates that it is male while the straight form indicates a female bearer (Wyman 1983a:75). A similar distinction holds true for lightning arrows or snakes held in the hands of figures; male snakes or Snake People are usually crooked, while their female counterparts are straight.

Male/female color symbolism is complicated in Navajo sandpainting, and many exceptions exist (see Reichard [1950:214–40] for a discussion of possible color combinations and their meanings). This is because sex pairing—that is, the powers that are dominant (male) and secondary or weaker (female)—vary from chant to chant. Usually, however, black or yellow symbolizes male figures in sandpaintings and blue or white symbolizes female figures; this holds true for the following chants: Big Starway, Nightway, Big Godway, Navajo Windway, Hand Tremblingway, Beadway, and half the paintings in Plumeway (Wyman 1983a:75). Another common arrangement, seen in the Shootingway and Beautyway, is black and blue for males, white and yellow for females (Wyman 1983a:75).

THE SANDPAINTING AS A SACRED, LIVING ENTITY

The sandpainting is considered to be a sacred living entity.[8] The Anglo perception of a sandpainting as an artistic achievement misses the true meaning and cultural significance of the sandpainting. The physical beauty of the depicted image is insignificant in comparison to the ceremonial accuracy and sacredness of the depicted forms. The emphasis of the sandpainting is on process, the dynamic flow of action, and on its ability to summon power through the process of its creation and use.

In the next chapter, I will explain how the order inherent in the repetitive annual motions of the cosmos is reflected in the Navajo emphasis on dynamic order, or orderliness, which must be continually recreated through time. The concept of the sandpainting as a sacred, living entity is based upon the Navajo emphasis on continual movement and regeneration. This philosophy underlies the creation and use of the sandpainting, as well as all aspects of Navajo ritual.

Much has been written about the sacred, powerful, living qualities of the Navajo *jish,* or medicine bundle (Frisbie 1987). As defined in the "Medicine Men's Association Letter to Museums, March 1, 1979," the *"jish* is a sacred living phenomena[*sic*];[9] a source as well as a repository of sacred power" (in Frisbie [1987:421]). The extent to which *jish* is considered to be a living entity is illustrated by the following passage: "That *jish* is like a person . . . it should be exercised so it doesn't lose its life. Without use, its power declines; that bundle becomes lonely. To lock up a *jish* for a long period of time would be like if I locked you up in a closet for thirty days and didn't let you come out. You would be weakened from the experience and would need to be renewed and strengthened" (MN, in Frisbie [1987:103]).

The sandpainting is considered to be equally alive despite its more transitory nature. This emphasis on active process rather than on static product explains the nature of the painting itself. The completion of a sandpainting may take from one to ten hours, but only minutes pass between the painting's completion and its use, and this time is spent not in aesthetic appreciation but rather in a final check of the accuracy of the depiction. The completed painting is much more than the sum of its parts: its power is derived from its state of completeness. Once it has been completed, it is far more powerful, and therefore more dangerous. Reichard (in Newcomb and Reichard 1975:22) described the sense of urgency after the painting has been completed:

> Up to now no obvious attention has been paid to time. . . . But now that it is finished . . . there is a note, if not exactly of haste, nevertheless of an application and bustle, not noticeable before. The painting must be used. It is powerful. The longer it lies the more likely it is that someone may make a mistake in its presence, therefore the Chanter will put all in a position to imbibe its good, he will do all he can to prevent error, which is the same as harm.

The sandpainting, as a sacred, living entity, must be treated with proper respect; this explains why the painting is subject to ritual disposal after use and why it is crucial that the remains of the painting not come into contact with domestic animals and that these remains be allowed "to return unmolested to the earth" by natural processes (Reichard 1950:343).

Because the painting is a living entity, replete with power and sacredness, one must not act disrespectfully in its presence. The chanter helps to remind people of the painting's sacredness by explaining various aspects of the image: "While they are making the sandpainting, the chanter tells whoever is sitting there why the forms are as they are. He explains not just the meaning, but also how they came to be" (Consultant A). This explanation helps all those present to maintain the proper frame of mind, which is crucial to the efficacy of the ceremonial.

Ideally, everything surrounding the ceremonial must be done in a consciousness of harmony, from the time of inception when the immediate family visits relatives to notify them of the ceremonial, indirectly seeking their aid, until the moment when the patient is allowed to wash on the fourth day following the close of the ceremonial. Everyone has the responsibility of participating with a "good heart." Through proper actions and correct thoughts, those present help the patient by *hózhǫ́ ntséskees,* or "thinking in beauty" (Harry Walters, personal communication, 1990).

This means that all those who are present not only during the use of the sandpainting but also at its creation should participate or watch in the correct spirit. A good heart means clearing the mind of everyday worries and preoccupations and substituting thoughts of sacredness, respect, and the true meaning of the prayers and the myths behind them. As we will see in the next chapter, sacred space must be recreated through time; so, too, the proper frame of mind and heart must be continuously created. It is not enough to think of the ceremony's meaning at its inception and then to allow your thoughts to drift back to the new pickup truck you want to buy so that you can drive to the Navajo Fair in Shiprock in two weeks. Ideally, one should focus throughout the ceremony on the meaning of the words in the prayers.

Navajos do not always deal directly with disruptive elements at a ceremonial. A good example of this is the way drunken individuals are treated. Because ceremonials are a social occasion, alcohol, although forbidden, is often present, particularly at the large ceremonial performances. At a Male Shootingway in 1989 I saw a highly intoxicated Navajo in the ceremonial hogan while the sandpainting was being made. I later asked the chanter's son why his father had not forced the drunken man to leave. He explained, "When my father performs a ceremony, he concentrates very hard. He thinks only of the ceremony and gets himself into a harmonious, peaceful state of mind that he must concentrate to keep because there are so many distractions. If he got angry at the drunken man, my father's peaceful state of mind would be disrupted."

The son's wife added, "Navajos respect the individual. Nobody wanted to tell him [the drunken man] to leave because that isn't respectful. And something inside him drew him to the ceremony. He was supposed to be there and maybe it will help him to change. A seed might have been planted to help him see another way. It isn't our place to turn anyone away."

Navajos weigh the potential costs of disruption. The chanter must strive to keep his tranquility and concentration, while those present hope that a disruptive person will be calmed and healed by the powers invoked at the ceremony. In the situation just described, the individual ultimately was forced to leave by a member of the patient's family because he became too disruptive of everyone else's frame of mind, so that his presence threatened to destroy the air of solemnity and sacredness, which would have had an effect upon the outcome of the ceremonial itself.

The concept of continuous, regenerative movement is also reflected in the nature of the sandpainting image; this image is not fixed or bounded in space or in time but rather is fluid and dynamic. As I will explain later, space extends both horizontally and vertically so that the powers of the sacred light phenomena located in each of the four directions, as well as the powers of the heavens and the earth, are drawn into the painting for the purpose of healing. Time, as well, is compressed so that powerful mythic events of the past coexist with the present for the restoration of harmony and well-being.

The significance of order and symmetry of form in the sandpainting image cannot be overestimated. Illness, as we have seen, results from a disruption of universal order and balance, and ceremonials work by restoring order to the spiritual, emotional, mental, and thus physical realms of the patient's life. Through the ceremonial the patient's perception of the world is altered. The sandpainting plays a major role in this restructuring of reality by bringing the chaotic under control as it replaces disorder with order.

One of the fundamental characteristics of any sandpainting is the pain-staking order in which the image is laid out: tape measures and yardsticks ensure that forms are equidistant and equivalent in size; taut string assures the straightness and perfect alignment of figures and shapes; cans and even wire cookie-cutter-like patterns are pressed into the sand to make sure that forms are identically shaped. The placement of the first symbol is the subject of much deliberation so that successive forms will have sufficient space to expand outward with the regularity they require. It is especially important that directional symbolism be equidistant and identical in shape and size, for only then can it summon the powers of the four directions into the painting for the purpose of healing. Balance and symmetry are *essential* for the proper invocation of these supernatural presences. A great deal of consideration, for instance, goes into the placement of the four shallow bowls of water at the base of Sky-Reaching-Rock (plate 5), in order to be absolutely certain that the "lake" in each directional quadrant has the proper orientation and is equidistant from the base of this supernatural rock. This is linked to the concept of interrelated totality (which will be discussed at greater length later): each part is an essential component of the whole, playing a crucial role in the realignment of the patient to the balance and order inherent in the cosmos.

Earlier, I discussed the Navajos' recognition of thought as creative and attractive and their understanding that things must exist in the mind before they can manifest themselves in the outer world. As any doctor will attest, a patient who actively believes in his healing has a much greater chance of recovery. By interacting with complex images of a supernatural world wherein miraculous events are possible and even commonplace, the patient begins to accept the possibility of his healing. The sandpainted image is a means of projecting the mind through time and space, allowing the patient to rise above present limitations and to bring forth desired results. The sandpainting focuses the mind on order, symmetry, and sacred healing power, bringing into action the powerful force of the human imagination.

The sandpainting is unusual as performative ritual art because of the lengthy period that goes into its preparation before its ritual use. Although the effect of participation in the sandpainting's creation is not explicitly acknowledged as healing or beneficial, clearly, this creative process is profoundly powerful for the participants.

The creative endeavor,[10] by its very nature, is one of bringing order out of chaos. To create order one must think about order. Conversely, as order is established on the hogan floor in painted images, so too order becomes uppermost in the thoughts of all those who are present. As they carefully measure the alignment and positioning of each form and figure, they cannot help but think about the orderly universe they are creating in sand, thus deriving a deeper understanding of one of the key principles of the universe.

Spider Woman taught the allegorical string figures, such as the one depicted in plate 7, to the Navajo to help them "keep our thinking in order" and thus also keep "our lives in order" (a Navajo father, in Toelken [1979: 96]). The activity of making the sandpainting requires the same kind of total concentration and also brings the principle of order to a conscious level of awareness, thus becoming a healing activity in and of itself.

The chanter and his helpers focus their energies, for as long as eight to ten hours, on the restructured, orderly reality they are participating in bringing forth. In so doing, they become at one with the work at hand, losing themselves in a state of creative flow. I have seen this state of rapt attention in the faces of the assistants. The helpers, completely involved in their task, are transported to a higher state in which the physical and spiritual become one. However, this is not in any way a trance state, for they remain clearly in touch with the here and now; anyone who has watched a sacred sandpainting being made remarks on the lighthearted banter that goes on in the hogan. But all creative endeavors necessitate mindfulness, a state of intensely focused awareness in which there is an element of losing the egocentric self and of giving one's self completely to the endeavor.

There is clearly a devotional, meditative component that goes into the creation of the sandpainting, for it is a shared activity in which all are contributing toward a higher purpose, namely, the creation of a restructured reality. Through their joint efforts, this previously inaccessible world located in a space-time frame far removed from everyday reality will become accessible to the patient and to all who are present. As the workers create the portion of the painting in front of them, their inner gaze is fixed on the mythic, supernatural landscape or figures to which they are giving expression.

Part of the sacred beauty and power of the sandpainting—its presence—derives from the spirit that is brought to it during its creation; those who participate in its making are aware of fulfilling this responsibility. At the same time, participation in this process cannot help but enrich them, for they are using their gifts in support and affirmation of the spiritual values that underlie the ceremonial. Clearly, all who are engaged in this creative endeavor must feel a certain level of spiritual fulfillment from having contributed to the restoration of harmony and balance in the cosmos.

How do Navajos themselves view the sandpainting designs? Wyman (1983a:79–80) observed that Navajos derive satisfaction from the correctness of the depiction because this determines whether it will "work as a sacred tool to attract the supernatural beings depicted in it." He went on to say that although there is nothing we would understand as an aesthetic value judgment concerning sandpainting in the vast recorded Navajo mythology, there is evidence for a concept of the beautiful. Wyman (1983a:79) paraphrased Ethel Albert's (1956:234) remarks:

> The notion that something could be useless but pretty or beautiful but bad is foreign to Navajo thinking. Anything that is good is good for something. It is as if the Navajo is convinced that beauty must work as a powerful instrument. It is likely that when the singer leans back with a sigh of satisfaction and silently observes the finished sandpainting, he is not only looking for mistakes that would interfere with its function but is also admiring its beauty.

This approach to beauty as playing an integral and useful role in healing is related to N. Scott Momaday's (1976:84) account of Native American attitudes toward the environment. Momaday explained that the "aesthetic distance" employed by the nineteenth-century "nature poets" to look at nature and to write about it was a notion completely alien to Indians because, in their mind, nature is not something they push away so that they can focus upon it from a distance. Nature, instead, is an element within which Native Americans exist as an integral part.

Similarly, in the Navajo mind, beauty and sacredness are so intertwined, with the latter overshadowing the former, that the inclination seldom arises for aesthetic contemplation. Of course, things that are created to please and to attract the gods should be beautiful and should meet the highest standards of physical excellence. For the Navajo, the sandpainting's beauty is expected, and therefore overlooked.

When I commented on the beauty of the sandpainted forms, Consultant A replied in a puzzled tone of voice, "I never thought of them that way." When Anglos look at sandpaintings, they see images of great beauty; when Navajos look at sandpaintings, they see images of sacred power.

However, before the painting has been completed and sanctified, moments do occur when the helpers pause briefly to consider their progress. Even though their overriding concern is the proper creation of a powerfully sacred entity, at a certain level, part of the satisfaction that they derive at this time must surely be aesthetic, particularly if we use Boas's definition of aesthetic as a certain standard of excellence that is demonstrated through the technical treatment and control of the processes involved. "The judgment of perfection of technical form is essentially an esthetic judgment," said Boas (1955:10). We must also release the culture-bound notion of the aesthetic as an expression only of individual creativity. This aspect of creativity is not a part of Navajo ritual images, for sandpaintings, the product of many hands and minds, severely limit creative expression in the depiction of sandpainting forms.

Two Navajo words relate to a concept of beauty: *nizhóní* and *hózhóní*. The former means "to be pretty, nice, beautiful, good-looking, attractive" and comes from the stem Øzhóní, "to be pretty" (Young and Morgan 1980:665), while the latter comes from the stem Øzhǫ́, "to be beautiful, peaceful, harmonious" (Young and Morgan 1980:459). Clearly, outer and inner beauty are related in Navajo thought. An experience that I had in April 1986 provides some insight not only into how sandpainting images are chosen but also into the nature of the intimate relationship between beauty and sacredness.

I was sitting inside a ceremonial hogan watching the preparation of a Male Shootingway sandpainting that depicted the Buffalo People. The patient was a Male Shootingway chanter himself (Chanter A) and, although another chanter (Chanter B) was conducting the nine-night ceremonial, the patient-chanter wandered into the hogan, pacing the floor and observing the sandpainting from all angles. In these unusual circumstances, the patient-chanter chose the specific paintings to be produced for his healing as well as directing their production. Between four and eight men and women worked on the sandpainting, at times laughing together or talking quietly. The chanter sat nearby watching their progress. The patient-chanter took a more active role by freely criticizing the work of the assistants, pointing with a weaving batten to specific figures and details that did not meet his standards. Accordingly, the responsible man or woman would patiently cover the offending form with tan sand and begin that portion again under the watchful direction of the patient-chanter. During this period of ceremonial preparation, the patient-chanter clearly directed more of the sandpainting's creation than did the chanter who was to perform the ceremonial.

When the patient-chanter was pleased with the forms produced, he uttered the word, "*Nizhóní.*" He was clearly feeling quite satisfied because the forms were stylistically, and thus ritually, correct. However, he was expressing much more than the limited Western notion of "beauty" or even "beauty as stylistic accuracy." Boas (1955:10) referred to the emotional response generated not by form alone, but by the close associations that exist between the form and the ideas held by a people. Although Boas was referring primarily to the ideas held by a cultural group, this concept also applies to individuals within the group, and especially to ceremonial specialists like Navajo chanters.

When I later asked the patient-chanter why he had chosen this particular sandpainting of the entire Male Shootingway repertoire of appropriate sandpaintings for this day of the ceremonial, he told me that the Buffalo People have a special meaning for him and for Chanter B, who was performing this ceremonial. This particular image evoked memories of stories that his parents had told him, memories of a former time. "Buffalo Pass [near Lukachukai] over there," he gestured toward his right, "was named for the buffalo. They used to be all around here." He went on to explain, "Because the buffalo are special to me and to the chanter [who is conducting this ceremonial] the Buffalo sandpainting is even more powerful." It soon became clear that this sandpainting had been chosen primarily for its emotive, evocative power. Using an emotionally charged sandpainting—one bearing not just cultural significance but deep personal significance as well—greatly enhances the curing process.

As this story illustrates, the process of the sandpainting's creation is one of bringing *hózhǫ́,* a state of blessed conditions, into tangible form. The patient-chanter was deeply satisfied with the orderliness of the sandpainting's unfoldment as the forms took their correct placement and shape. The physical beauty of the sandpainting was but the outer reflection of the sandpainting's inner beauty and sacredness.

✠ 4 ✠
Cosmological Order as a Model for Navajo Philosophy and Life

As my understanding of the components of Navajo ritual images and the philosophy behind these images increased, I found that specific visual images indexed key aspects of Navajo philosophy. In trying to see this relationship from a broader perspective, I realized how cosmological order serves as a model for Navajo philosophy, which in turn is expressed visually in ritual images.

In his detailed, comprehensive analysis of the Male Shootingway ceremonial, McAllester (1980:199–237) found that myth and ritual reiterate such pervasive aspects of Navajo philosophy and worldview as duality, pairing, alternation, reciprocation, progression, and sequence. He concluded, "There is plentiful evidence of a universe ordered down to minute detail."

Cosmological order serves as a model for Zuni philosophy as well. M. Jane Young (1988:95) hypothesized that "the order apparent in the cosmos acts as a paradigm for the Zunis, a model for conceptually organizing their visual and verbal art." This means that the Zunis' perceptions of the motions of the sun, moon, and stars, as well as their temporal and spatial concepts, serve as an organizing principle for such diverse expressions as ritual poetry and figures carved on rocks and mesa walls and in caves surrounding the pueblo.

The increasing interest in the study of indigenous astronomical systems has added a new dimension to studies of Native American cultures by demonstrating the influence of perceptions of cosmological phenomena on their ways of organizing the world. Both Gary Urton (1981), in his field work in the Quechua-speaking village of Misminay, Peru, and Von Del Chamberlain (1982), in his study of ethnohistorical records of the Skidi Pawnee, discovered that these groups perceive a patterned mirroring between the celestial and terrestrial spheres. The people of both cultures arrange their physical surroundings to reflect their perceptions of the heavens. Thus, the Skidi Pawnee sometimes arranged their villages in terms of celestial constellations, while the inhabitants of Misminay build footpaths and canals that mirror the intersecting axes of the Milky Way. On a more abstract level, in both groups celestial entities and phenomena are integrated into cosmology in a consistent and coherent pattern that underlies many earthly activities, such as agriculture and socioreligious practices.

The approach taken in this book is that cosmological order—that is, Navajo conceptions of time and space, as well as perceptions of solar, lunar, and stellar motions—serves as a model for Navajo philosophy. Not only does their cosmological outlook form an organizing principle for the Navajos' ritual images and procedure, but also what Anglos call cosmological bodies and phenomena (which are Navajo Holy People) possess the ability to influence human thought and conduct.

THE REFLECTION OF COSMOLOGICAL ORDER IN NAVAJO THOUGHT

Agricultural groups, such as the Zunis, devote most of their attention to the apparent recurrent motion of the sun, which they call "Our Father the Sun" (Young 1988:95–96). While the sun is vitally important to Navajo thought, the Navajos consider the various components of the heavens to be of equal importance and usually do not single out any one celestial entity for symbolic parentage.[1] Instead, it is much more common to hear Navajos say, "The sky is our father" (Yádiłhił nihitaa'). The sun may be the main subject of a sandpainting, but more commonly it is but one component of a night sky consisting of stars, sun, and moon.[2]

Although the apparent daily motion of the sun is responsible for the four cardinal light phenomena, its annual motion is not significant for the Navajo. It is easy to understand why a people as geographically dispersed as the Navajo would focus on the annual motion of constellations rather than on that of the sun: constellations appear at about the same time within the approximately 18 million acres of reservation and lease lands (Wyman 1983a:11), while the annual motion of the sun along the horizon varies with location.

Traditionally, it is the annual appearance of specific constellations and, in some cases, the moon that marks the beginning of the winter ceremonial season during which the Night Way can be performed, the time when certain stories can be told, the time when planting should begin and cease, the quality of the harvest and the weather conditions at the time of harvest, and the appropriate time for the hunting of certain animals.

The order inherent in the repetitive annual motions of the cosmos is reflected in Navajo thought with its emphasis on dynamic order, or orderliness, which must be continuously recreated through time. Creation itself occurred *nizhónígo,* or "in an orderly and proper way." (The enclitic *-go* at the end of the word means "in that way" and denotes a continuing process.) Rather than being a static quality, orderliness must be continuously recreated just as the constellations reappear annually and move in their established patterns and as the sun moves daily across the sky.

The pervasive concepts of motion and regeneration also find expression in the transitory nature of sacred space, which must be resanctified with each use. The Navajo hogan stands in sharp contrast to the Zuni kiva: while the hogan doubles as both everyday living space and the site of ceremonial activity, the kiva, with its permanent altars, remains separate from family dwellings. Ceremonies mark the transformation of the hogan from the site of everyday living to the place of ceremonial activity.

A remark of Consultant A illustrates the significance of duration in the definition of sacred space. We were discussing the physical boundaries of the sacred space around the consecrated hogan. When I described the space between the doorway of the hogan and the set-out mound about six feet to the east of the doorway as *hodiyiin,* consecrated space in which domestic animals must not be allowed, she corrected me: "To say 'sacred space' makes it sound permanent when it isn't. *Hodiyiin* really means 'it is in the state of being blessed' or 'at this moment in time it is blessed.'" Thus, sacredness, with regard to space, must be continually renewed.

The concept of regeneration/resanctification is also embodied in the treatment of the chanter's *jish,* or medicine bundle, which requires renewal "to bring life back into those things" (Navajo consultant, in Aberle [1966:199]). Nightway masks (also considered to be *jish* because of polysemic and synecdochic features of the word *jish* [Frisbie 1987:12–13]) must also be refurbished before they can be used in a ceremonial; again, we see the principle of regeneration and renewal through resanctification.

Cosmological order is also reflected in the Navajo conception of wholeness; inherent in this view is the understanding that each part or facet is interrelated and equally necessary to the totality. A basic element of this concept is the understanding that the completed entity is much more powerful than the sum of its parts; power derives from the state of completeness. As we will see later, this is a major reason why the completed sandpainting is so powerful.

One model for this concept is the annual cycle of the earth with its seasonal changes (caused by its tilt toward or away from the sun): each part of this cycle has a unique and vital role, and no part is more important than any other because each is necessary to the whole. In Navajo thought, the entire year is much more powerful than the sum of the seasons because it represents the completion of a cycle. Similarly, each of the four times of day and each of the four stages of life is valued as an equally important and essential part of the whole, with the completed cycle being most powerful of all.

Complementarity and the number four are important aspects of this concept of order and wholeness—interrelated totality—in Navajo thought. What Anglos call the pairing of opposites Navajos conceptualize as the halves of a whole, with each half necessary for completeness. As Consultant A explained, "When you say 'opposites' it sounds like each part is whole by itself. It misses the point because you need to include them both." The fundamental distinction between male and female has already been discussed. Other examples of such essential, complementary pairs are life-death, night-day, and dawn–evening twilight. Later in this chapter, I will explain how the four Sacred Mountains "keep each other in check" by embodying the principle of balance, for they are conceptualized as two pairs.

The pairing of *hózhǫ́,* all that is good, beautiful, and harmonious, with *hóchxǫ́,* that which is evil, ugly, and worthless, could be considered to be a reflection of cosmological order at a very abstract level. Rather than having a fixed, absolute moral quality, these terms are better conceptualized "as temporary, although cyclically reappearing, points in an ongoing process" (Farella 1984:36). For example, when one kills an enemy in war, the death is *nichxóní* but the act is not immoral; the heroism displayed is, in fact, *nizhóní* (Farella 1984:35). (In this example, *nichxóní* means contaminating and therefore, ugly, while *nizhóní* means beneficial and therefore, beautiful.) Each is necessary for the existence of the other and gains meaning from its complement; they are two halves of the same whole.

The number four is often perceived as two pairs and also plays a key role in the establishment and maintenance of order. Just as a pair is composed of the halves of a whole rather than of independent opposites, the four components represent four equally essential parts of the whole. There are four kinds of corn (white, yellow, blue, and variegated) and four kinds of Sky People (Sky, Sun, Water, and Summer); attempts to overcome evils or to create new things are usually unsuccessful three times and successful the fourth (Matthews 1897:74, 93, 95, 110); to announce their presence supernaturals commonly give their call four times, beginning with a faint sound that becomes increasingly nearer and louder (Matthews 1897:104). This emphasis on pairing and the number four is reflected in Chanter A's categorization of the eight major Navajo constellations into four male/female pairs, with each pair representing a successively older age of one's "walk through life" (see tables 4.1 and 4.2).[3]

Related to the concept of wholeness, or interrelated totality, is another important Navajo concept, that of increase/augmentation. In the story of Navajo Creation, each of the successive lower worlds was more ordered than the one(s) before it. The First World, inhabited by insects, was the most chaotic and was characterized by confusion, uncertainty, and error (Reichard 1950:16). Each subsequent upward migration toward emergence onto the earth's surface led to greater stability, order, and knowledge.

The progressive quality of the upward migration embodies this concept of increase/augmentation. The previous hemispheres are described as being superimposed, with each higher hemisphere being "larger than the one below it since the characteristics of the lower were imitated and added to, and the whole was magically enlarged" (Reichard 1950:14).

Many scholars (Reichard 1950:349–51; Kluckhohn and Wyman 1940: 76–104; McAllester 1980:234) have observed the kind of augmentation of ritual activity that occurs during the latter days and nights of Navajo ceremonials; this means that an increase in activity leads to several climaxes,

Table 4.1. Chanter A's Constellation Categories

Life Stage	Male	Female
Babyhood	Náhookǫs bikạ'ii (Big Dipper)	Náhookǫs ba'áadii (Cassiopeia)
Adolescence	Dilyéhé (the Pleiades)	'Átsé'ets'ózí (Orion)
Adulthood	Hastiin Sik'ai'í (Corvus)	'Átsé'etsoh (front part of Scorpius)
Old age	Gah heet'e'ii (tail of Scorpius)	Yikáísdáhí (the Milky Way)

Table 4.2. Chanter B's Constellation Categories

Directional Association	Paired Constellations		Unpaired Constellations
	Male	Female	
East			Yikáísdáhí
South			Hastiin Sik'ai'í
West			Dilyéhé, 'Átsé'etsoh
North	Náhookǫs biką'ii	Náhookǫs ba'áadii	
No Directional Association	Sǫ'tsoh	Cane of 'Átsé'etsoh	
	Gah heet'e'ii	'Átsé'ets'ózí	

each of which incorporates ideas from all that went before, together with many new ritual developments. These ceremonial climaxes are so important that the last day is called *bijį* (its day) and the final night is called *bitł'éé* (its night).[4] This Navajo concept of increase through accumulation is particularly evident in the four cardinal light phenomena, which are associated with all acts of creation and are described in Navajo creation myths as "giving birth" to various Navajo supernaturals.

Figure 4.1 and plate 2 illustrate sequential views of the Navajo cos-

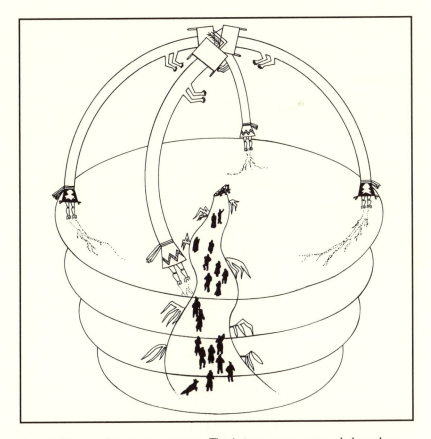

Fig. 4.1. The pre-Emergence universe. The beings emerge upward through a sequence of previous worlds to arrive eventually at the earth's surface. According to some accounts, the present world is the Fourth World, while others hold that this is the Fifth World.

mos, including the Emergence and Creation, as my Navajo colleagues described it. Significantly, Chanter A objected to the depiction of pre- and post-Emergence events in a single diagram. The underworlds are not mentioned in the Blessingway myth, which is the cornerstone and beginning of Navajo chantway ceremonials; because the underworlds are associated with witchcraft, it is wrong to connect them with the present world. Figure 4.1 portrays the three previous worlds—many Navajos believe there were four previous worlds—and the present world. The beings had no definite form and were slowly transformed, as they progressed upward through a hollow reed, passing through successive worlds, into human beings. The sun, moon, and stars had not yet been created and the only light came from Dawn Boy, Daylight Girl, Sunset Girl, and Darkness Boy, who are represented in human form at each of the four directions.

Plate 2 illustrates the present world after the Emergence. In the center is the lake that filled the Place of Emergence. The four cardinal light phenomena are once again represented in the form of four Holy People who are intimately connected to the four Sacred Mountains, the four directions, the four sacred plants, and the four times of day, which are represented in trapezoidal form. Over the earth lie four sky layers. The sun, moon, stars, and an opening to the sky beyond, the skyhole (*yáyóhokáá'*), are found in the highest level, called *hahadonzeh*. Various thunders and winds live in all four layers.

THE SACRED MOUNTAINS

Another view of the world bounded by the four Sacred Mountains is illustrated in figure 4.2, an interpretation that focuses on the earth as a sacred, living being. As Haile (1970a:16) explained, the Sacred Mountains were placed at the cardinal points to strengthen the earth, and the inner forms of these mountains had the capability of giving names to one another. In sunwise order (that is, from east to south, west, and north) the Sacred Mountains are Sis Naajiní (Blanca Peak), Tsoodził (Mount Taylor), Dook'o' oosłííd (San Francisco Peaks), and Dibé Nitsaa (Hesperus Peak).

The Navajo name of the Sacred Mountain of the south can be translated as Tongue Mountain; in the Blessingway myth it is the tongue of the inner form of the earth. The Sacred Mountain of the north is the heart of the earth's inner form (Haile 1970a:18). Between these two lies the earth's "breathing means," or diaphragm.

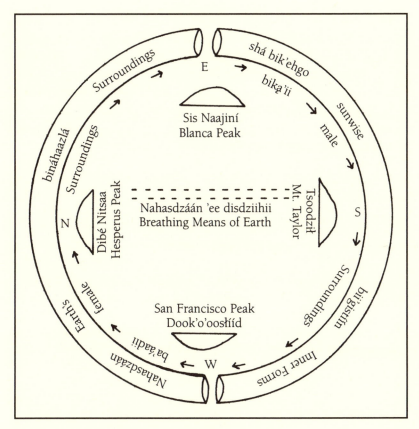

Fig. 4.2. The four Sacred Mountains. (Adapted from Haile [n.d.]. Courtesy Special Collections, University of Arizona Library.)

Harry Walters explained that the earth's diaphragm is Hogback, a geological fault that lies between Shiprock and Farmington, while its mouth is Gobernador Knob (Ch'óol'į́'í). (The Sacred Mountains are shown on the map in figure 1.1) He continued,

Each of the Sacred Mountains and the four directions have their own Holy Person who is either male or female. They are each paired. The Holy Person of the East is Talking God and is male and is paired with hogan God who is female and represents the West. Born-for-Water is the Holy Person of the South and is female[5] and is paired with Monster Slayer, the Holy Person of the North, who is male. There are pairs of Mountains within the four Sacred Mountains, and

chi

they face each other and keep each other in check. There is a word which talks about all this: *ałch'jsilá,* which means "balance."

Thus, the Sacred Mountains play an active role in maintaining the dynamic order of the universe. Not only are these mountains alive individually but they also exist as a single entity. Once more, we see evidence of a universe whose parts are grouped into complementary pairs with both halves necessary for completion. Power derives from the wholeness and completeness of the entire group—in this case, the totality of the four Sacred Mountains.

WIND AND INNER FORMS

Two other concepts essential to the Navajo view of an ordered, structured universe are those of *nłch'i,* or the Holy Wind, and the inner forms. After the Emergence onto the earth's surface, wind and inner forms were placed within all living things as a source of life, movement, speech, and behavior (Haile 1943b:76–83).

Rather than being an independent spiritual agency that resides within the individual, like the Western notion of the soul, Holy Wind is a single entity that exists everywhere and in which all living beings participate (McNeley 1981:52–53). The concept of the Holy Wind has far-reaching implications. First, it exists as an underlying element that unifies beings and phenomena that Anglos perceive as distinct and isolated entities: deer, bison, spiders, stars, clouds, and piñon pines share the unifying element of the Wind, which exists within all of them. This means that all living beings are related and that nothing exists in isolation. Inherent in this relationship is a sense of kinship with other living beings and of the reciprocal responsibilities that accompany kinship. This means that the earth and the animals and plants that live on it (as well as the sky with its entities and phenomena) are related to and will provide for humankind as long as humanity recognizes and carries out its reciprocal responsibilities toward the other beings and phenomena of earth and sky.

Furthermore, breath and speech are intimately related to the concept of Holy Wind. *Nłch'i* also refers to air and thus involves the act of breathing. Because *nłch'i* has a holy quality not acknowledged in Western culture (McNeley 1981), the act of breathing is a sacred act through which the individual participates in an ongoing relationship with all other living beings. This is why it is possible for the patient in a ceremonial actually to breathe in the life-giving power of the sun outside the hogan, as described in chapter 3.

The intimate relationship between speech and breath—and thus, the life principle—makes the speech act sacred. Words have a sacred, creative power and the ability to summon forth that which is uttered. In Navajo Creation stories, the Holy People spoke, sang, and prayed the world into existence (Klah 1942:56–60; Witherspoon 1977:15–16).

Finally, because of the essentially unitary nature of the Holy Wind, it is the same force that animates the Holy People themselves with life, movement, speech, and behavior. Individual human beings therefore have "direct access to the thought and speech of the Holy Ones" (McNeley 1981:54).

The inner form, or *bii'gistíín* ("one who lies within it" or "an inanimate object lies within"), is a being independent of the object it happens to occupy (Haile 1943b:68, 69). As Haile explained, the entity or phenomenon itself is not animated but a humanlike personification, a soul, is placed within it. Human beings also have inner forms. Because of the inner form concept, the sun's disk (*shá*) is quite distinct from its carrier (*jóhonaa'éí,* who carries a round object here and there in daytime). Significantly, a solar eclipse is called *jóhonaa'éí daaztsá* (who carries a round object here and there in daytime died), which means that it is the inner form of the sun that has died rather than the (unanimated) sun disk itself (Haile 1943b:68).

Because each person has an inner form and participates in the omnipresent Holy Wind, each has a Holy Person located within. Harry Walters (personal communication, 1990) explained that people contact these inner beings by breathing; therefore, the human voice box—the means of breathing and of speech—is where the Holy Person lives. Just as the inner form is independent of the entity it occupies, so too this inner Holy Person is not a part of people's physical being. This conceptualization embodies the sacredness of Holy Wind: the reason why the acts of breathing and speaking are sacred is because the *diyin dine'é,* the Holy People, are everywhere, within everyone.

With the peace that comes of the realization of oneness with the universe comes the responsibility to live as the Holy People live, by treating one's fellow creatures on this planet with the same respect that one would have toward oneself. As we will see in chapter 7, the "Mother Earth, Father Sky" sandpainting is so powerful precisely because it stands as the visual embodiment of this fundamental relationship, reconnecting the individual to all other living beings of the earth and of the sky.

THE TEMPORAL MARKERS OF THE NAVAJO UNIVERSE

After the beings had emerged onto the earth's surface, there was a need for an orderly division of time. In chanter Frank Mitchell's version of Blessing-way, First Man addressed this issue, saying,

> "This particular [thing, the sun] in [the light] of which we will be moving about, does as yet not exist. . . . Nor [do] the time periods which are to intervene between each other from now on. . . . That by which . . . [day and night] are to be recognized has not as yet had our attention. At present we are merely continuing our working [period] without established order, whereas there is as yet no resting period . . . concerning these plants, the means of specifying the time of their action and of putting on their different colors [the seasons] is still an unsettled matter. . . . The time too in which those on the upper side [the heavenly bodies] will move about is a point to which you should also give your attention" (in Wyman [1970a:366]).

In this speech, First Man was proposing an orderly arrangement of time periods—a succession of day and night for labor and rest, a winter and summer season for growth and harvest by which the Earth Surface People could sustain themselves. He also called for regularity in the movements of stars and constellations across the heavens. From the passage quoted above, it is clear how fundamental the repetitive annual motions of the cosmos are to the Navajo conception of order. In response to First Man's speech, four sets of markers were created to divide and organize time: the sun and moon, the seasons, the constellations, and the cardinal light phenomena.

Jóhonaa'éí, the Sun, and Tł'éhonaa'éí, the Moon

First Man appointed He-Who-Returns-Carrying-One-Turquoise to carry the sun disk, Jóhonaa'éí, and He-Who-Returns-Carrying-One-Corn-Kernel to be the bearer of the moon disk, Tł'éhonaa'éí. These two entities represent the first set of complementary pairs, the stronger, male sun and the weaker, female moon.

Another primary contrast, that of birth and death, came into existence because of the sun bearer's demand for payment for carrying the celestial disk across the sky. He says, "I will not go down without a man's death. Every time I make this journey, let a man's death occur accordingly" (Frank Mitchell, in Wyman [1970a:379]). In return, he agrees, "You [will] see whatever you may presently be doing on its [the earth's] surface, I will keep all of that visible for you, and wherever movable things occur, I will keep all of them recognizable for you" (Frank Mitchell, in Wyman [1970a:379]). The moon carrier, when asked his opinion, says,

"I am now in control of this night [part]! . . . births in the future including any and every kind of birth will mostly occur at night, births will be more frequent at night.[6] That will be a cause for rejoicing. Oppositely too, deaths will occur only at night" (Frank Mitchell, in Wyman [1970a:380]).

The sun and moon, in addition to supplying illumination, provide the orderly arrangement of time periods proposed by First Man: the light of the sun marks the beginning of day; its disappearance marks the end. The moon is in charge of nightly events as well as vegetation and the monthly cycle. The sun's movement along the horizon is responsible for the seasons, which are marked by the appearance of specific constellations.

The Seasons: *Hai*, Winter, and *Shį*, Summer

Traditionally, the Navajo divide the year into only two seasons of approximately equal length. Again, complements are paired. The two seasons are represented in figure 4.3. This sandpainting from the Upward Reachingway depicts a central figure with the darker sky of winter to his left and the lighter summer sky to his right; constellations sparkle in each oval of sky.

The division of the year into twelve months may also have been superimposed on traditional Navajo concepts. This may be why only some of the months have specific constellations associated with them. Four of the months were said to have feather headdresses composed of the following constellations: November (Nłch'its'ósí, Time of Slender Wind) had Hastiin Sik'ai'í (Old Man with Legs Ajar) as its feather; December (Nłch'itsoh, Great Wind) had 'Átsé'etsoh (First Big One); January (Yas Niłt'ees, Crusted Snow) had Yikáísdáhí (Awaits-the-Dawn); and February ('Atsá Biyáázh, Baby Eagle) had Gah heet'e'ii (Rabbit Tracks). In July (Ya'iishjáátsoh, Great Seed Ripening), Dilyéhé (which has no agreed-upon English translation) appears in the early morning (Sandoval [Hastiin Tlo'tsi hee], in O'Bryan [1956:16–21]).

Chamberlain's (1983) identification of these constellations varies slightly from O'Bryan's. The following constellations rise heliacally—that is, they first appear in the morning sky before the sun comes up—at the following times: in November, Hastiin Sik'ai'í (Corvus) appears (O'Bryan identifies this as Orion); in December, 'Átsé'etsoh (the front of Scorpius, or at least Antares) is visible; in January, the brighter part of Yikáísdáhí (Milky Way) begins to

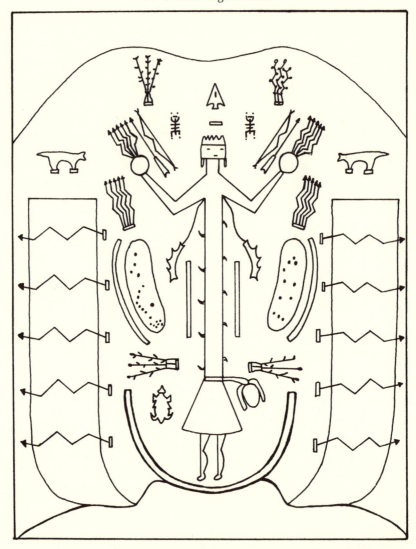

Fig. 4.3. "The One Who Controls the Rain," Upward Reachingway Evilway. (Adapted from a painting collected by Newcomb; singer, Bit'ahnii Bidághaa'í, 1936. Courtesy Wheelwright Museum, P21 #8.)

appear like false dawn; in February, Gah heet'e'ii (the tail of Scorpius) appears (O'Bryan identifies this as a star cluster under Canis Major); and by July Dilyéhé (the Pleiades) is visible before the morning light (Chamberlain 1983:52).

The traditional Navajo year follows the rhythm of the seasons as natural, cosmological order directs specific activities associated with each month for all forms of life on earth. The year begins with *Ghąąjį'* (October), which marks the "dividing of the seasons": *hai* not only means "winter" but also means "the parting of the seasons," signifying the division between winter and summer. (The information on the seasons is based on material developed by Andy Bia in Roessel [1981:108-111]). In *Ghąąjį'* the leaves turn to orange and yellow; animals grow shaggy winter coats and prepare for hibernation; birds migrate or store food; humans prepare for winter camp by harvesting and storing corn and other food and collecting wood and warm clothing. *Níłch'its'ósí* (November) is the month for hunting and for the gathering of grass and plant seeds that will be ground into flour for bread cakes to be eaten in the winter. The sun's light grows dimmer as the winds become colder and frost and snow increase. *Níłch'itsoh* (December) is a time of heavy snow and intense wind as both animals and humans hibernate or seek shelter. Traditionally, planting sticks are prepared this month so that the wood will be smooth and well-seasoned when planting time arrives in the spring; women tan hides and make moccasins. Winter games—moccasin games and string games (See Plate 7)—are played to develop right thinking; stories are told to instruct children in the right way to live; and winter ceremonials are held. In *Yas Niłt'ees* (January) there are more ceremonials; preparations are made for the planting of corn; coyotes breed. *'Atsá Biyáázh* (February) is the month of changeable winds as the "first chief of the winds" shakes the earth to awaken sleeping plants, bears, lizards, and snakes, and the first plants emerge from the earth. The ground and ice crack, as do the eagle's eggs. This is the last month in which it is proper to tell the sacred stories. In *Wóózhch'ííd* (March) white thunder begins to sound for summer rain as all living beings awaken from their long winter rest: animals give birth; birds sing once again in the canyons; and leaves burst forth. Ceremonials are held to bless the fields in preparation for planting.

T'ą́ą́chil (April) begins *shį́*, summer, and is a time of growth and emergence as the days grow longer and warmer and the sun's light becomes stronger. Baby birds grow feathers; the sheep grow more wool; and plants sprout. Early *T'ą́ą́tsoh* (May) is planting season, a time of rain and spring snow, wind, and thunder. Flowers blossom, plants produce pollen, and young birds learn to fly. In *Ya'iishją́ą́schchilí* (June) the stories, songs, and prayers center on agriculture. *Ya'iishją́ą́tsoh* (July) is a time of gathering seeds and guarding fields and of asking the earth and the Holy People to bless the plants; the deer give birth. In *Bini'ant'ą́ą́ts'ózí* (August) wild fruits—strawberries, cholla berries, and yucca fruit—are gathered. The final month of the year, *Bini'ant'ą́ą́tsoh* (September), marks the beginning of harvest as the first foodstuffs are stored for the coming of winter.

Not only are specific activities associated with the months marked by the arrival of these constellations, but also, in some cases, the quality of the constellation's appearance is of great significance. Tł'aii (in Newcomb [1966:206]) explains that the appearance of Hastiin Sik'ai'í (Corvus) in the eastern sky at harvesttime predicts the quality of the harvest: if the stars in this constellation appear full and bright, there will be an abundant harvest of well-ripened crops with fair weather for the harvest; however, if the stars are faint and flickering, the harvest will be poor, yielding little food for the winter and spring.

The seasons divide the year into halves, each with its own characteristics. In *hai,* winter, the earth and the beings that live on its surface rest or die; in *shį́,* summer, the earth and its inhabitants become active once more as they are restored to life. Changing Woman, who embodies the earth's powers of rejuvenation, goes through the same cycle of old age and restoration to beauty and youth, while Sky goes through his own seasonal changes. Again, we see the concept of dynamic order, or order being continuously recreated through time, as well as the pairing of complements, both essential to the order of the Navajo universe.

Sǫ', Stars and Constellations

Chanters A and B identified the eight major Navajo constellations recognized today as Náhookǫs biką'ii, the Big Dipper; Náhookǫs ba'áadii, Cassiopeia; Dilyéhé, the Pleiades; 'Átsé'ets'ózí, Orion; Hastiin Sik'ai'í, Corvus; 'Átsé'etsoh, the front part of Scorpius; Gah heet'e'ii, the tail of Scorpius; and Yikáísdáhí, the Milky Way. Figure 4.4 illustrates these constellations on the body of Father Sky, after a sketch in Haile's unpublished field notes. A catalogue of Navajo stars and constellations is presented in table 4.3.

These constellations are almost identical with those from the Western tra-

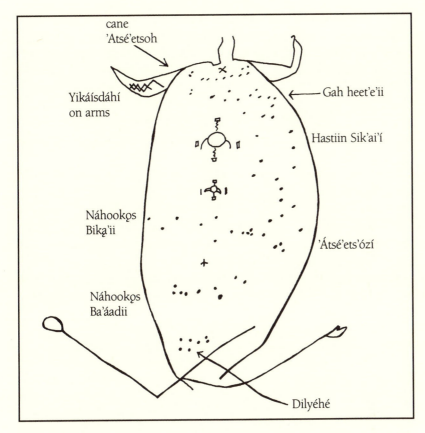

cane
'Atsé'etsoh

Yikáísdáhí
on arms

Gah heet'e'ii

Hastiin Sik'ai'í

Náhookǫs
Biką'ii

'Átsé'ets'ózí

Náhookǫs
Ba'áadii

Dilyéhé

Fig. 4.4. Father Sky. (Adapted from Haile [n.d.]. Courtesy Special Collections, University of Arizona Library.)

dition. Figures 4.5–4.8 compare Navajo constellations (as drawn by Chanter A)[7] with their Western counterparts.

The Big Dipper and Cassiopeia revolve around the almost motionless star called Polaris, forming a universal reference point that is visible at all times of the year in the northern hemisphere. The Navajo names for these constellations translate as the Male One Who Revolves and the Female One Who Revolves, a reference to their movement around Polaris, which is thought of as the source of their illumination. Plate 8 depicts the two as the Male and Female Revolving Ones.

Dilyéhé, the Pleiades, is a small but distinctive cluster of six easily visible

Table 4.3. A Catalogue of Navajo Stars and Constellations

Name	Translation	Identification	Sources[a]
PRIMARY CONSTELLATIONS			
1. Náhookǫs biką'ii	The Male Revolving One; Whirling Male; Cold Man of the North	Part of Ursa Major, including the Big Dipper	A,B,D,E/G-P; S/O; L/B; FF; S/H; K/W; N; T; W; Y; B
2. Náhookǫs ba'áadii	The Female Revolving One; Whirling Female	Cassiopeia	A,B,D,E/G-P; L/B; FF; S/H; N; B K/W; S/O; W; Y; L/B
3. Dilyéhé	(No agreed-upon translation)	The Pleiades[b]	A,B,C,D,E/G-P; L/B; FF; S/H; K/W; N; S/O; T; W; Y; B
4. 'Átsé'ets'ózí	First Slim One	Orion	A,B,D,E/G-P; L/B; FF; K/W; S/O; S/H; T; W; B
5. Hastiin Sik'ai'í	Man with Legs Ajar	Corvus	A,B,D,E/G-P; FF; S/H; B
6. 'Átsé'etsoh	First Big One	Front part of Scorpius	S/O; L/B; W A,B,D,E/G-P; S/H; L/B; FF; K/W; S/O; W; B
7. Gah heet'e'ii	Rabbit Tracks	Tail of Scorpius stars in Canis Major	A,B,D,E/G-P; N; K/W; B FF; S/O; W; S/H
8. Yikáísdáhí	Awaits-the-Dawn	Milky Way	A,B,D,E/G-P; FF; S/H; K/W; N; S/O; W; B
SECONDARY CONSTELLATIONS			
1. Sǫ'hots'ihi	Pinching Stars; Fighting Stars	Aldebaran and the lower branch of the Hyades[b]	S/H; T; FF; S/O; K/W; B
2. Baalchini	—	—	S/O
3. K'aalógii	Butterfly	—	FF; N; S/H

Table 4.3. Continued

Name	Translation	Identification	Sources[a]
4. Dahsání	Porcupine	—	FF; S/H; N; K/W
5. Shash	Bear	—	FF; S/H; N; K/W; B
6. Shash łichí	Red Bear	—	FF
7. 'Iiʼniʼ	Thunder	—	FF; N; S/H; B
8. Tłʼitsoh	Big Snake	—	FF; K/W
9. Bisolyehe	Ram	—	D/G-P; K/W; FF
10. Łeitsoh	Horned Rattler	—	S/H; N; B
11. Nashi-taythli	The Crown	—	K/W
12. Dont-whutsǫ	Two Stars Hooked Together	—	K/W
13. Tsétah dibé	Mountain Sheep	—	FF
14. Haashchʼééshzhiní	Fire God (Black God)	—	S/H
15. Naayééʼ Neizghání	Monster Slayer	—	S/H; N
16. Tóbájíshchíní	Born-for-Water	—	S/H; N
17. —	Corn Beetle	—	S/H; N
18. Tązhii bikéeʼ	Turkey Tracks	—	K/W
19. —	Flash Lightning	—	S/H; N
20. Naalʼeełí	The Ducks	—	S/H; N
21. —	Red Heavens	—	S/H, N
22. Tsídiiłtsoii	Lark Who Sang His Song to the Sun Every Morning	—	N
23. Mąʼii tsoh	Wolf	—	N
24. ʼAtsá	Eagle	—	N
25. Naʼashǫʼii	Lizard	in Scorpius	N
26. Átséʼetsoh bigish	Cane of the First Big One	—	FF
27. —	Southern Cross		K/W
28. —	Harvester	—	N

Table 4.3. Continued

Name	Translation	Identification	Sources[a]
SINGLE STARS AND PLANETS			
1. Sǫ'tsoh	Big Star	Venus	A,B,E/G-P; S/H
	North Star	Polaris	Y
Sǫ'doo ńdízídí	Morning Star	Venus	Y
2. —	North Star	Polaris	A,B,C,D,E/G-P; M; N; Y; S/H; S/O; FF; L/B, K/W
3. Mą'ii bizǫ	Coyote Star	—	A,B,D,E/G-P; N; M; K/W
Sǫ'dondizídí	No-Month Star	—	FF
4. —	Red Star (Fire of the Twin Stars)	Canopus	S/O; FF; S/H
		Antares	K/W
5. Sǫ'biįh	Deer Star	Aldebaran[b]	L/B; K/W
6. Hayoołkáał 'ats'os	Dawn Feather	—	FF
7. Nahodeełt'iizh 'ats'os	Feather of the Southern Blue	—	FF
8. Nahootsoii 'ats'os	Feather of the Evening Twilight	—	FF
9. Chahałheeł 'ats'os	Feather of Darkness	—	FF
10. Sǫ bidee'	Horned Star	—	K/W
11. Tah'zhuni	Smoky Star	—	K/W
12. Sǫ'eh'dekah	Out of Sight Star in the East	—	K/W
13. Sǫ'bokho'i	Large, Bright Stars Scattered over the Sky	—	S/H; FF

[a]Key (Consultant/Ethnographer): L/B = Little Salt/Brewer (Brewer 1950); FF = Franciscan Fathers (1910); S/H = Son-of-the-Late-Cane/Haile (Haile 1947c); K/W = Klah (T'ai)/Wheelwright (Klah 1942); N = Newcomb (1967); S/O = Sandoval/O'Bryan (O'Bryan 1956); T = Tozzer (1908); W = Wyman (1970a); Y = Yazzie (1971); B = Begay (1990); A,B,C,D,E/G-P = Chanters A,B,C,D,E/Griffin-Pierce (Griffin-Pierce 1987).
[b]The open cluster of stars, the Pleiades and the Hyades, and the bright star Aldebaran belong to the constellation Taurus.

stars with a fainter seventh star; seven stars are usually depicted in Navajo renderings.[8] Plate 7 depicts a Navajo woman making a string figure of Dilyéhé with the Pleiades behind her in the sky.

Orion, whose Navajo names translates as the First Slim One, is a conspicuous winter constellation composed primarily of a quadrangle of bright stars bisected by three stars that form a belt.[9]

Corvus (the Crow) has a Navajo name that means Man with Legs (or Feet) Ajar. This constellation forms a quadrilateral figure located in a fairly dark part of the sky; most Navajo renderings include four stars.[10] Corvus appears in the sky above the Navajo stargazer in plate 6.

The large fishhook shape of Scorpius, a summer constellation in the southern sky, is easily identifiable.[11] The Navajo (as well as the Skidi Pawnee [Chamberlain 1982]) divide Scorpius into two constellations: 'Átsé'etsoh, the First Big One, is the front of Scorpius, while Gah heet'e'ii, Rabbit Tracks, is the tail of Scorpius. Scorpius also appears in the sky in plate 6.

Yakáísdáhí, the Milky Way, is a universally known "landmark" in the sky because of its continual presence and conspicuous appearance, owing to the multitude of distant stars that compose this whitish ribbon.

The underlying theme of the story of stellar creation is the interplay of order and disorder. While the Navajo recognize specific orderly groupings of stars in the heavens, which were carefully placed by the Holy People, they consider other stars to exist without patterning, in a state of disorder, as a result of the impulsive actions of the trickster and philosopher, Coyote.

As with the other temporal markers, the stars were created for a purpose: not only were they to provide light in the heavens for those times when the moon was absent or waning, but also they were to provide seasonal and nightly markers for agricultural, hunting, and ceremonial activities. Their creation, as part of all Creation, was intended to unfold nizhónígo, or "in an orderly and proper way," as discussed above. However, Coyote, "patron of disorder" (Consultant G), intervened by disrupting both process and product.

Black God is generally considered to be the creator of the constellations; he is also known as Fire God because he is responsible for all fire, including the fire in the stars that is the source of their light. When diyin dine'é entered the hogan of Creation, "the sky and earth lay on the floor of the hogan with heads pointing eastward, the sky on the south, the earth on the north side. Both had received the 'breath of life' with various winds, though they were not 'dressed' yet" (Haile 1947c:1).

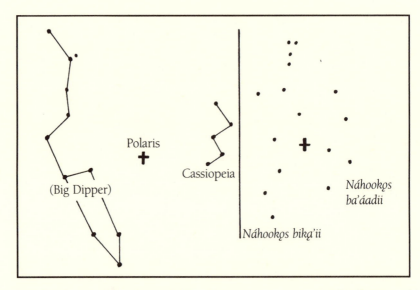

Fig. 4.5. The two Náhookǫs and their Western counterparts, the Big Dipper and Cassiopeia. (Adapted from a drawing by Chanter A.)

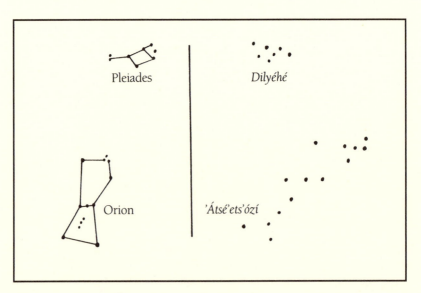

Fig. 4.6. Dilyéhé and 'Átsé'ets'ózí and their Western counterparts, the Pleiades and Orion. (Adapted from a drawing by Chanter A.)

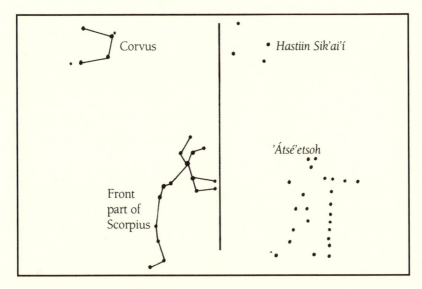

Fig. 4.7. Hastiin Sik'ai'í and 'Átsé'etsoh and their Western counterparts, Corvus and the front part of Scorpius. (Adapted from a drawing by Chanter A.)

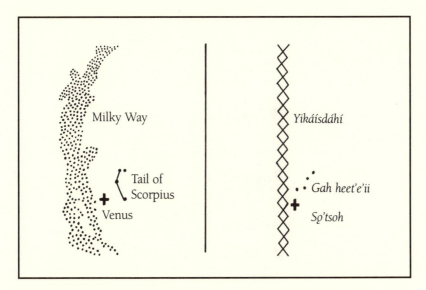

Fig. 4.8. Gah heet'e'ii and Yikáísdáhí and their Western counterparts, the tail of Scorpius and the Milky Way. (Adapted from a drawing by Chanter A.)

In Haile's (1947c:1–4) version taken from Upward Reachingway, Black God entered the hogan with Dilyéhé (the Pleiades) lodged at his ankle. When he stamped his foot vigorously, the constellation jumped to his knee. Another stamp of his foot brought it to his hip. He stamped again, bringing the constellation to his right shoulder. The fourth and final time he stamped his foot, the Pleiades lodged along his left temple where, he said, "it shall stay!" Thus, Dilyéhé is located on Black God's mask (see figure 4.9). In Haile's work, this constellation appears on Black God's left cheek (Haile 1947a) and on Black God's temple (Haile 1947c:3). In my experience, the Pleiades is usually not visible on Black God's mask, either in Nightway sandpaintings of Black God that I have watched being made or on the mask worn by the Black God Impersonator.[12] Chanter D explained that this is because Black God's face represents the entirety of the heavens, and the Pleiades is very small in proportion to the entire sky.

Black God's feat of placing Dilyéhé where he wanted it confirmed to the supernaturals in the creator group that he had the power to beautify the "dark upper," as they called the sky, by producing and placing constellations. Moving in the sunwise circuit, Black God first positioned Corvus in the east. In the south, he placed Horned Rattler (Haile does not list Western equivalents for all the constellations he mentions), Bear, Thunder, and

Fig. 4.9. Black God's mask. (Adapted from Haile [1947c:3].)

'Átsé'etsoh (the front part of Scorpius). In the north he placed the Big Dipper, Cassiopeia, Orion, the Pinching or Doubtful Stars (Aldebaran, lower branch of the Hyades), Gah heet'e'ii (which Haile identifies as a star cluster under Canis Major, but which today is generally identified as the tail of Scorpius); and finally the Pleiades. Because none of these constellations could shine without an igniter star to furnish their light, he added *bikǫ'*, an igniter. Finally, he sprinkled the heavens with the Milky Way.

Black God, weary from the process of creation, was resting when Coyote snatched Black God's fawnskin pouch, which contained the remaining unnamed and unplaced star crystals. Coyote then flung these stars into the night sky where they were scattered at random instead of forming the orderly patterns of constellations for which they had been intended. According to Haile's (1947c:4) consultant, "That explains why only the stars put there by Fire god [Black God] have a name and those scattered at random by Coyote are nameless."

Suddenly, Coyote took one remaining crystal and deliberately placed it in the south. This Coyote Star, Mą'ii bizǫ, was the source of confusion and disorder just as Coyote intended it to be. Accounts disagree on the identity of this "Monthless Star," so called because it is in the heavens for less than a full month, as well as on whether it is one star (Haile 1947c:8, 1981a: 129; Klah 1942:58; O'Bryan 1956:21; Consultant G) or three (Matthews 1883:214).

While some accounts agree that Black God was in charge of the creation of the stars (Haile 1947a:29–30, 60–61, 1947c:1–2, 1981a:128–29), others say that First Man and First Woman or other Holy People were responsible (Klah 1942:39, 66; Matthews 1883:213–14, 1897:223–24; O'Bryan 1956:20–21; Yazzie 1971:21; Newcomb 1967:78–88; Chanter A).

Although accounts differ concerning the identity of the supernaturals responsible for the creation of the stars, all versions do share the underlying theme of the universe as an orderly system. The order inherent in the cosmos was meant to serve as a pattern for proper behavior in both general and specific ways. "Laws," or rules for proper conduct, were symbolized in such constellations as Gah heet'e'ii (the tail of Scorpius), whose seasonal movements determined the periods when hunting would be allowed (Newcomb 1980:197). Similarly, the two Náhookǫs, the Male and Female Ones Who Revolve (the Big Dipper and Cassiopeia), represented a married couple that encircled Polaris, the fire in the center of their hogan; these two constellations, along with Polaris, represented laws against two couples living in the same hogan or doing their cooking over the same fire, as well as the mother-in-law avoidance law to be followed by her son-in-law. (These constellations are depicted in plate 8; the constellations as a cultural text will be explored at greater length in chapter 6.)

The Four Cardinal Light Phenomena

In addition to the sun and moon, the seasons, and the constellations, the four cardinal light phenomena constitute a fourth and final set of markers for the division of time. As noted above, the four cardinal light phenomena are results of the sun's apparent daily motion. These phenomena are the four directions and the times of day and colors that are linked to them. A Navajo does not think of the east without envisioning *hayoołkááł,* Dawn, and the white color of the sky at this time of day. Next is *nahodeełʼiizh,* which is usually glossed as "horizontal blue" or "blue haze" in reference to the band of relatively darker blue that lies on the horizon at midday; this light is associated with the south. *Nahootsoii* follows and literally means "around the area becomes yellow," although this word is usually translated as "evening twilight"; it is linked to the west. Finally, *chahałheeł,* darkness, is associated with the north and with the blackness of the night sky. These four phenomena are conceptualized as two pairs: Dawn and Twilight, Midday and Night. Once more, we see the pairing of complements so fundamental to the Navajo worldview.

Although the sun's apparent movement across the heavens results in the four cardinal light phenomena, in the story of Navajo Creation the prototypes of these light phenomena existed in the underworlds long before the creation of the sun and moon, which took place in the present world. Various translations describe them as "cloud columns," "pillars of light," "clouds of light," or simply "mists." The four lights are described as "mating" and as "giving birth" to various Navajo supernaturals, and are associated with all acts of creation. According to some accounts, First Man and First Woman themselves were created from the boundaries of pairs of these light phenomena.

When First Man unrolled his sacred medicine bundle, the source of creation and animation for all beings, the bundle was covered with "sheets" of the four cardinal light phenomena. After unrolling the four sacred jewels, he placed supernaturals in human form upon them. "Over these he spread [sheets of] dawn, evening twilight, sunlight [instead of horizontal blue of the south], a spread of darkness" (Slim Curley, in Wyman [1970a:111]).

In the drypainting in figure 4.10, Father Sky is held in place by these

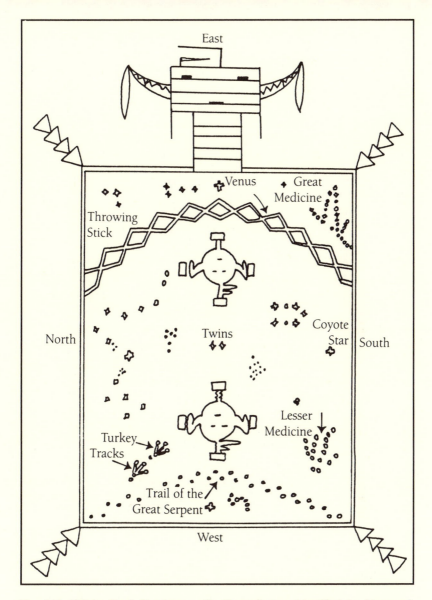

Fig. 4.10. "Night Sky," Blessingway (?). Constellations identified by Newcomb (Bit'ahnii Bidághaa'í): crossed lines represent the Milky Way, above which are Rabbit Tracks, the Throwing Sticks, and the Great Medicine. The Twins are near the center, and the Coyote Star is in the south. Below it is the Lesser Medicine and from south to north along the west runs the trail of the Great Serpent. The Western Star is near the Pleiades. The Turkey Tracks point southeast. The North Star is in the north with the Big Dipper (and Cassiopeia, which Newcomb omits in her description). If this painting belonged to Blessingway, it would be made of materials other than sand. (Adapted from a painting collected by Newcomb; singer, Bit'ahnii Bidághaa'í, 1936. Courtesy Wheelwright Museum, P1#15.)

cloud columns.[13] However, in this visual representation, instead of one color existing over each corner of the world, the colors are stacked so that each corner contains all four colors of cloud. The masked face of Father Sky also depicts these four cardinal light phenomena: the yellow of evening twilight covers his chin, the blue of the midday sky lies across his nose, the black of night lies under his eyes, and the white of dawn covers his forehead.

Although the four clouds of light could create life, they remained lifeless themselves (as did other natural phenomena) until the present world, when an inner form from First Man's sacred medicine bundle was placed within each of them as their life principle to vitalize and personalize each phenomenon (Wyman 1970a:381–82).

The most vivid depiction of the cardinal light phenomena is in a sandpainting from the Male Shootingway known by chanters as "The Dawn" and more commonly called "The Skies." It may be represented in trapezoidal or keystone form; as Chanter A explained, in the most elaborate version of this painting (the keystone form) both the Pathway to the Heavens and the Opening to the Heavens are symbolized (see plate 3).

The keystone version of "The Skies" also depicts the inner beings of each phenomenon. In plate 3, four keystone shapes represent the four light phenomena; within each stands its inner form. Beginning with the east, the white of dawn contains its inner form, Dawn Boy. To the south, Blue Sky Man stands within the keystone form of the blue of the daytime sky. To the west is the yellow form of evening twilight with Yellow Evening Light Girl. Finally, in the north, darkness is spread with the beings of Darkness—the stars and constellations of the night sky and Darkness Girl.

The same or similar beings as those of the cardinal light phenomena were placed within the mountains created in the cardinal directions of the present world to animate them and to give them life. Plate 2 depicts the inner beings of the four light phenomena emerging from the Sacred Mountains. Father Berard Haile (in Farella [1984:104–5]) elicited (and recorded in Navajo) the following description of the intimate relationship between the cardinal light phenomena and the Sacred Mountains:

> Sisnajiini mountain [Blanca Peak] already stood there, here on the east side. On the south side stood Mt. Taylor, on the west side San Francisco Peak, on the north side La Plata range it was found.[14] This (thing) that rose as a white column in east time and again, is the inner form of sisnajini by which it breathes and this we know is the dawn. In the west (the rising column) is the inner form of San Francisco Peak by means of which this breathes. This, we see is evening

twilight. When they joined the one from the east, you know, the people had made it daytime. (The column) from the south, the inner form of Mt. Taylor by which it breathes is, we know, the sky blue. The one from the north, the inner form of Perrin's Peak by which it breathes, is really the darkness, they say. This, when it would meet the one from the south, they had made (it) the night. Here towards the south stood a mountain yellow in color, and right opposite, towards the east there was a dark mountain. So you see that was the condition of their country.

Figure 4.11, adapted from Haile's notes, shows the inner forms of the cardinal directions with the four Sacred Mountains lying at their feet. The names of these inner forms differ according to sex and generation in pub-

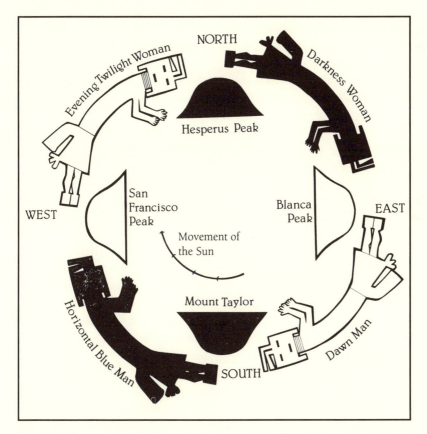

Fig. 4.11. The inner forms of the cardinal points with the Sacred Mountains. (Adapted from Haile [in Wyman 1970a:2].)

lished Navajo accounts. The chanter who worked with Haile (1943b:70–71) calls the inner form of the white dawn "Dawn Man," whom we see lying in the east with Blanca Peak, the Sacred Mountain of the east, at his feet. To the south is Horizontal Blue Man with Mount Taylor; to the west is Evening Twilight Woman with San Francisco Peak; and to the north lies Darkness Woman with Hesperus Peak, the Sacred Mountain of the north, at her feet.

THE HOGAN AS A MODEL OF THE NAVAJO COSMOS

As noted in the passage from Haile quoted above, the light is the inner form of its respective mountain, "by means of which it breathes." This means that the Sacred Mountains are living beings animated by the life force of the cardinal light phenomena. The mountains can also be viewed as the hogan, or "place home" (*hoo* "place" and *-ghan*, "home"), for each of the light phenomena (Farella 1984:105).

Some Navajos conceive of the earth's surface as being covered by an enormous transparent hogan of the older, conical, forked-pole style (see figure 4.12), with the Sacred Mountains as its cornerposts. Talking God stands at the doorway, which faces east, while Calling God is at the west. The hogan is a living entity, with the smokehole as its breathing hole; this is where prayers emerge and rise to the heavens.

The first hogan, constructed after the Emergence into the present world by the *diyin dine'é* near the rim of the Emergence Place, was not only the site for the creation of many elements of the present world, but also a model of the cosmos. It was in the hogan of Creation that Black God produced and placed the stars in order to beautify the "dark upper" or sky (Haile 1947c:2).

Both the shape of the hogan and the required directional movement within it are associated with the sun. The hogan was built in the shape of the sun because "the sun being the source of heat, light, and protection from the evils abroad at night symbolizes the qualities that were desired for the home" (Newcomb 1940:23–24). The doorway faces east to catch the blessing of the first rays of sunlight (Jett and Spencer 1981:17). The Navajo word for east, *ha'a'aah,* reflects the order inherent in the repetitive diurnal motions of the sun, for this word means literally "a solid roundish object [the sun] moves about regularly." The required directional movement after entering the hogan is the sunwise circuit, which also reflects a recognition of the motions of the heavens.

The hogan has been called a master encoding (Farella 1984:87), or a

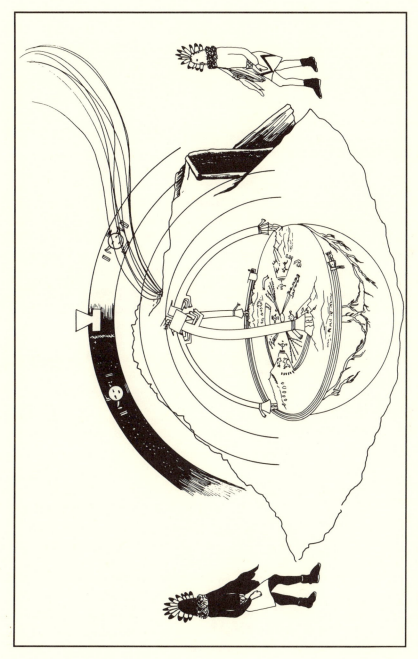

Fig. 4.12. The post-Emergence universe with hogan. Talking God stands at the east (facing the door of the hogan) while Calling God stands at the west. Prayers rise to the sky through the smokehole.

diagram of the Navajo cosmos. The first hogan was conceived, planned, and constructed by the *diyin dine'é* who decreed that the Earth Surface People should follow the plan of this first hogan with its posts at the four cardinal directions and east-facing doorway. The main poles of the hogan are to be picked up in the sunwise order, with two stones of the sacred jewel associated with each direction embedded in the ground next to each pole. Sacred jewels are condensed symbols intimately related to sacred colors, directions, places, and entities (see Reichard 1950:208–13).

Although the hogan is never physically subdivided, it is conceptually divided according to directional orientation: four forked upright posts are named for each of the directions (Witherspoon 1983:532) while the interior space is divided into areas that include the eastern, southern, western, and northern recesses, and possibly "sky center," an area in between the fireside and the western recess (Jett and Spencer 1981:23).

One Navajo eloquently explained the sacredness of the hogan:

> The hogan is built in the manner of this harmony. The roof is in the likeness of the sky. The walls are in the likeness of the Navajo's surroundings: the upward position of the mountains, hills, and trees. And the floor is ever in touch with "the earth mother."
>
> The hogan is comprised of white shell, abalone, turquoise, and obsidian, bringing the home and sacred mountains into one sacred unit. The home is also adorned with the dawn, the blue sky, the twilight and the night—the sun in the center as the fire. . . .
>
> The hogan is a sacred dwelling. It is the shelter of the people of the earth, a protection, a home, and a refuge. Because of the harmony in which the hogan is built, the family can be together to endure hardships and grow as a part of the harmony between the Sacred Mountains, under the care of "Mother Earth" and "Father Sky" (Louis 1975:3).

The hogan, with its directional divisions, is such a fundamental encoding of the Navajo worldview that the Tsaile campus of Navajo Community College used it as the master plan for the placement of various campus buildings. Harry Walters (personal communication, 1990) explained that, in their desire to have Navajo education parallel Navajo ceremonial life, the college planners used the activities associated with different parts of the hogan as a guide for the location of student activities that were related to traditional activities carried on within the hogan:

> The South side of the hogan is associated with things needed to make a living—weaving, silversmithing—so along the south side of campus is where

classrooms for teacher education and animal science are located. The West is associated with social relations. Changing Woman made clans in the West; it's where you sit [in the hogan] when you visit or sleep. Grandfathers tell their stories on the west [side of the hogan]. So anthropology and sociology and dormitories are on the west side of campus. The North is for reverence: you prepare the Nightway mask and anything used in ceremonies on the north side [of the hogan]. So this is where anything that deals with the environment—science, math, geology, biology—is taught [on campus]. The fireplace and cooking area is in the center of the hogan so the kitchen and dining room are located in the center [of the campus].

Figure 4.13 depicts the directional division of the hogan with the inner beings, colors, and mountains associated with each of the four directions. However, this diagram represents much more than a list of spatio-temporal

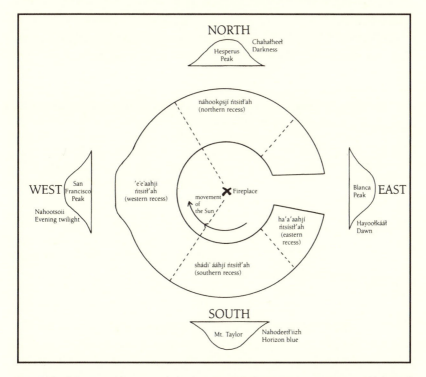

Fig. 4.13. Schematic diagram of the hogan with directional associations. (Adapted from information in Witherspoon [1983:532]; Jett and Spencer [1981]; and Mindeleff [1988:plate XC].)

associations, for just as the Sacred Mountains are animated with life force, so too are the directions themselves. The east is associated with the Dawn and Talking God, who represents knowledge, wisdom, philosophy, hard goods, the pursuit of discipline, and striving (Harry Walters, personal communication 1990). Consultant A told me, "The East says, 'I am birth; I am new life; I am a new day; I am all these good things,' so you pray to that. The directions are very much alive. They are the places where sacred things happened, the places where the mountains live."

GUIDANCE FROM THE TEMPORAL MARKERS

As previously discussed, each living thing has an inner form and Holy Wind placed within it through which it has the capacity to live, think, speak, and move; Holy Wind is also the means of communication between all elements of the living world (McNeley 1981:1). Messenger winds from the inner forms of various natural phenomena based in the four directions inform, advise, and protect people and also report back on their behavior (McNeley 1981:30). When Changing Woman and the other *diyin dine'é* departed after completing Creation, they left gifts and instructions about the correct way to live. These Holy People are based in the cardinal directions, and thanks to the messenger winds they are all-knowing.

Because celestial entities, particularly Earth, Sky, Sun, and Moon, were endowed with inner forms and with the capacity to live, think, speak, and move, they had a means of guiding and regulating human life (McNeley 1981:28). The Sun regulates the cardinal light phenomena, for its apparent diurnal motion determines the sequence of these phenomena. The Dawn appears before the Sun; the Sun journeys over horizontal Skyblue; Evening Twilight follows the Sun; and the Sun returns to the east under the Darkness (Wyman 1970a:372). Specific patterns of thought and behavior are associated with each time of day. In chanter Frank Mitchell's version of Creation (in Wyman [1970a:370]), Coyote, in his role as native philosopher, discusses how the cardinal light phenomena are to guide the Earth Surface People: "Offerings made . . . [at dawn] will all be holy, and in the future young men and women who are to come into being will all be put in shape [so that] he [or she] who has walked in . . . [the dawn] will enjoy every [possession]." Coyote goes on to say that while daylight is good as a time to carry out the plans made at dawn, it can bring either good or ill fortune. Deaths that occur at this time are the payment required by the sun carrier for his travel: "Concerning . . . [daylight] although good to some extent it will remain two-sided. Whereas it will be a protection particularly 'for one's journeys, bad things [deaths] will repeatedly occur in that time . . . [so that] half of it will be good, the other half will not be good" (in Wyman [1970a:370]).

The third light phenomenon, twilight, is a time of bringing people together again; thus, travel during that time is not proper.

"The . . . [twilight] will also be good, and offerings too will be made in that time, it will be the time of bringing [people] together again. Should any of you not act properly, should anyone disbelieve and continue [travel] through it, that also will not be quite proper" (in Wyman [1970a: 370]). The period of darkness, however, has more of whatever is bad. It is during this time that the Moon's demand for deaths as payment for his journey across the sky must be satisfied. "As for . . . [darkness], only a small portion of it will be good. Merely the resting part in this time period, in this small point only will conditions be good. Otherwise, there will be more of whatever is bad [death] in this time than in the others. And should you desire this . . . [time] above the others [that is, sleep too much], you will suffer want of everything. That is the purpose of these things" (in Wyman [1970a:370]).

Coyote instructs the Earth Surface People on appropriate behavior for each time of the day associated with the cardinal light phenomena. By following these instructions for moderation, order, and balance, and by heeding other advice and warnings from the *diyin dine'é,* which are relayed by messenger winds, one can ensure that one's life will be marked by prosperity and abundance.

The Navajo saying "Yá'át'eehgo nijgha łí" is an admonition to "walk in a good and orderly way, always." This phrase embodies the ideals of Navajo philosophy discussed in this chapter by referring to the order inherent in the cosmos. Each day this order recurs in the form of the four cardinal light phenomena; the order of the year is manifested in the earth's hibernation in winter and restoration to life in summer, as well as in the annual appearance of specific constellations at their expected time. Both the Navajo hogan and sandpaintings encode this cosmological order. "Yá'át'eehgo nijgha łí" is a reminder to live in a way that shows respect to the *diyin dine'é,* the Holy People, by doing one's part to continually create anew the order that they created originally in the universe.

✤ 5 ✤

The Navajo Heavens in Visual Image
and Verbal Narrative

Through the sandpainting, one enters a powerful mythic world suspended in time and space. This ability to fuse temporal and spatial realms and to make the here and now coexist with the mythic past helps explain the sandpainting's power and the transformation of the one-sung-over from observer to actor as she is taken from the context of a family hogan into a mythic world where miraculous events are commonplace.

The conceptualization of time as cyclical is shared by traditional North American cultures. This experience of time is in direct contrast to the linear progress-oriented temporal concepts of modern Western culture. Because the past coexists with the present, the past is accessible to Native Americans in a way that it is not to Westerners. The recitation of the mythic episodes through prayers, songs, and ritual procedures is understood to be an actual—not a symbolic—reenactment (see Brown [1982] for a discussion of the Native American cyclical perspective of time).

Barre Toelken (1976a:31) explains the cyclic nature of Navajo time in his description of a Navajo weaver who, "instead of standing on a straight ribbon of time leading from the past to some future point, stands in the middle of a vortex of forces" with which "she negotiates," looking "to the past for patterning, for advice and wisdom. . . . Time *surrounds* her." This circular approach to time, which is a fundamental quality of Navajo thought on an everyday basis, plays a key role in the intensification of experience during ritual.

Robert Plant Armstrong (1981:14–15) coined the phrase "affecting presences" to describe works with "indwelling" power "which own some kind of ability—of efficacy of affect." These objects, he explained (Armstrong 1981:5–6), are both objects and subjects: they are made of materials through the same processes as other things are made, but because people's behavior toward them endows them with presence, they are treated as human subjects. These works exist in a state of ambiguity, and it is in the energy of the interplay of existing as both object and subject that the power or energy of works of affecting presence is found.

Sandpaintings clearly possess the kind of power and energy that makes them "affecting presences." The Navajo consider them to be sacred, living entities; sandpaintings derive this power from their ability to compress time and space and from their completeness, a concept fundamental to Navajo philosophy.

The rich visual and verbal symbols in a Navajo ceremonial refer to past and present at the same time, resulting in the intensification of experience. This compression of emotion is similar to that which M. Jane Young found in Zuni pictographs and petroglyphs and features of the landscape. Young (1988:153) explained that the Zuni images derive their affecting presence from "their ability to evoke stories of the myth time and consequently to make the past coexistent with the present."

This evocative ability is precisely what makes the sandpainting images so profoundly powerful. When the patient sits upon the painting in the center of the hogan, not only is he deriving comfort from the present ritual ministrations of a trusted and highly respected chanter, but also he is stepping back into a mythic time and place in which the protagonist of the myth, with whom the patient is now fully identified, receives supernatural assistance that lifts him far above any danger, rendering him immune to evil forces.

Prayers uttered by the protagonist of the myth are given voice again in the sacred hogan. These prayers, characterized by great lyricism, beauty, and dignity, return the patient to a state of harmony and health:

By holy means I go about,
Because I am Holy Young Man I thereby go about,
Now Sun's feet are my means of travel,
Now Sun's legs are my means of travel,
Now Sun's travel means are my means of travel,
Now Sun's body is my means of travel,
Now Sun's arm is my means of travel,
Now Sun's mind is my means of travel,
Now Sun's voice is my means of travel,
Now Sun's eyes are my means of travel,
Now Sun's hair is my means of travel,
Now Sun's plume is my means of travel.
After I have ascended Dark Mountain it is pleasant . . . [in front of me] . . .
    pleasant . . . [behind me] . . . as thereby I go about,

Now because I am long life now happiness I thereby go about,
  in a holy way I thereby go about . . .
Because I have ascended Pollen Mountain I am thereby reseated, now to you, my
  relatives, I have returned! Yours, my relatives, I have returned to be! All of you,
  my relatives, are rejoicing! Mutually, folks of my relationship, pleasant again it
  has come to be!
Pleasant it is . . . [behind me] . . . as thereby I go about,
Pleasant it is . . . [in front of me] . . . as thereby I go about,
Pleasant it is below me as thereby I go about,
Pleasant it is above me as thereby I go about. (Blue Eyes, in Haile's unpublished
  manuscript of the Male Shootingway, pp. 179–81).

The strength of the myths lies in their ability to reach through time with themes that are both universal and eternal. Not only do these messages have vital import for the patient and her specific situation, but they also have larger meanings that, in the process of reenactment through prayers and songs, tell of the ultimate realities of existence. Everyone can relate to the overcoming of vast difficulties to reach a perspective of personal wholeness, and thus holiness, through identification with an ideal world characterized by inner and outer beauty, balanced and harmonious conditions.

Rain Parrish, former curator at the Wheelwright Museum of the American Indian and herself a Navajo, described the compelling power of the mythic odyssey of a chantway ceremonial. She explained that the plots of these stories express ideas:

> about natural laws that help us understand ourselves. They recount our adven-
> tures and misadventures. Sometimes we, ourselves, actively court dangers so
> that we may learn. Whatever the provocation, the hero or heroine's deliverance
> is achieved through the miraculous intervention of the supernaturals. This is
> the restoration of harmony and well-being, acquired through careful knowledge
> of appropriate ritual actions and powers (Rain Parrish, in Wheelwright Museum
> exhibition brochure [1985]).

The power of the mythic drama is evoked at the time of drawing the sandpainting image as well as during its ritual use. Certain sandpainting forms stimulated the narration of songs associated with them. For example, when Chanter A, in a nontraditional setting (an interview held in a building rather than in a ceremonial hogan), was drawing the constellations in a pencil drawing of Father Sky, he began singing passages from the accompanying ceremonial prayers; rather than prefacing these narrative songs with explanatory statements, he simply sang as a direct response to particular images, images that fit Young's (1988:122) description of "metonyms of narrative": visual images that "stand for and call forth the verbal recitation." She (1988:153) explained that "the power of these depictions" derives from their ability to refer to past and present *at the same time*, intensifying experience through the metonym of narrative. In the words of Robert J. Smith (1975:99), such visual/verbal interaction results in a "tremendous compression of both emotion and concepts."

The sandpainting is an example of visual/verbal interaction because the visual symbols index key episodes in the mythic odyssey of the chantway ceremonial to which the painting belongs. In a sacred sandpainting several time periods are collapsed into a single moment: first, there is the present moment, that of the actual ceremony being performed over the patient; then, there is the first time the ceremony was given on earth by the Holy People; there is also the moment in which the commemorated episode occurred in the accompanying chantway myth; and, finally, the moments marked by the occurrence of mythic events that lie outside the narrative of the specific ceremonial being performed.

The Navajo ceremonial system is loosely interrelated through a highly complex body of Navajo mythology.[1] The most detailed account of the general origin myth is found in Blessingway, which tells the story of the lower worlds, the Emergence onto the earth's surface, and the Creation. Branching off from the origin myth are the various origin legends of specific ceremonials, which relate the ceremonial to the story of the Emergence and Creation and recount the mythic odyssey of a hero or heroine as he or she interacts with the Holy People who give the ceremonial to the protagonist for the benefit of humanity.[2]

Some myths share a fairly large portion of their stories and later diverge, while others include only one episode common to two myths. The supernaturals usually point out to the hero, as part of his ceremonial tutelage, the connections between this chantway and another. The same characters often appear in several myths; the Hailway people appear both in the myth of Hailway and in that of the Great Star Chant. For this reason, non-Navajos have observed that such recurrent characters link the myths into one complex system. However, much of the systematic, coherent quality of the myths and their relationship to one another has been artificially imposed by the anthropologists who collected them. In his extensive work with contemporary Nightway chanters, James Faris (1990:65) pointed out that "writing them [episodic events in different narrative accounts] down has indeed frozen them—not a quality characteristic of the dynamic phenomena that is Navajo healing activity."

The chantway myths—not an oral literature in the sense of performance—are seldom, if ever, related in their entirety as unified narratives except at the prompting of anthropologists. Instead, chanters focus on the oral features of specific chantway ceremonies, songs, and prayers. This led Edward Sapir and Harry Hoijer (1942:574) to observe, "It is the songs that the narrator has in mind and much in the story is constructed from them." Faris (1990:28) found that "the specific details of Nightway practice are not learned from the recitation of the narrative, but are learned . . . from observation in the case of specific healing practices and material constructions [such as sandpaintings], and by listening and repetition in the case of songs and prayers."

The power of a particular sandpainting image to heal is far more important than its coherent presentation of a mythic episode. This is why few sandpaintings are narrative in the sense that they illustrate specific episodes in the myth. There is no way to predict what mythic details will find visual expression in the sandpainting and what details will be omitted. For example, although the Navajos are always preoccupied with the water supply and, in the story of Beadway, a spring is supposed to lie within the plaza around which the Eagles' pueblolike dwellings are built, there is no such spring in the sandpainting "The Home of the Eagles" (Reichard 1977:82).

Rather than being illustrations, sandpainting images use symbolic devices to indicate action and characters. Someone who is familiar with the outline of the ceremonial's origin myth and the visual "language" used to represent specific supernaturals and plot action can "read" paintings in which cardinal episodes of the myth may be presented in symbolic form. However, because healing efficacy takes priority over mythic narrative, sandpaintings more commonly depict symbols associated with the ceremonial or with the etiology of illness connected to the ceremonial. This is also why the versions handed down by different chanters vary in the emphasis they place upon particular details. Different chanters pass on those sandpainting details which they find to be most effective in healing. Thus, some sandpaintings may emphasize a specific episode that, in another version, is only of secondary importance. The ability of a sandpainting image to heal is far more important also than the realism with which its individual components are portrayed. This is why the constellations in sandpaintings are *symbolic* rather than literal representations of star groupings and should be interpreted as such.

Constellations do not carry the heavy functional load for the Navajo that they did for such groups as the Caroline Islanders in Oceania (Gladwin 1970), for whom remembering specific forms in perfect alignment was a matter of navigational life and death. While constellations are a part of Navajo life, the Navajo no longer use them as their ancestors might have done, in their migration from Canada or on a daily basis for local hunting trips. Furthermore, the constellations are not a part of the "ceremonial core" of the Navajo. Father Berard Haile (1947c:5) addressed this issue when he said, "As starlore is not prominently mentioned in the legends, the few that know treasure it as distinctly personal knowledge." Thus, even in Haile's time—he conducted his astronomical field work in 1908—the knowledge of the constellations was not a significant part of chantway stories (compared to other features). Haile (1947c:1) also remarked that most chanters do not possess astronomical knowledge. This is why the representation of constellations in sandpaintings is often idiosyncratic, why no two chanters draw the constellations identically. Wyman (1970a:339) observed that in the prayers of Blessingway, the cornerstone of Navajo ritual, chanters can mention as few or as many of the constellations in the creation of the sky as they desire.

It is important to remember that what remains is only the fragments of astronomical knowledge; it is impossible to assess whether one chanter's view was idiosyncratic or representative of a larger body of knowledge that has been lost. Since most of the anthropologists who recorded sandpaintings had no astronomical training themselves and occasionally misidentified sandpainting constellations, we see the constellations recorded in these reproductions through two filters: the possibly idiosyncratic view of one Navajo chanter, and the untrained eye of the ethnographer. For this reason, it is more appropriate to focus on the eight major Navajo constellations recognized today, rather than on more obscure constellations mentioned in the literature by only one or two chanters.[3]

The "variation" apparent to non-Navajos in the depiction of the constellations is not significant enough to warrant concern among Navajo chanters (Griffin-Pierce 1987:152–54). While some depicted constellations are rec-

Table 5.1. Visual Formats of Constellations in Chantway Sandpaintings

Chant	Father Sky (with/without Mother Earth)	Night Sky	Stars Reflected in — Oceans	Stars Reflected in — The Skies	Star Map	As Background/with People	Earth & Sky (not as figures)	Individually	In Summer & Winter Skies	Big Stars
Hailway		X								
Waterway			X							
Male Shootingway	X			X						
Nightway								X		X
Plumeway	X									X
Beadway						X				
Earthway	X									
Upward Reachingway									X	
Big Starway[c]	X				X			X		X
War Prophylactic Rite[a,b]					X		X			
Hand						X				X
Tremblingway[a,b,c]										
Blessingway[a,b]	XX					X				

[a] Drypainting (may be made of materials other than sand).
[b] May be made on buckskin (or cloth substitute) instead of on a background of sand.
[c] Some or all sandpaintings are made after sundown.

ognizable because they coincide with the form seen in the heavens, most are symbolic interpretations. Again, the painting's ability to heal takes priority over realism of representation. For these reasons, I believe that to focus on the "accuracy" of constellation representation in the sandpainting reproductions is an inappropriate analytical exercise.

Table 5.1 summarizes the visual formats and chantway ceremonials in which stars, constellations, and the heavens are depicted in Navajo sandpaintings. It is important to remember that these are *non-Navajo* categories of depiction, which I use merely to clarify the discussion of these images.

FATHER SKY

Star maps may appear on the body of Father Sky; this format is found in sandpaintings from the Male Shootingway (plate 4), the Big Starway (fig. 5.1), the Plumeway (fig. 5.2), and the Earthway (fig. 5.3). Father Sky is also depicted in the painting in figure 5.4; the chantway derivation of this painting is uncertain (Wyman 1952:58, 74–76, 80–81).

Wyman (1983a:107) noted that although some Navajos say that the sandpainting of Mother Earth and Father Sky together may be used on the last day of any ceremonial, he considers this to be unlikely because this usage has been recorded only for the Shootingways (plate 4) and once for the extinct Earth chant (fig. 5.3) (compare Reichard [1977:45]). When Father Sky is depicted alone in the Big Starway (fig. 5.1), he tends to have keystone-cloud-shaped hands and feet. His white-masked face denotes that the body is controlled by spiritual forces (Wheelwright 1988:142). The Plumeway "Father Sky" (fig. 5.2) has five big stars on his body. Of the three chantways about which a significant amount of information has been recorded—Male Shootingway, Big Starway, and Plumeway (also known as Downway [Haile 1947c:frontispiece, 41–42] and the Feather Chant [Reichard 1950:322; Wheelwright 1946b:9–15])—two are usually performed according to Holyway—Male Shootingway and Plumeway (Wyman 1983a:23). (Because so little is known about Earthway [Wyman 1983a:151], this chant will not be included in this discussion; because of the uncertain derivation of figure 5.4, this painting also will not be discussed.) A similar feature in the narratives of Male Shootingway and Plumeway is a sky visit to the hero's (in Wheelwright's [1946b:9–15] version of Plumeway) or heroes' (in all versions of the Male Shootingway) father, the Sun, which may be why both have sand-

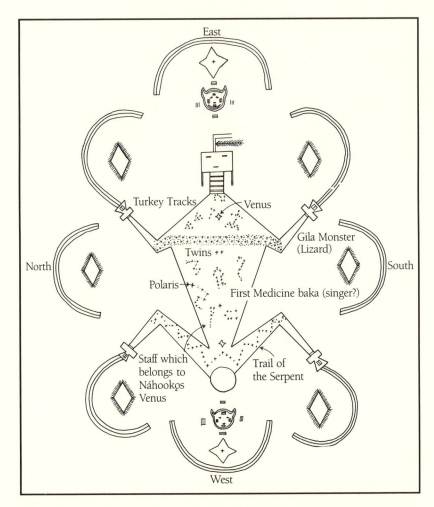

Fig. 5.1. "Father Sky," Big Starway Evilway. Constellations identified by Newcomb (Bit'ahnii Bidághaa'í): near the neck lies the Pleiades, under which are (north to south) Turkey Tracks, Rabbit Tracks, Venus, and the Lizard (Gila Monster). The Twins are below the Milky Way, which lies across the breast and arms. In the north are the two Náhookǫs with Polaris; the staff of Náhookǫs biką'ii lies to the west. In the center is the first "medicine-baka" (singer?), south of which is Hastiin Sik'ai'í (Corvus). (Adapted from a painting collected by Newcomb; singer, Bit'ahnii Bidághaa'í, 1935–36. Courtesy Wheelwright Museum, P8#16.)

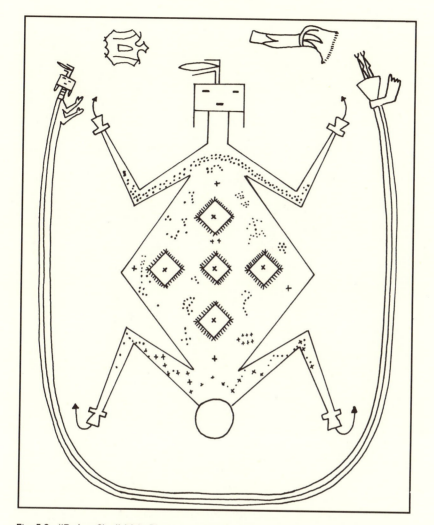

Fig. 5.2. "Father Sky," Male Plumeway. (Adapted from a painting collected by Newcomb; singer, Adeetsa Begay, 1929. Courtesy Museum of Northern Arizona.)

paintings depicting Father Sky, where the Sun lives. The Plumeway "Father Sky" painting, however, does not depict the Sun while the Male Shootingway version does. Otherwise, the narrative portions of these two chants stress different topics—Plumeway emphasizes game, hunting, and the origin of agriculture, while the Male Shootingway describes the exploits of the Sacred

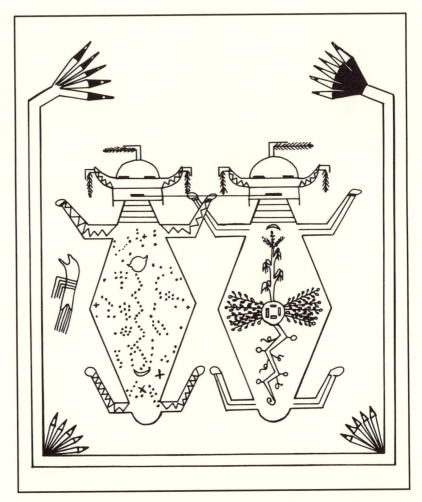

Fig. 5.3. "Mother Earth, Father Sky," Earthway. (Adapted from a painting collected by Oakes; singer, Charlie Tsosie, 1946–47. Courtesy Wheelwright Museum, P20#7.)

Twins. Plumeway is rarely performed today, but the Male Shootingway remains popular and is one of the most frequently performed chants (Wyman 1983a:22).

The other Father Sky image, that of the Big Star Chant, belongs to the Evil Chasing or Evilway form of this chant and is used for a divination rite. The story (Wheelwright 1988) recounts the adventures of a family who are aided

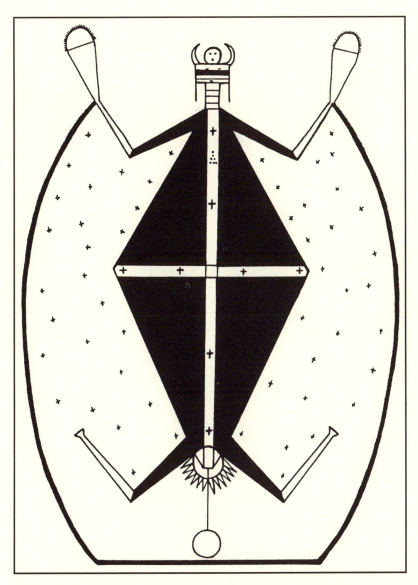

Fig. 5.4. "Father Sky," Blessingway (?). The vertical broad white stripe is the spine of the Sky with Venus and the Pleiades; the horizontal white stripe is the Milky Way with the Moon below the tail of Father Sky. The points on the tail are the twelve men who never die, the months. These twelve men are also called "the spirits of the wind, the sun, the moon, the rain, the rainbow, pollen, everlasting life, lightning, heat, cold, stars and the clouds, all things that are in the heavens, except the pollen which blows on the wind and is the symbol of life" (Wyman 1952:75). If this were a Blessingway painting, it would be made of materials other than sand. (Adapted from a painting collected by Wetherill; singer, Yellow Singer [Sam Chief], 1910–18. Courtesy Wheelwright Museum, P1#13.)

by Big Star and the Star People who teach them the ceremonial, which they bring back from their sky visit to heal the Earth Surface People; the events from which the Big Star ceremonial derives are the encounters of the younger brother. Big Star teaches the hero's older son the male form of the ceremony; his wife, the female form; and his younger son, the Evil Chasing form (Spencer 1957:126). The "Father Sky" sandpainting (fig. 5.1) belongs to the Evil Chasing form of the Big Star ceremonial. One feature common to the stories of these three chantways is a sky visit by the hero or heroes.

Although Wyman (1983a:23) classified Plumeway as a Holyway ceremonial, he noted (1962:87) Reichard's (1950:329) remark that she would expect the Feather Chant (Plumeway) to be an Evilway ceremonial because of its exorcistic emphasis. One procedure characteristic of an Evilway ceremonial is the use of sandpaintings at night. The documentation accompanying the Plumeway "Father Sky" does not indicate if this painting is created at night. The remarkable similarity between the Big Star Chant "Father Sky" (fig. 5.1) and the Plumeway "Father Sky" (fig. 5.2)—the same distinctive body shape (different from other Father Sky forms) and accompaniment by big stars (around the Father Sky of the Big Star Chant and on the body of the Plumeway Father Sky)—leads me to believe that the Plumeway "Father Sky" might be performed in an Evilway form of this ceremonial (it is known that the Big Star Chant "Father Sky" is performed according to Evilway).

THE SKIES

A depiction of the constellations that belongs exclusively to the Male Shootingway is "The Skies." This painting, described in the last chapter, is referred to by chanters as "The Dawn" and is illustrated in plates 2 and 3 and in figure 5.5. The four trapezoidal (fig. 5.5) or keystone forms (plates 2 and 3) show the sky at four times of day as the sun passes "through the hours of the day" (Wyman 1983a:109). The association of subdivisions of the day (symbolized by specific colors) with directions is known as the day-sky sequence (Reichard 1950:163, 190). As previously explained, the "Skies" painting is a visual representation of the four cardinal light phenomena—the white of dawn in the east, the blue of day sky in the south, the yellow of evening in the west, and the black of darkness or night in the north.

In the Male Shootingway story (Reichard 1977:42), the first paintings the

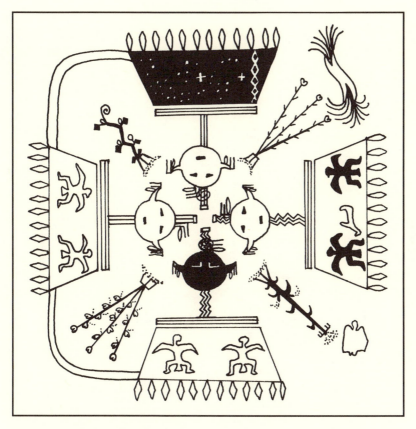

Fig. 5.5. "The Skies," Male Shootingway. (Adapted from a painting collected by Newcomb; singers, Klahtso's sons, before 1930. Courtesy Wheelwright Museum, P4#3.)

Sun showed his children, the Sacred Twins, were those of the skies with domesticated plants, the skies without plants, and the Sun's house.

STARS AS BACKGROUND FOR OTHER FIGURES

A third mode of representation is to depict constellations as a background for other figures; this format is followed in sandpaintings from the Hand Tremblingway (fig. 5.6) and from Beadway (fig. 5.7) and in a drypainting from Blessingway (fig. 5.8).

The Hand Tremblingway Evilway painting (fig. 5.6) is made just after

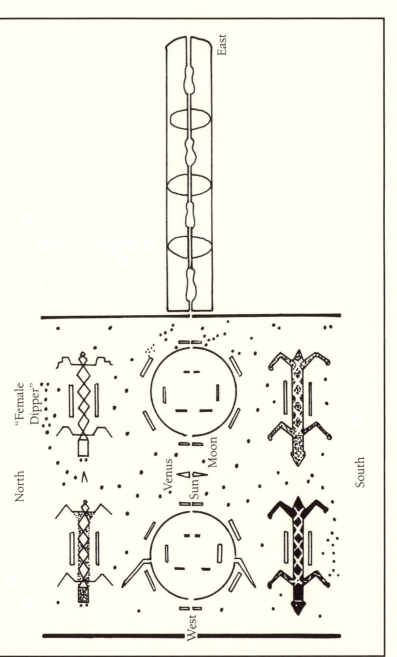

Fig. 5.6. "Gila Monsters," Hand Tremblingway Evilway. Constellations identified by Oakes (Willie Yazzie): the Big Dipper is south of the black (southwestern) Gila Monster, and Cassiopeia is north of the white (northeastern) Gila Monster. The Pleiades lie northeast of the Moon (the round form without horns) and Orion is east of the Moon. Unlike most paintings, this one would be made after sundown, on a white buckskin (or white cloth) pegged down over a platform of brown sand; it would be made of sand and meal. (Adapted from a painting collected by Oakes; singer, Willie Yazzie, 1946–47. Courtesy Wheelwright Museum, P17#11)

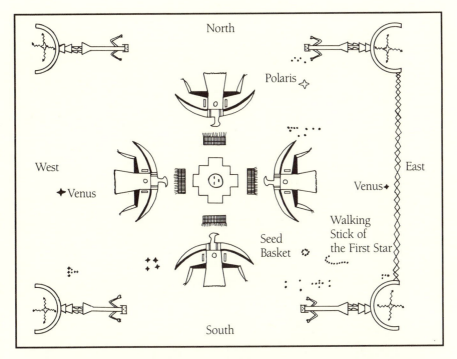

Fig. 5.7. "Home of the Eagles," Beadway. Constellations identified by Wetherill (Sam Chief) (in Wyman 1952: 109–12): Rabbit Tracks at southeast; west of Rabbit Tracks, Scorpius ("first star"; Wetherill does not identify Rabbit Tracks as the tail of Scorpius); north of Scorpius, "the walking stick of the first star"; west of Scorpius, "the seed basket"; west of the south Eagle, Corvus; at southwest, the Pleiades; north of the east Eagle, Ursa Major (which includes the Big Dipper); north of Ursa Major, Cassiopeia. (Adapted from a painting collected by Wetherill; singer, Yellow Singer [Sam Chief], 1910–18. Courtesy Wheelwright Museum, P19#14.)

sundown, on a white buckskin or white cloth. Here the constellations serve as a background for the Gila Monster, the deity of Hand Trembling divination. Kluckhohn found a variant of this sandpainting (also with constellations) made for the Holyway version of Hand Tremblingway (Kluckhohn and Wyman 1940:182). One of Kluckhohn and Wyman's informants (1940: 183) explained that "the stars [in figure 5.6] afford protection."

The constellations in the Beadway sandpainting (fig. 5.7) made by Yellow Singer (Sam Chief) and collected by Louisa Wetherill between 1910 and 1918 are particularly appropriate because this painting is an illustration of

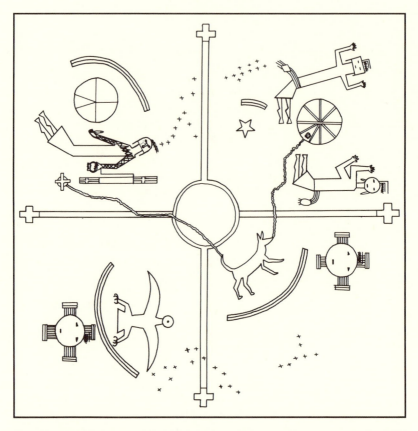

Fig. 5.8. "First Man Group," Blessingway. As a Blessingway painting, this would be made of materials other than sand. (Adapted from a painting collected by Henderson; singer, Bit'ahnii Bidághaa'í, 1938. Courtesy Wheelwright Museum, P1A#10.)

the homes of the Eagle People in the land beyond the sky that is described in the Beadway story. The figures that stand at each corner atop a rainbow are "the props that hold up the heavens, the men that never die,"[4] while at the center, we see the four "eagle men" whose heads point toward "the opening into the heavens" located at the center of the painting (Wyman 1952: 110). The chanter Miguelito recounted the myth of Beadway for Reichard (1977); the paintings of Beadway present a more continuous narrative than do the paintings of most chants. This painting is described at greater length later in this chapter.

The Blessingway drypainting in figure 5.8 was recorded in 1938 from chanter Bearded Bit-ahni by William Henderson and depicts First Man, First Woman, Black God, and Coyote. This painting is called "First Man Group (First Family)." It is subtitled "Coyote Steals the Fire": Coyote and the First People suffered intensely from the cold until Coyote stole fire both for himself and for the benefit of humanity; Coyote burned his tail in the process, which is why even today his tail is tipped with black (Newcomb 1967:138-50). A line of fire stretches from the fire symbol, the cross near Black God's left hand (in the upper lefthand quadrant), to Coyote's tail and from Coyote's nose into the hogan of First Man and First Woman (in the upper righthand quadrant). Chanter E said that the constellation in each quadrant belongs to the Holy Person in that particular quadrant; therefore (moving clockwise from the upper righthand quadrant) we see First Man and First Woman's constellation, followed by those of Coyote, Eagle, and finally Black God. These are clearly metaphoric constellations: Black God's constellation, the Pleiades, and First Man's and First Woman's constellations, the Big Dipper and Cassiopeia, are not drawn as they usually are in Navajo depictions.

In contrasting the three examples of constellations-as-background, we can see that these chants have relatively little in common. The Hand Tremblingway is usually performed according to Evilway, and the only reason suggested by Kluckhohn and Wyman (1940:183) for the presence of stars in the painting is protection, which is needed in an Evilway chantway sandpainting. In Beadway, a Holyway ceremonial, constellations are an integral part of the background for the homes of the Eagle People; thus, constellations serve as an illustration of the story. The constellations in the Blessingway meal-and-pollen painting enhance the narrative but are definitely not a major feature of either the story or the painting.

THE HAILWAY NIGHT SKY

Constellations are also depicted in the "Night Sky" painting unique to Hailway (fig. 5.9). Here the heads of twelve Storm People bearing the distinctive Sun's house stripes line the rectangular night sky on which are depicted the constellations. Wheelwright (1946a:3–45) and Reichard (1944a:3–155) recorded the two published versions of this myth from Tł'aii presumably at different times. The "Sky" or "Universe" painting (fig. 5.9) was made on the ninth day of the ceremonial to represent the sky supported by twelve cyclones or Storm People who support the sky and "move everything in it"

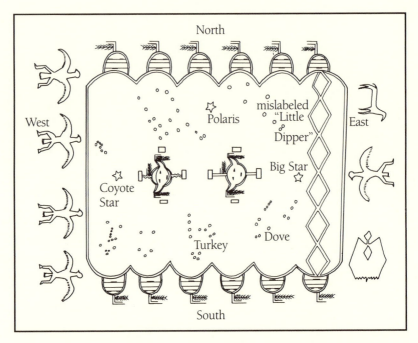

Fig. 5.9. "Night Sky," Hailway. Constellations identified by Newcomb (Tł'aii): the Milky Way is the zigzag path in the east; in the north are the Big Dipper and "the Little Dipper" (which is actually Cassiopeia); in the south are Rabbit Tracks, Hastiin Sik'ai'í, the Turkey, and the Dove; at the west are the Coyote Star and the Pleiades. (Adapted from a painting collected by Newcomb; singer, Hastiin Tł'aii, before 1933. Courtesy Wheelwright Museum, P2#16A.)

(including the constellations) (Wheelwright 1946a:29,192). The Hailway, at least as practiced by Tł'aii, is no longer performed (Wheelwright 1946a:3; Wyman 1983a:23).

STARS REFLECTED IN THE OCEANS

We see the reflections of the constellations, rather than their actual images, in the eastern and western oceans in a painting from Waterway (fig. 5.10), also known as the Rain ceremony (Haile 1979:144). Náhookǫs biką'ii (the Big Dipper) appears briefly to ask the hero and his wives, "Whence do you come?" and to tell them they do not have far to go, in Wheelwright's (1946a:62) version of the story. The depiction of the constellations could be

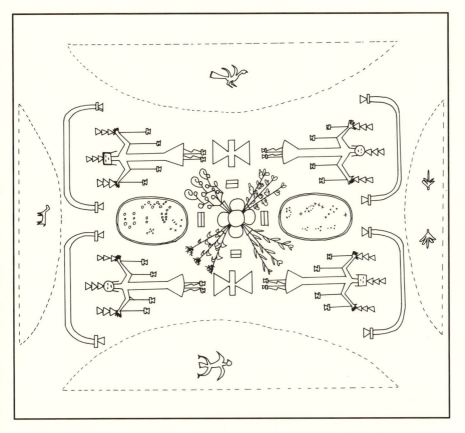

Fig. 5.10. "Rain People," Waterway. (Adapted from a painting collected by Newcomb; singer, Bit'ahnii Bidághaa'í, 1938. Courtesy Wheelwright Museum, P3A#4A.)

a visual acknowledgment of this assistance from Náhookǫs biką'ii; it is more probable that this painting, the second-day sandpainting of a Rain ceremony by the singer Furhat (Bit'ahnii Bidághaa'í (collected by Newcomb in 1938), is an illustration of the earth's surface after the Emergence with an emphasis on water sources. In the center is the Emergence lake; four Rain (Cloud) People stand on mountaintops indicated by double clouds-meeting-earth; mists (also a source of water) surround the painting; and, in two large bodies of water that probably represent the eastern and western oceans, we see constellations reflected. By depicting the constellations, the chanter was able to represent aspects of both earth and sky, creating a sense of balance and

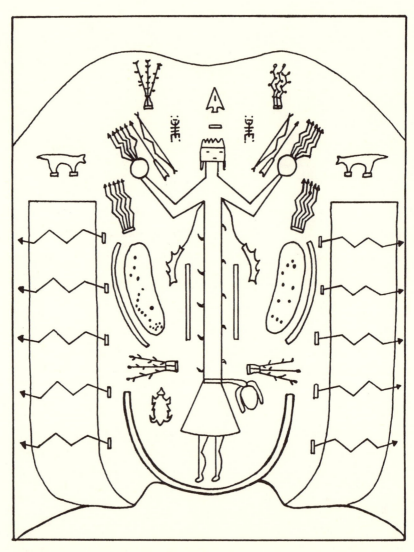

Fig. 5.11. "The One Who Controls the Rain," Upward Reachingway. (Adapted from a painting collected by Newcomb; singer, Bit'ahnii Bidághaa'í, 1936. Courtesy Wheelwright Museum, P21#8.)

wholeness. Unfortunately, few Waterway paintings have been recorded because this chant is no longer practiced (Wyman 1952:32).

WINTER AND SUMMER SKIES

A painting from Upward Reachingway Evilway depicts "The One Who Controls the Rain" (fig. 5.11). This painting, collected by Newcomb in 1936, was also created by the singer Furhat; it is another Emergence painting. Obvious similarities exist between the Waterway sandpainting (fig. 5.10) and this Upward Reachingway sandpainting (fig. 5.11): both depict beings that are responsible for rain, the mountaintops on which clouds gather, the four sacred plants, and the constellations on blue and black ovals. Newcomb's documentation (Wheelwright Museum Sandpainting Reproduction Catalogue, n.d.), however, says that the ovals in the Upward Reachingway painting represent the winter and summer skies rather than the eastern and western oceans. When I showed this painting to Chanter E, he interpreted the blue and black constellation-bearing ovals as Mother Earth and Father Sky. An underlying similarity among these constellation depictions and interpretations is pairing for balance and completion: blue and black, the eastern and western oceans, the winter and summer skies, and Chanter E's interpretation of Mother Earth and Father Sky. Again, we see the pervasive Navajo emphasis on complementary pairing for wholeness and holiness.

EARTH AND SKY

A "Mother Earth, Father Sky" image from the War Prophylactic Rite (fig. 5.12) is quite different from previous images of these subjects. In a painting unique to this ceremonial, the Earth and Sky take the form of adjoining rectangles instead of bodies with overlapping hands and feet. When Maud Oakes collected this painting in 1942 from singer Jeff King, he told her, "This painting . . . is for warriors, to give them the strength and protection of their Earth Mother and Sky Father" (Oakes, Campbell, and King 1969:55). The drypaintings of the War Prophylactic Rite illustrate the myth of Monsterway, especially the portion entitled "Where the Two Came to Their Father." This tells the story of the obstacles overcome by the Sacred Twins in their journey to their father, the Sun. A depiction of the constellations is quite appropriate for this story in which the Sun's home plays a major role. The constellations depicted in this painting are described later in this chapter.

east

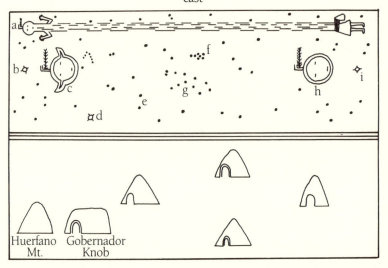

Fig. 5.12. "Earth and Sky," War Prophylactic Rite. Constellations identified by Oakes (Jeff King) are, from east to west: "Milky Way Man, Boss Sparkling Star of the East, the white Sun, the yellow Coyote Star, the seven Eastern Stars, the seven stars of the Pleiades, the twelve stars of the Dipper, the Moon, and the Big White Star of the West." It is unusual that the Sun would be white instead of blue. "This painting . . . is for warriors, to give them the strength and protection of their Earth Mother and Sky Father" (Jeff King). This painting would preferably be made on buckskin and executed in cornmeal; ground flowers; the pollen of flowers, plants, and trees; and charcoal. (Adapted from a painting collected by Oakes; singer, Jeff King, 1942. Courtesy Wheelwright Museum, WPR 14.)

STAR MAPS

The star map (fig. 5.13) is unique in being the only painting devoted entirely to a map of the sky. The chanters with whom I worked even questioned whether it was an actual sandpainting. Wyman (1983a:109) described this star map as follows: "A unique painting of a star map said to be for Big Starway is among the rather offbeat creations of Sam Chief in the Wetherill Collection." Wetherill's description of this painting (in Wyman [1952:47]) identifies the constellations and says, "This is the heavens Didelgay [Dilyéhé, the Pleiades, the hero of the Big Star Chant, according to Wetherill] told the people about after his return from the skies." The two star maps that occupy the entire field of the sandpainting—the Beadway "Home of the Eagle

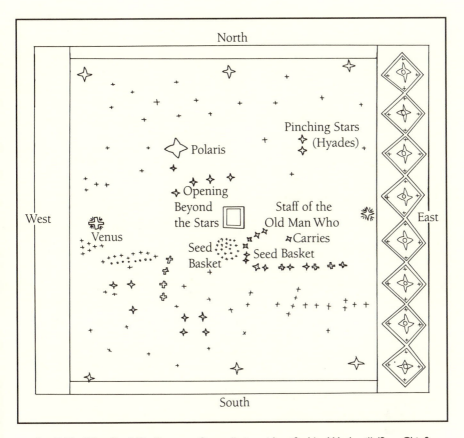

North

Pinching Stars
✧ (Hyades)
☐ Polaris

✦✦✦
✦ Opening
Beyond
the Stars ☐   Staff of the
Old Man Who
Venus   ⋈ Carries
Seed 　　 ⋈ Seed Basket
Basket

West   East

South

Fig. 5.13. "The Sky," Big Starway. Constellations identified by Wetherill (Sam Chief) (in Wyman 1952:47): "East: Milky Way . . . south of center, circular patch . . . 'the seed basket'; east of it, 'the staff of the old man who carries the seed basket'; south of the latter, Orion; west of Orion, Scorpius; . . . large star at west . . . Venus; south of Venus, the Pleiades; north of Venus, 'the rabbit tracks' . . . ; east of the latter, Cassiopeia; north of the latter, Ursa Major . . . ; two stars east of it, the pinching stars (center double stars in the lower branch of the Hyades)." (Adapted from a painting collected by Wetherill; singer, Yellow Singer [Sam Chief], 1910–18. Courtesy Wheelwright Museum, P8B#14.)

People" painting (fig. 5.7) and this Big Starway painting (fig. 5.13)—are both products of Yellow Singer (Sam Chief). Sam Chief's sandpainting designs have been described as "undoubtedly idiosyncratic" and decidedly unorthodox" (Wyman 1983a:45); I feel that they are probably not accurate reproductions of ceremonial sandpaintings. (They are also the only two sandpaintings that include a Seed Basket constellation, which makes me believe that this is a metaphoric rather than an actual constellation. Once again, it is important not to read more into these sandpainting interpretations of the sky than is actually present.)

INDIVIDUAL CONSTELLATIONS

In paintings from two chants we see Dilyéhé (the Pleiades) depicted in isolation from other constellations; this is the only constellation in the sand-

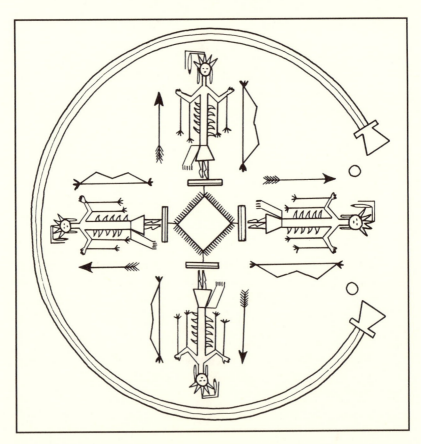

Fig. 5.14. "Star People and Blue Star," Big Starway. The Star People represent the Big Dipper. (Adapted from a painting collected by Armer; singer unknown, 1929. Courtesy Wheelwright Museum, P8B#1A.)

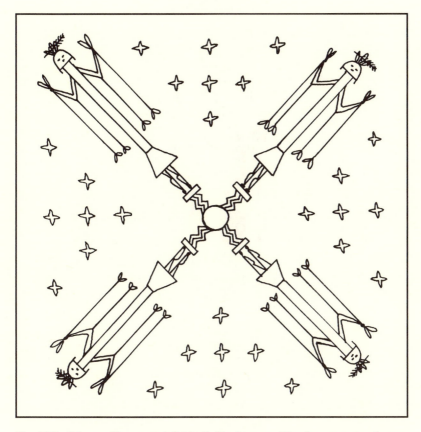

Fig. 5.15. "Human Figures and Spirits," Big Starway. The four groups of seven stars represent Dilyéhé (the Pleiades). (Adapted from a painting collected by Wetherill; singer, Yellow Singer [Sam Chief], 1910–18. Courtesy Wheelwright Museum, P8B#12.)

paintings I have studied that is depicted alone in star form. Náhookǫs biką'ii (the Big Dipper) is depicted in the form of people in figure 5.14; this painting is discussed later in this chapter. In a painting from the Big Star Chant (fig. 5.15), another of Sam Chief's works, the group of seven stars represents "tracks made by Didelgay [Dilyéhé, the hero of the story] when he came back to heal his people. They are still in the heavens and are called the boy chasing an arrow" (Wetherill, in Wyman [1952:46]). In a detail from a Nightway painting (fig. 5.16), we see a far different depiction of Dil-

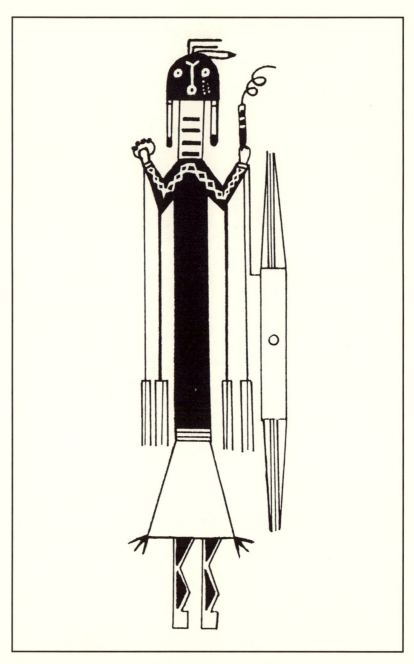

Fig. 5.16. Black God, detail from Nightway painting. (Adapted from a painting collected by Newcomb; singer, Hastiin Tł'aii, before 1933. Courtesy Wheelwright Museum, P11#9.)

yéhé: here it is depicted on the mask of Black God. The association between Black God and the Pleiades will be discussed in the next chapter.

BIG STARS

A final style in which stars are depicted in sandpaintings is in the form of big stars (fig. 5.17). When stars are the main theme of the painting, they are either lozenge-shaped or square-bodied (oriented like a diamond) and are bordered with short rays of all colors, or else they are four- or eight-pointed stars. Big stars appear in paintings from the Nightway, the Plumeway, the

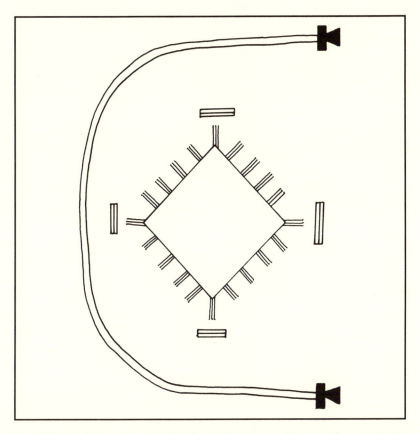

Fig. 5.17. "Big Yellow Star of the West," Big Starway. (Adapted from a painting collected by Armer; singer unknown, 1929. Courtesy Wheelwright Museum, P8B#4.)

Hand Tremblingway, and the Big Starway. These stars seem to have no Western counterpart in the night sky. Big stars will be discussed at greater length in the next chapter.

THE HEAVENS IN CHANTWAY NARRATIVES
AND SANDPAINTINGS

Now that I have explored the visual contexts in which the heavens appear, I will integrate these visual depictions from the sandpaintings with verbal accounts from chantway narratives to present a composite view of the Navajo heavens.[5] Wheelwright's (1988) version of the Sǫ'tsojí, or Great Star Myth; Reichard's (1977) version of the Yoo'ee, or Beadway; and the sandpaintings collected by Wetherill (in Wyman [1952]) furnish the most graphic account of the celestial realm with its inhabitants, hostile birds of prey and infinitely powerful yet friendly Star People, and also give some sense of how the heavens are structured. Newcomb and Reichard's (1975) version of the Na'at'oyee bikạ'jí, or the Male Shootingway, vividly describes the Sun and his house; sandpaintings from this ceremonial are the primary context for the depiction of the constellations. Constellations play a role in two chantway myths: the Big Dipper in Haile's (1932) Chiricahua Windway and the Pleiades in Wetherill's (in Wyman [1952]) version of the Big Star Way (an entirely different story from Wheelwright's Big Star Way).

The Structure of the Heavens and the Star People:
The Myth of the Great Star Chant

The myth that presents the most vivid account of the heavens belongs to the Sǫ'tsojí, or Great Star Chant, which is seldom performed today.[6] In this dramatic and beautiful story, the hero, Younger Brother, was transported to the sky after being tricked by Coyote, who wanted Younger Brother's wife. The hero arrived in the sky world by means of a supernatural rock, which grew until it reached the circular opening to the sky. However, the sky retracted each time he tried to step off the rock until he offered black *n'itł'iz*, powdered jet, to the eastern sky. The rock then sank back to earth, leaving Younger Brother in the country of the sky. Thus, the hero was not allowed to set foot in this sacred realm until he presented an offering, a show of respect to the *diyin dine'é*.

What did Younger Brother see when he looked around at his celestial surroundings? The sky opening from which he had emerged was at the center of a circle of long dwellings in the sacred colors (the hogan in the east is white, that to the south is blue, the hogan to the west is yellow, and the one to the north is black). Surrounding these dwellings, which belonged to hostile birds of prey, was a concentric, outer circle of homes in the same colors.

While Younger Brother was trying to absorb the new surroundings in which he had so suddenly found himself, the Eagle People, Hawk People, and Buzzard People, who lived in the inner circle of dwellings, crowded around him, peering at him with great hostility. They did not understand him when he spoke to them.

The hero found an opening in the crowd and left these hostile beings for the outer circle of dwellings, where he encountered the Star People. In sharp contrast to the birds of prey, the Star People were friendly and understood his speech. They expressed curiosity over his sudden appearance and mysterious means of transportation. "How did you get up to this place?" they wanted to know. "No Earth People should ever come this high in the sky."

Younger Brother felt he could trust them and told them of his intense desire to find a way down to earth again. The Star People were concerned about his welfare, and one of them warned the hero to stay in the black hogan near where they stood. "You should not go off alone because there are many bad people around," he explained.

The Star People took Younger Brother inside the black hogan, telling him, "This house belongs to Sontso, the Great Black Star. The people here are all your friends."

Younger Brother responded by calling them Diné [the Navajo's name for themselves, meaning "The People"] as he looked around at them with a sense of kinship. Thus, a kindred feeling was established between those on earth and these powerful, benevolent Star People.

The impression of similarity between the Earth Surface People and their celestial counterparts was strengthened when the latter served Younger Brother food "just like what he had below on the earth," which they ate along with him. As they shared this act of hospitality and peace, the Star People reassured him, "We will help you reach the earth again."

They described the inner circle of dwellings with their inhabitants: "The Eagle People own the white hogan which was the first dwelling that you reached when you came to the sky. The blue hogan in the south is the home of several kinds of Hawk People: the Chicken Hawk, the Grey Hawk, the Grey Barred Hawk, and two other smaller hawks. The Yellow-Winged or Yellow-Tailed Hawks live in the yellow hogan. And in the black hogan in the north live the Black Eagle, the White-Headed Eagle, the Buzzard, and the White Eagle.

"Now you are in the hogan of the Black Star People. The Blue Star People live in the blue hogan to the south, the Yellow Star People live in the hogan to the west, and the White Star People live in the hogan to the north."

Younger Brother looked around at each kind of Star People, observing that the Black Star People were dressed in black flint, the Yellow Star People in yellow flint, the Blue Star People in blue flint, and the White Star People in white flint. Then he noticed a fifth kind of Star People, the Many-Pointed Star People, who lived overhead, and were dressed in flint of all colors.

After this description of Younger Brother's immediate surroundings, the Star People explained, "As soon as you arrived in the sky, everyone knew that you were here and that you belonged to the earth because the Wind told us."

The Black Star People added a warning, "Don't go near the place where you came up from the earth. Stay with us and you will be safe, and, when we think you are ready to go back to the earth, then you can go to the opening."

Younger Brother, compelled by the Wind, repeatedly disregarded such warnings not to wander. He had to be rescued from his first adventure but in a second adventure he was victorious through his own efforts.

At this point, he began a lengthy apprenticeship in ceremonial learning under the tutelage of Sontso, the Great Black Star. He learned the Great Star ceremony and returned to earth to take revenge on Coyote. After teaching the ceremony to his own people, he and his brother departed to live with the Star People.

Now let us look at the sandpaintings that refer to these events.[7] Plate 5 is a photograph of an actual sandpainting, made at the Wheelwright Museum, with the magical Sky-Reaching Rock that transported Younger Brother to the heavens. (Although this painting is from the Male Shootingway, the supernatural rock is the same as the one in the story of the Great Star Chant.) As can be seen from the photograph (and as described earlier), when reproduced for a sandpainting ceremony, the rock is a three-dimensional cone measuring nine to twelve inches in height and about six inches in diameter at the base, tapering to about five inches in diameter at the top. The top is concave, forming a base for the chanter's abalone shell of chant infusion. Sky-Reaching Rock is made of clay carefully kneaded into shape. It is significant that when earthly mountains are depicted in sandpaintings, they are ephemeral mounds made of sand, constructed with the sandpainting and then destroyed with it. This sculptural representation, however, is permanent: the clay cone is saved as part of the Male Shootingway chanter's ceremonial equipment. This difference clearly emphasizes the distinction between the terrestrial and celestial realms.

The opening to the heavens, surrounded by the circle of long dwellings in the sacred colors, is depicted in the center of the sandpainting in figure 5.7.[8] The sun lies at the center of this skyhole. The long bars (in white, turquoise, yellow, and black) around this opening are the houses of the Eagle People, with fringes of smoke issuing from them. The inhabitants of the sky world— the Eagle Men—stand behind their homes. These men have white bodies with white and red wings fringed in black; red, blue, and yellow stripes on their breasts; red stripes on their hearts; and black thighs with yellow calves and feet. At their sides, between their wings and legs, the Eagle Men are protected by rainbow bars or sundogs.[9] In the corners are the men who support the heavens. (The constellations in this painting will be described in the Beauty Chant section of this chapter.)

The opening to the heavens is depicted in two other sandpaintings: according to Chanter A, the four keystone shapes of the Male Shootingway painting called "The Skies" (plate 3) represent this opening; the center of the Big Starway painting (fig. 5.13) also represents the opening to the heavens. Wetherill (in Wyman [1952:47, 110]) referred to the skyhole as both "the opening beyond the stars" and as "the opening into the heavens." To the latter description she added, "The eagle people and their houses are beyond the heavens so we cannot see them, the rest we can see" (in Wyman [1952:110]).

This impression of layered heavens coincides with Reichard's description of these two higher realms of the universe. She (1950:17) explains that

> The sky is a world just like this one; in it Sun, Moon, and stars are visible to us as they move through the space between the world hemispheres. Above the stratum into which we look, the heavenly bodies have their home, living much like the people on earth. The better-known Thunders also live in the sky realm.
>
> The Land-beyond-the-sky is inhabited by extra-powerful storm elements— Winter, Pink and Spotted Thunders, Big Winds, and Whirlwinds. They run a school for novices learning the ritual of the Male Shooting, Hail, Water, and Feather chants; the pupils are conducted thither and back by other gods.

The Star People, who play such a prominent role in the story of the Big Star Chant, are depicted in several sandpaintings and in several different guises. First, we see the Star People, including the Great Black Star, depicted as four-pointed stars;[10] they sit in the hogan of the Great Black Star in figure 5.18. In this painting from the Great Star Chant Evil Chasing ceremonial, the Black Star is next to the entrance at the black point that is toward the east. The spatulate objects are the ceremonial knives of the various stars; these knives are connected by their paths to the different stars that use them and are of the same color as the stars to which they belong. Thus, we see the Great Black Star to the east with his black flint knife, the Blue Star with his blue knife to the south, the Yellow Star to the west with his yellow knife,

Fig. 5.18. "Black Hogan of the Star People," Big Starway. (Adapted from a painting collected by Oakes; singer, Edwin Martin, 1946–47. Courtesy Wheelwright Museum, P8C#1.)

and the White Star with his white knife to the north. Younger Brother sat in the center, and the Stars taught him their songs and prayers.

A big, or great, star may also be depicted as an individual diamond-shaped entity, such as the large Yellow Star of the west with a fringe of rays, blue, white, black, and red (fig. 5.17).[11] In this Big Starway painting, rainbow bars surround the star at the four cardinal points while a rainbow guardian encircles the star, ending at the eastern opening with a black raincloud symbol.

Star People as well as specific constellations may also be depicted in human form in sandpaintings. As was explained previously, humans are made from the same elements as the stars.[12] The stars are depicted in human form to remind people of the relationship and its accompanying kinship responsibilities.

When stars are depicted in human form, they may represent the Star People in general or specific constellations. In Big Starway paintings, two constellations—Náhookǫs Biką'ii (the Big Dipper) and Dilyéhé (the Pleiades)—are represented as people. In the painting in figure 5.14 we have already seen Náhookǫs Biką'ii in human form. At the center of the painting, blue water with a yellow pollen edge symbolizes the glitter of the stars. White lines lead to the rainbow bars on which the four Star People representing the Dipper whirl about the central body of water, which is located on earth. As previously explained, the Navajo name for this constellation is translated as "The Male One Who Revolves" or "Whirling Male"; this is why the stars are said "to whirl" about the central image.

As we have seen, the *diyin dine'é,* Holy People, can be benevolent or dangerously destructive depending upon the context. In Wheelwright's version of the Big Star myth, the Great Black Star, though powerful, is characterized as a benevolent being who forgives the hero's transgressions and generously shares his ceremonial knowledge for the benefit of those on earth. However, a painting like the one shown in figure 6.4, made for the purpose of banishing evil dreams and fear of darkness, depicts a more malevolent manifestation of a star similar to the Black Star. The dichotomy between apparently conflicting characterizations of the same entity exemplifies the point that the *diyin dine'é* possess dangerous power, which they can exhibit at will. The star in this painting—the Great Blue Star—obstinately refused to emit light or to travel a given path; instead, it willfully roams wherever it desires, sending forth little "imps" with arrows on their heads to annoy people who travel at night. In her description, Newcomb characterized all stars as "more or less evil," adding that the Black Star and its companion, the Blue Star (fig. 6.4), are feared most of all because they cannot be seen as they move through the sky (since they do not emit light). To these stars is attributed all of the sickness and accidents that befall those who are abroad at night. Furthermore, if someone travels often at night without falling into such trouble, this person is said to be guarded by evil spirits.

Another large star, also from the Big Star Chant, but one with a more positive connotation is shown in figure 5.19. Here we see five spirit rays issuing from a white five-pointed star while arrows fly around it. Unfortu-

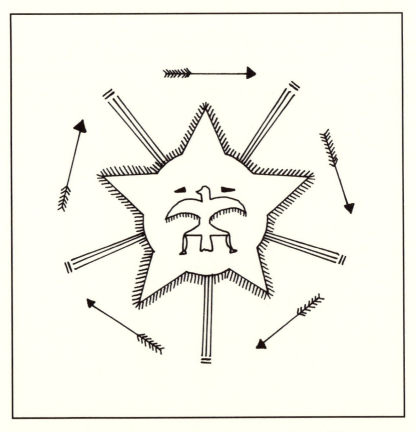

Fig. 5.19. "Five Pointed Star and Blue Bird," Big Starway. (Adapted from a painting collected by Newcomb; singer, Hastiin Tł'aii, 1930. Courtesy Wheelwright Museum, P8#6.)

nately, this painting lacks an extensive description; however, the bluebird seen on the star is symbolic of peace and happiness. This bird, generally beloved by the Navajo, is a herald of the dawn as well as a manifestation of Talking God, who told the hero of the Night Chant that he would appear among the Navajos as a bluebird. The feathers of the bluebird are required for many ceremonies. Because the bluebird is depicted on the face of this star and because the star is white, a color signifying innate goodness and sacredness, this star has a more beneficent interpretation.

The Creation of the Constellations: The Upward Moving and Emergence Way, Blessingway, and (Wetherill's) Beauty Chant Story

Few chantway myths actually include the origin of the constellations. Two myths that mention the constellations by name are the Upward Moving and Emergence Way, the story of prehuman beings as they moved upward through the various underworlds and finally emerged onto the earth's surface, and Blessingway, which focuses on post-Emergence events.

The story of stellar creation from the Upward Moving and Emergence Way (Haile 1981a) is nearly identical to the story presented in chapter 4. The Blessingway account goes into less detail regarding the placement of the constellations, but Wyman (1970a:339) does mention the following constellations: the Big Dipper, the Little Dipper,[13] the Pleiades, Orion, Corvus, Scorpius, stars under Canis Major, and the Milky Way.

Another of the few chantway myths to describe in detail the placing of the constellations is found in Louisa Wetherill's (in Wyman [1952:112]) "Beauty Chant Story."[14] This account, which accompanies the painting shown in figure 5.7 (as the depiction of the opening to the heavens), is quite different from the two previous accounts of the placement of the constellations:

> The first man and the first woman made the sun and hung it in the heavens with a spider web. Then they made the stars and hung them in the heavens; then they made the rainbows and put them in the corners of the heavens. Then they said to each other, "If we do not build a prop for the heavens they will fall down; what shall we build it of?" So they thought and thought, and then the man said, "We will make four men of *mirage stone*—and put them at the corners of the heavens on the rainbows, and they can hold the heavens up." So they made them, and they hold the heavens up, and they never die.
>
> Then after they had made the sun, moon, and stars, and all the things in the heavens and the earth, with the aid of their son in the heavens, the man went

to the house of the sun in the east and the woman went to the house of the sun's wife in the west. We cannot see them now but we can see their shadows and their fires at night. The great bear is the shadow of the man, and *Cassiopeia* is the shadow of the woman, and the north star is their 'fire. *Scorpio* is the shadow of the chief of the good natured people, who died of old age; the walking stick is his walking stick; the basket is what he eats from; the rabbit tracks are what he eats. *Corvus* is the blue bottle fly that carried the news over the heavens; the *Pleiades* are their ants, the yellow ants, the black ants, the little black ants, the cicada, the badger, and the blue coyote, that came from beneath the earth; after they died they went up there to live.

The blush of dawn [the Milky Way] is some bread that the first girl was making when the first boy stole it and ran with it to the east, so it is there now. The war gods of the stars are four guards that the first man and the first woman made to guard them while they slept while they were on the earth, and when they stretched the earth they set them up at the four corners to guard the earth. Their names are the big black star, the big blue star, the big yellow star, and the big white star.

The Sun's House: The Myth of the Male Shootingway

The epic myth of the Male Shootingway focuses on the Sacred Twins, Slayer-of-Alien-Gods (known more commonly as Monster Slayer) and Child-of-the-Water (known as Born-for-Water), describing their conception, birth, travels, and adventures as they acquire ceremonial powers.[15] In this myth, we get a somewhat different glimpse of the heavens than in the Sǫ'tsojí or Great Star Chant. The Male Shootingway provides us with a characterization of Sun, his house, Changing Woman's house, and constellations on the body of Father Sky and in the form of the night sky.

The mother of the Twins is Changing Woman, one of the most fascinating and appealing of the *diyin dine'é*. Although she is often paired (as a contrastive complement) with Sun, she is never drawn, unless the representation of Earth in sandpaintings can be said to symbolize her. With her powers of senescence and rejuvenation, she symbolizes the annual cycle of the earth, which renews itself in spring and gradually dies with the coming of winter, only to begin anew the pattern of seasonal rebirth the following spring.

One day, soon after she reached puberty, she went to gather seeds and met a magnificent being dressed in white who was elevated some two feet above the ground on a white horse with a white bridle. This was the Sun, a being so handsome that women dared not look at him because they felt so inferior. The Sacred Twins resulted from the union of Sun and Changing Woman.

The Twins were curious about their father, and in response to their questions, Changing Woman told them, "Far away your father lives. Between here and there every conceivable danger lies. Now go to sleep and think no more of it."

They felt driven to seek their father, Sun, who lived with his acknowledged wife in the sky. The Twins had to pass a series of trials in order to prove their parentage. As Reichard (1950:472) said, "Apparently so many children claimed him as their father that only the severest tests could prove their legitimacy."

Despite almost insurmountable supernatural obstacles, the Twins survived. After Wind carried them over the final obstacle, Sliding-Sand-Dune, the Twins crossed a red mountain, then a glittering mountain, an abalone mountain, a whiteshell mountain, and finally a turquoise mountain, all belonging to the Sun. Not far from the blue mountain stood their father's house. Immediately, they recognized this magnificent dwelling as that of the Sun because of its unparalleled beauty and its distinctive four colors, white at the east, blue at the south, yellow at the west, and black at the north.

The Sun's house was guarded by two Winds, Thunders, a pair of Snakes, and a pair of Bears. Located on the shore of the eastern ocean, this pueblo-style house was made of turquoise. Rooms branching off from the central room served as showrooms for Sun's wealth: to the south a room housed his flocks, stores of blankets were stacked in a room to the west, while to the north were farms and corn (Stephen 1930:93).

At each side of the house were twelve rattles composed of precious stones to sound and give forth lightning to herald Sun's arrival. Clothing and weapons were hung upon pegs on the walls while, on a special peg, Sun hung the sun every night.

The Sun hurled the Twins against spiked, barbed flints of the same precious stones as those that composed his rattles. Each of these flints (which resembled a trumpet) folded on itself, crushing its victim. However, the Twins were protected by life feathers given them by Spider Woman. When the Flints touched the life feathers they drew back, leaving the Twins unharmed. The Sun subjected them to further tests: the poison of the sphinx-worm; a freezing test on a small rocky island; exploding agate in a sweatbath. By surviving, they proved that they were indeed the Sun's children.

After acknowledging his children, the Sun asked them why they had come. "I will give you horses of all colors, the mule which becomes mirage, even the sheep with the thin-bladed horns which is the one I cherish most. I will give you my precious stones. Did you come for dark clouds with male rain, dark mist, female rain or the mirage which turns into a gray-bellied burro?"

"Yes, Father, all those things are precious, and the Earth Surface People would much like to have them, but that is not why we have come. We came about these monsters, the Monster-Evil, Horned-Monster, Kicking-Off-Rocks, Throwing-Against-Rocks, Tracking-Bear, Eye-Killers, and the others. They eat up all people and they cannot flourish on earth. We want obsidian armor, shoes, clothes, and headdress and lightning arrows in order to overcome the earth monsters."

Sun then bowed his head in sorrow, his eyes filling with tears. After a few minutes, he looked up at his children, saying, "I suppose it can't be helped, but those are my children just as you are. Nevertheless let it be done."

After clothing them in flint armor and providing them with the most powerful of songs, sacred food, and incomparable weapons, Sun tested the Twins about their knowledge of geography and showed them where to descend. The Twins then encountered a series of complicated and dangerous adventures through which they gained ceremonial power and knowledge, which they taught to the Earth Surface People.

At Sun's request, the Twins and other *diyin dine'é* tried to persuade Changing Woman to move to the magnificent new home on an island in the Pacific Ocean that Sun had built for her. Slim Curley described this dwelling:

> A house had been built for her, designed in various colors on the outside, and inside a ladder had been provided [like a Pueblo house]. At this ladder a rattle had been set which would shake to let it be known that people had entered. White shell had been spread out and the floor space was white shell. In various places her footprints of white shell had been placed. And along the shore [of the Pacific Ocean] white shell [food] had been washed on the banks with turquoise, abalone, and jet. The purpose of this was that she would live by the strength of this food. And too a white shell cornstalk and a turquoise cornstalk were set at her entrance and were made as uprights of the entrance. Their purpose was to make all things known to her. Pollen flowed down on the one to the east and on the one to the west. So at the tip of the one a bluebird regularly gave its call, at the tip of the other a cornbeetle regularly called. One would call regularly in the morning, the other at noon, one in the evening, another at midnight, and one at dawn. They had been made to do just that (in Wyman [1970a:219]).

A painting of the western ocean, where Changing Woman's home was built, is depicted in figure 5.10.[16] This painting is of particular interest because it is the only one that depicts the reflection of stars rather than the stars themselves.[17] Here, we see the eastern and western oceans reflecting constellations of stars.

After Changing Woman acceded to the request of the delegation of *diyin dine'é*, Holy Man (as Monster Slayer was now called in this version of the myth) continued to seek out forbidden territory and to obtain further ritual knowledge and equipment. Holy Man and his brother then traveled with Holy Woman and Holy Girl to Dawn Mountain where the Twins left the women. Holy Man and his brother visited the Sun in order to acquire more ritual information and equipment, including the "Dawn" painting ("The Skies," plate 3 and figure 5.5) and the "Earth and Sky" painting (plate 4). After their return, they described all that they had learned to the women. This knowledge was too powerful for Holy Girl, and when the Sun's house was described to her, she had "a fit" (described as the origin of fits and spells). By stepping and pressing, the Twins restored her as the Sun had shown them. Holy Girl was now strong enough to hear the description of the "Earth and Sky" painting and the painting "The Dawn."

The Twins continued their quest for supernatural adventure, adding to their store of ceremonial knowledge, which they ultimately shared with the Earth Surface People. When they returned to the sky, they took the sacred paraphernalia, including the sandpaintings. Holy Man and Holy Boy (Monster Slayer and Born-for-Water, respectively) explained this by saying, "The original articles [cannot] be replaced, repaired, or duplicated, whereas the symbols of the originals made of earthly materials [can] be secured and made by all those who learn the chant, and [will] thus be available to all the Earth People who [need] them" (in Reichard [1977:73]).

As they ascended, the Sacred Twins said, "We will be living in the sky where the same places exist with the same names as those on the earth." Once again, we see the concept of the sky as the celestial counterpart to earth.

Now let us examine how the heavens described in this myth are presented in visual form.[18] The "Dawn" painting was described in the last chapter because it depicts the sky at four different times of day and the cardinal light phenomena. The well-known "Mother Earth, Father Sky" painting is also performed for the Male Shootingway.[19] The acquisition of these paintings has also been described.

Plate 3 depicts the "Dawn" painting, more commonly known as "The Skies." As previously noted, the skies are represented at various times of day, as the sky changes with the sun's passage across it. The four keystone forms that symbolize the Skies surround the Sun and Moon, and Yellow and Black Winds, which are clustered at the center of the painting. Proceeding sunwise, at the east lies the white sky of dawn; to the south is the blue of the midday sky; the yellow of the evening twilight sky lies in the west; and, finally, to the north is the black sky of night glittering with constellations.

The other painting acquired by the Twins is the famous "Earth and Sky" painting, more commonly known as "Mother Earth, Father Sky." This painting, depicted in plate 4, includes the eight major constellations recognized today by the Navajo. Reichard (1977:45) recounts a legend about this painting that does not belong to the Male Shootingway. The female Earth and the male Sky quarreled and decided to separate. "[The Sky said,] 'I will send no more rain to you.' As a result there was a great drought on earth. The streams dried up and all the vegetation was dying. Then Mother Earth asked for a reconciliation which was made. The rains fell once more and the plants grew and furnished food. This picture shows the reconciliation between Sky Father and Earth Mother."

Figure 5.12 depicts another image of the Earth and the Sky, one that is unique and appears only in the War Prophylactic Rite. Although this painting is from a chant other than the Male Shootingway, its myth, known as "When the Two Came to Their Father," also tells the story of the Sacred Twins as they journeyed to seek their father, the Sun. In their quest, they acquired ceremonial power with which to aid the Earth Surface People. This painting, executed in cornmeal, ground flowers, and the pollen of flowers, plants, and trees, rather than in sand, depicts the sky with its constellations and stars overlying the earth. At the top of the sky (which is at the eastern edge of this painting) lies Milky Way Man (a); to the west are the Boss Sparkling Star of the East (b), the Sun (c), the yellow Coyote Star (d), the Seven Eastern Stars (e), the Pleiades (f), the Dipper (g), the Moon (h), and the Big White Star of the West (i). On the earth are the six Sacred Mountains (the four Sacred Mountains, plus Gobernador Knob and Huerfano Mountain), each with its own door oriented to the west.

In addition to these images of the sky at various times of day and the Sky deity himself, the Sun's house is depicted in a visual image (fig. 5.20). Rather than a sandpainting, however, this depiction is usually a large replica of the Sun's house, measuring some six feet in length and five feet in height (if the chanter does not own or cannot borrow a Sun's house screen, he may substitute a sandpainting of the house). This visually impressive screen only

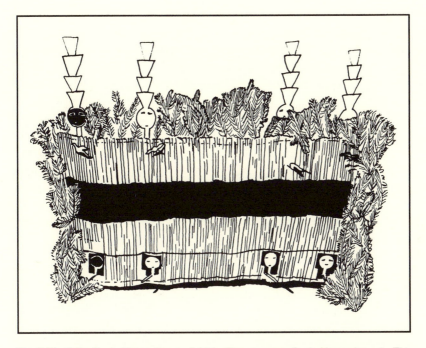

Fig. 5.20. "The Sun's House Screen," Male Shootingway, Sun's House branch. This replica of the Sun's house measures some six feet in length and five feet in height. The four bands of color across the screen are, from bottom to top: yellow, blue, black, and white. The yellow band at the bottom represents evening twilight and the home of Yellow Wind; directly above this, the blue band symbolizes the daytime sky and the color of the Sun; black, the next layer, stands for the darkness of night and the home of Dark Wind; and, at the top, white symbolizes dawn and the color of the Moon.

appears in this particular branch—the Sun's house branch—of the Male Shootingway.

The Sun's house screen is a stage set made of vertical wooden rods, or laths, bound side by side. Four wide stripes are painted on this screen: yellow, at the bottom, represents evening twilight and the yellow home of Yellow Wind; blue, above the band of yellow, symbolizes the blue of the daytime sky and the blue of the Sun; black, the next layer, stands for the darkness of night and the home of Dark Wind; at the top, white symbolizes the white of dawn and the color of the Moon.[20]

The four *diyin dine'é* (Holy People) who are symbolized in the colors of the screen—Yellow Wind, Black Wind, Moon, and Sun—appear as painted wooden disks at doorways near the ground where they are surrounded by rainbows and guarded by snakes of contrasting color. During the ceremonial, these snakes issue forth from and draw back into the doorways.

The same four *diyin dine'é* are represented again at the top of the screen; over their heads stand cloud symbols in the form of inverted wooden triangles. In front of these four deities, small birds, with bodies of yucca root and wings and tails of wood, hang suspended on strings and fly about during the ceremony when connecting threads are pulled by assistants hiding behind the screen. These helpers also blow reed whistles to imitate the chirping and trilling of the birds as they fly about; these assistants are also the source of the snakes' movement at the base of the screen. This screen appears on the afternoon of the fourth day and on the fifth night, at the midpoint of the ceremonial when the focus shifts dramatically from exorcism and protection to the complementary processes of invocation and blessing (McAllester 1980:206).

A large sandpainting is completed in front of the screen, and the sandpainting ceremony is performed for the patient. The screen, the sandpainting, and the costumes of the impersonators are dismantled, and singing goes on until dawn.

Each morning after the fifth night, the Sun's house screen is reassembled and sandpaintings are made, for a total of four sandpaintings (one each on days five, six, seven, and eight of the ceremonial). On the eighth and final day, the chanter chooses the last great sandpainting to be drawn, from the repertoire of sandpaintings appropriate to this chant. "The Earth and Sky" painting is one of the possible paintings that he can choose, but this one can only be made on the final day of the chant. Regardless of which sandpainting is chosen, in the long form of this ceremonial (the Male Shootingway can last two, five, or nine nights), the patient's face is painted in the four broad Sun's house stripes. (This procedure is described in chapter 7) Her body is painted with other symbols of the Shootingway, identical to those on the bodies of the *diyin dine'é* represented in the sandpainting. The emphasis now shifts from pleas for protection to statements that the supernaturals have helped to restore the energy of the patient who has also become the protagonist in the story of the Male Shootingway (McAllester 1980:209).

From the images presented thus far as well as the myths they symbolize and, in some cases, narratively illustrate, we have gained some understanding of the Navajo heavens. It is a land reached by supernatural means: the

Sacred Twins travel there on rainbow and lightning but mortals such as Younger Brother, in the myth of the Great Star Chant, may reach it by supernatural means such as Sky-Reaching Rock. The celestial realm consists of two layers: the Sky World, in which are located the Sun, Moon, and Stars, and the Land-Beyond-the-Sky, inhabited by supremely powerful storm elements. The lower realm of the heavens, the Sky World, is inhabited by hostile birds of prey as well as the Star People and constellations. Here, too, is the magnificent house of the Sun, home to a being so powerful that his passage through the skies completely alters their appearance. We have seen the skies as they change with the Sun's passage in the painting known as "The Skies," as well as the Sky deity himself paired with his complement, the Earth.

We are now ready to explore the heavens in greater depth through a body of traditional narratives that lie outside the chantway myths related in this chapter. We will see how the constellations of the night sky operate as a cultural text by evoking a corpus of oral literature that provides moral guidance for how people should live their lives.

✛ 6 ✛

The Constellations as a Cultural Text

Navajo constellations, as well as features of the earthly landscape, have the power to evoke traditional narratives by conceptually linking the mythic past with the physical present. Not only do these terrestrial and celestial features fuse the past and present into a state of coexistence, but they also evoke the underlying moral component of these narratives.

As Keith Basso (1984:45) demonstrated among another Athabascan group, the Western Apache, geographical features of the physical landscape serve as "indispensable mnemonic pegs on which to hang moral teachings." When a Western Apache sees a particular mountain, the name of the mountain evokes a particular historical tale having moral significance. In this way, "the land makes people live right" (Mrs. Annie Peaches, in Basso [1984:2]).

This is also true for the Navajo. For example, the outcropping of lava rocks southeast of Mount Taylor is well known as Yé'iitsoh Bidił, The Blood of the Monsters, slain by the Sacred Twins as they proved their supernatural heritage to their father, the Sun, while at the same time they made the world safe for humankind. Sky-Reaching Rock, which transported Younger Brother to the heavens, is located near Mount Taylor.[1] Knowledge about celestial phenomena serves a similar function as a set of visual reminders of key values: the stories associated with constellations provide moral guidance, reminding the Earth Surface People to adhere to the values essential to the establishment and maintenance of harmony in their lives and in the universe. The constellations serve as powerful symbols because they are universally visible. First Woman, in Newcomb's (1967:83) version of Creation, implies that the stars are an important cultural text when she says, "When all the stars were ready to be placed in the sky First Woman said, 'I will use these to write the laws that are to govern mankind for all time. These laws cannot be written on the water as that is always changing its form, nor can they be written in the sand as the wind would soon erase them, but if they are written in the stars they can be read and remembered forever.'"

In chapter 5 I discussed the heavens as they are portrayed in sandpainting images, which draw together earthly and celestial three-dimensional space into a two-dimensional format, and in chantway narratives, which vividly recount supernatural events. In this chapter I will explore another kind of cultural text besides sacred sandpaintings and their accompanying chantway narratives—celestial constellations. Star groupings, the most striking features of the celestial "landscape," indeed operate as cultural texts as their appearance in the night sky evokes tales and myths, which nearly always possess an underlying moral component.

The tales associated with the constellations form a fascinating body of Navajo oral literature because, with the exception of the story of stellar creation, these stories lie outside the ceremonial core, the corpus of chantway narratives. As previously explained, starlore is not prominently mentioned in the legends, and only a few chanters have this knowledge (Haile 1947c:5). Thus, even in Haile's time, astronomical knowledge was not a significant part of chantway stories, and therefore was not a necessary part of a chanter's nonmaterial property.

Before examining the stories associated with the constellations, it is important to understand something about the primary contexts for astronomical knowledge among the Navajos: divination, and Evilway and Holyway sandpaintings.

STARS AS A MEANS OF DIVINATION

Stargazing, *déest'íí,* is used to determine the etiology of illness, the source of misfortune, or the location of missing objects. The patient may contact a stargazer, *déest'íí'íí'tíní* (depicted in plate 6), before he hires the chanter to perform a ceremonial.

There are several kinds of diagnosticians, or diviners, among the Navajo: hand tremblers, listeners, and stargazers. All of these, in contrast to chanters, acquire power through personal contact with the supernatural and perform their rituals in a trance state. Thus, the stargazer is technically a shaman, while the chanter is technically a priest, in the sense of having learned standardized ritual through apprenticeship to an older chanter (Lessa and Vogt 1979:301). Because shamanism, by its very nature, is a far more individualistic enterprise than chanting, the following descriptions of stargazing ritual are far from standardized.

In some cases, the stargazer gazes through a crystal at a star of the first magnitude (*déest'íí 'áshłééh* [Young and Morgan 1980] means "to do stargazing"). The colors that are refracted through the prism indicate the answers to the questions posed by the diagnostician, who then relays this information to the patient. The specific information regarding causal factors indicates not only the cause of the illness—and thus which particular chant needs to be performed—but also what sandpaintings, branches, and subrituals need to be performed for the restoration of the patient to a state of health and harmony.

Matthews (1887:387), one of the first ethnographers of the Navajo, reported only that the patient and his friends determined "what particular rites are best suited to cure the malady." More was known about diagnosis when the Franciscan Fathers (1910:365) described the various forms of divination and mentioned "divination by sight (*dest'í*) . . . or star reading (*sótsóji*)." Morgan (1931:390–91) was the first to stress the distinction between chanters (whom Morgan refers to as "shamans"), who know the myths behind the ceremonials and are responsible for their performance, and diagnosticians, who reveal the cause and prescribe the cure of illness.

> A man is sick. A stargazer is called in. He comes into the hogan. The patient is there. Others are there. He talks to the patient and others. They discuss the illness. The fire is put out. The stargazer chants, then he says, "Everyone must close his eyes. No one must move or speak. Everyone must concentrate on the illness and try to see something." The stargazer takes a man from the hogan, and walks away some distance. He performs movements with his body. Any horses or sheep are frightened away. When there is no noise, the stargazer places a crystal or stone on his hand. He chants. He prays to the Gila monster. He does not pray to a lizard, but a lizard beyond the lizards, a larger one. Then the stargazer holds out his arm and hand in line with the moon or some star, and gazes unwinking at the crystal. Soon he sees something. He closes his hand upon what he has seen in the crystal. Also there may seem to be a line of light which is "lightning" from the star to the crystal or to the ground around him so that the ground appears light. The stargazer sees the hogan and the sick man, even though his back is turned to it. . . . He sees a man, or a bear, or a coyote, or perhaps the head of a coyote, or perhaps the bear is biting the patient. Then he goes back to the hogan. The fire is lighted. He asks what the others have seen. This is talked about. He tells what he has seen. . . . If the illness is serious the stargazer will prescribe a ceremony and the shaman[2] who can give it (Morgan 1931:394-395).

Haile (1947c:38–39) stated that in the opinion of men like the late Slim Curley stargazing was developed during the Fort Sumner period. Haile does not describe stargazing as an elaborate ritual; "Usually . . . group gazing is not frequent, and the individual star gazer is unaccompanied at night, making his report in the morning" (Haile 1947c:39).

Wyman (1936:244) provided a description of events inside and outside the hogan during one stargazing ritual. He first described the procedure inside the hogan.

In the complete ritual the diagnostician first makes a sandpainting in the dwelling . . . about two feet in diameter. It represents a white star with four points toward the cardinal directions. Between the points of the star are four heaps of sand representing mountains, the southeast mountain being white, the southwest blue, the northwest yellow, and the northeast black. Around the whole, with an opening to the east, is a zig-zag line representing lightning. Then the diagnostician makes ready the dried and powdered lenses from the eyes of the five nightbirds with keen sight who acted as lookouts in the legend of how stargazing was first made known to the people. He dips the tip of his finger in this material and then draws it along his lower eyelids. It is similarly applied to the patient, to the one man who will go out with the stargazer to assist him, and to anyone else present who is "smart" and may be able to assist by seeing something. The eyes of the five birds mentioned are the main ones, but eyes of other birds may also be used if available. Then the fire is covered and from now on the people who remain inside do not move or make any noise, but they concentrate and try to see something in addition to that which is seen by the diagnostician, sometimes gazing at a star through the smokehole. . . . [The stargazer and another person then leave the hogan to do the actual stargazing.] Outside he [the stargazer] prays the star-prayer (*sǫ'dízin*) to the star-spirit, asking the star to show him the cause of the sickness. Then he begins to sing star-songs (*hotsǫ' biyiin*) and while singing gazes fixedly at a star or at the light of a star reflected in a "glass rock" or quartz crystal which he holds in his hand. Soon, it was said, the star begins to "throw out a string of light and at the end of this the star-gazer sees the cause of sickness of the patient, like a motion picture." If these strings of light are white or yellow the patient will recover; if red, the illness is serious or dangerous. If the white light falls on the house and makes it as light as day around it, the patient will get well. If the house is seen burning or in darkness he will die. If a certain medicine man is the proper one to cure the sickness the star will throw a flash of light in the direction of his home, or on his body if he is present. Places faraway may be seen. After the diagnostician has obtained enough information in this way he returns to the house and tells what he has seen. If anyone else has seen anything, his experience is also considered (Wyman 1936:244–45).

The prayers addressed to the stars establish a kin relationship between humans and these *diyin dine'é,* Holy People. Stargazer A explained that he asks four questions to diagnose illness, each addressed to a different star that he calls "my maternal grandchild." Thus, he first faces the east and addresses the morning star, *sǫ'tsoh* (Venus), which he also calls the Big Black Star: "My grandchild, what is wrong with this person [the patient]?" The stargazer then faces south and asks the Big Blue Star (the remaining stars seem to be metaphorical ones with no identifiable counterparts in the night sky): "My grandchild, what can be done for this person?" Then the stargazer turns to the west and addresses the Big Yellow Star: "Grandchild, does this person's illness have anything to do with Navajo ceremonies?" Finally, the stargazer faces north and asks the Big White Star, "Grandchild, which ceremonies with which branches and subrituals will cure this person's illness?" Thus, the stargazer establishes a specific kin relationship with each of the stars he addresses, to show respect and to enlist their aid in the diagnosis of illness.

The same stargazer explained that another version of stargazing uses the sandpainting in figure 6.1. Prayers are addressed to the Big Jagged Star, the central figure of the painting: "Now that we know what is wrong with your child [the patient], we ask you to restore him or her to health and harmony." Here the diagnostician asks a particular stellar supernatural to come to the aid of the star's child, the patient.

How does one become a stargazer? Morgan (1931:39) explained that while "the ability to diagnose is not inherited," the diagnostician must have a proven ability to enter a trance. He or she then serves an apprenticeship under a practicing diagnostician. Stargazer A described what this process was like for him: "I learned from a woman who is the wife of a well-known medicine man in Lukachukai. I was her helper, and I slowly learned from her. After several years she told me, 'You are ready to go out on your own.' Now I have been a stargazer for fifteen years." Stargazer A indicated that while the individual must have an aptitude for diagnosis, the power of diagnosis resides in the crystal itself. When asked if he had to have an overview of all the ceremonies in order to prescribe the appropriate one for the patient, Stargazer A responded, "The crystal tells me if the patient needs a specific ceremony or a doctor or if I can help the patient myself with herbs. The power is in the crystal."

Haile (in Wyman 1970a:221–22) illustrated the power of rock crystal in locating missing children:

Now this Rock Crystal Talking God kept himself well posted on events by means of his dreams. In addition he would place twelve layers of rock crystal one above the other [like a magnifying glass]. By sighting through them [like a

Fig. 6.1. "Big Star," Hand Tremblingway Evilway. (Adapted from a painting collected by Oakes; singer, Bit'sui Dine Chili, Curly's grandson, 1946–47. Courtesy Wheelwright Museum, P17#15.)

telescope] he kept himself posted at the east, south, west, and north. . . . His two children were occupied in playing games . . . [Later] the children were missed. . . . Without a delay he looked . . . with his twelve rock crystal eyepiece . . . toward the west he realized that here they could be found. . . . Through an eyepiece of twelve rock crystals nothing is hidden.

Wyman's (1970a:222) footnote to this passage emphasized that this powerful crystal differentiates this Talking God from other Talking Gods: "Unlike others . . . he has his rock crystal eyepiece which enables him to detect everything, even to the ends of the earth and sky, of mountains and water."
    Reichard (1950:254) referred to the rock crystal held by stargazers as a

"symbol of illumination." Remington (1982:97-98) described how the star-gazer puts water or mucus from birds with the best eyesight on his lower eyelids and on those of the patient and the one who goes outside the hogan to help in stargazing. The stargazer prays and sings to the star-spirit while outside. Remington (1982:98) explained, "He gazes at the star, the star group, or the moon and holds the crystal out to reflect the light. A light beam comes down and lights up the crystal. The stargazer is illuminated, the hogan is illuminated, and the stargazer can see far away or back to the hogan, without looking."

Armer (1931:657) was the first to mention the sandpaintings used in stargazing rites. She objected to Morgan's (1931:390) claim that "diagnosticians do not use sand paintings." Some, although not all, stargazers do use sandpaintings. Stargazer A was the only consultant I worked with to recognize the sandpaintings used in divination that I showed consultants. The sandpaintings in figures 6.2 and 6.3 were produced by stargazers who are also chanters. Stargazer A explained, "They gaze through the crystal at stars in the sandpaintings."

In Newcomb, Fishler, and Wheelwright's book, Newcomb (Newcomb, Fishler, and Wheelwright 1956:23) discussed the sandpaintings used in stargazing: "These symbols of abstract powers [Mother Earth, Father Sky . . . the Gila Monster, the tornado], whose size and power is considered unlimited, are generally included in sandpaintings used for exorcism or diagnosing, and less frequently on those employed for restoration." She then discussed (Newcomb in Newcomb, Fishler, and Wheelwright 1956:25–26) the sandpaintings of the Star Chant:

> The Star Chant is one of the few Navajo ceremonies in which the sandpaintings are made at night. This is necessary, for the stars made with colored sand must be lighted and given spiritual power by the star shine of a particular star, which looks down through the opening in the roof of the medicine hogan.
>
> If the sandpainting consists of five stars, the largest is placed in the center, and the other four stand at the cardinal points. This central star represents the largest star to be seen through the roof opening while the ceremony is in progress, and the healing rites are supposed to be completed before this star disappears from view, as this is the one being interceded with in behalf of the patient. It may also be the one that is selected for a stargazing rite.
>
> In the Star Ceremony there are not many sky maps such as we find in the Hail Chant and in the Shooting Chant, nor are there any real constellation groupings. Each medicine man chooses one or more that he believes he can

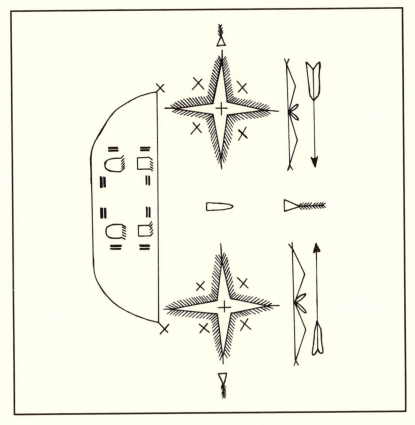

Fig. 6.2. "Spruce Hill Star Gazing Sandpainting," Big Starway Evilway. (Adapted from a painting collected by Armer; singer and date unknown. Courtesy Wheelwright Museum, P8B#10.)

influence, and then directs his ceremonial prayers and rites toward that particular one or group of stars.

Thus, we see that the astronomical knowledge of a stargazer may be based on an intimate relationship with one star or one constellation. This specific relationship contrasts with the more general knowledge of a Male Shooting-way chanter, who would be more likely to know something about all eight of the primary constellations recognized by the Navajo today. The chanter would have a greater overall knowledge of the constellations because it would be his responsibility to place them correctly in a sandpainting star

Fig. 6.3. "Corn Girl," Divinationway. (Adapted from a painting collected by Newcomb; singer, Bit'ahnii Bidághaa'í, 1930. Courtesy Wheelwright Museum, P22#2.)

map, such as the one that appears on the body of Father Sky. If a chanter
has been trained well, he should be able to relate stories about the specific
sandpainting images and their individual meanings.

STARS IN HOLYWAY AND EVILWAY CONTEXTS

As discussed in chapter 3, the degree of danger associated with a particular
Holy Person—recall that the stars are Holy People—varies with context.
While the primary ritual context (Holyway or Evilway) in which some entities are found may render them more "persuadable" or less so, it is important
to remember that these labels are context-dependent rather than absolute.

Thus, Reichard's (1950:470) description of stars as "undependable" and "feared" is accurate but incomplete. This characterization of stars as entities which "are feared by the Navaho" (Reichard 1950:470) is primarily based upon stars in their Evilway role, which emphasizes exorcism of evil rather than the attraction of good.

Newcomb (Wheelwright Museum Sandpainting Reproduction Catalogue, n.d.) confirmed Reichard's Evilway interpretation of stars: "All stars are more or less evil, but these two [the Great Black Star and the Great Blue Star of the Big Starway Evilway] which cannot be seen as they move through the sky, are feared most of all. To them is attributed all of the sickness, accidents and upset that happen to people who are abroad at night." Newcomb, like Reichard, was viewing stars in their Evilway context when she categorized them in their manifestation as big stars from the Big Starway and Hand Tremblingway chants, chants she classified as Evilway. Wyman (1983a:23) agreed on this classification of the Big Starway as being performed primarily, if not always, according to Evilway. Although Kluckhohn had heard of chanters who knew both Holyway and Evilway versions of the Hand Tremblingway, most of the examples of this chantway investigated by Kluckhohn and Wyman (1940:169) were also performed according to Evilway.

In the Big Starway, stars *are* the etiological factors; that is, stars cause the patient to suffer from a host of symptoms, such as the mental distress, insomnia, and bad dreams that characterize "ghost sickness" or bewitchment. This is the only chantway in which stars are the direct cause of illness; thus, stars are most dangerous in this context.

Although the sandpaintings of several chants contain stars, the Big Starway and the Hand Tremblingway are the only chantways whose sandpaintings feature stars.[3] The sandpaintings of the Big Starway depict particular stars, such as the Big Blue Star (fig. 6.4), which is described as "a . . . star which wanders about and shoots people with magic arrows to cause fevers and mental aberration" (Newcomb in Newcomb, Fishler, and Wheelwright 1956:15).

In Hand Tremblingway, a big star (fig. 6.1) is depicted "protected by eight rainbow bars . . . [and with] four points, two male with crooked lightning; two female with straight lightning. The little short lines radiate light" (Wheelwright Museum Sandpainting Reproduction Catalogue, n.d.). Hand Tremblingway is used for any illness caused by practicing or overpracticing hand trembling divination or stargazing, or otherwise becoming infected with overdoing of divination. Such illness may be manifested as tuberculosis, nervousness, mental disease, paralysis of the arms (from overdoing Hand

Fig. 6.4. "Blue Star," Big Starway Evilway. (Adapted from a painting collected by Newcomb; singer, Nahtol Hatile, 1930. Courtesy Wheelwright Museum, P8#11.)

Tremblingway), or impaired vision (from overdoing stargazing) (Wyman 1940:169). The paintings of Hand Tremblingway are made only on buckskin (Wyman 1940:172).

At the beginning of my research, I asked chanters about Reichard's (1950:470) characterization of stars as "feared." When I asked if this was true of all stars, every chanter and consultant answered with a resounding no. The "feared" nature of the Blue Star comes from its association with witchcraft (Harry Walters, personal communication, 1989).

With this understanding of the primary contexts for astronomical knowledge, let us now discuss each constellation and its associated interpretation.

NÁHOOKǪS BIKẠ'II AND NÁHOOKǪS BA'ÁADI

These were the only constellations that were consistently paired by all consultants, who agreed that Náhookǫs bikạ'ii (the Big Dipper) is male and Náhookǫs ba'áadii (Cassiopeia) is female; the Navajo names are translated as the "Male One Who Revolves" and the "Female One Who Revolves," respectively. It is significant that while relative size is a more salient trait from the Western perspective, with its quantitative emphasis—for example, the pairing of Ursa Major with Ursa Minor—the Navajo conceptualize such paired entities in terms of gender. As we have seen, such a qualitative distinction embraces a much wider range of complementary characteristics than relative size.

Chanters A, B, and E gave more extensive interpretations of these constellations than any that appear in the scholarly literature. Chanter A regarded them as a symbol of the Navajo home, or hogan, because these two star groupings revolve around Polaris, which represents the central fire in the hogan (fig. 6.5). Together, these constellations represent "old people" or "women folks," said Chanter A. "They tell us ·[by their example] to stay at home, to stay around your fire." Here the implication is that these constellations set a moral example for the Earth Surface People to remain at home to carry out their familial responsibilities.

Chanter A had offered a slightly different interpretation of these same constellations at an interview held three months previously. Then he had referred to the two Náhookǫs as leaders, as sources of wisdom and knowledge always available to the Earth Surface People; they are also visual reminders to leaders on earth that they must always be willing and ready to help their people.

Chanter B offered another interpretation. For him, this pair of constellations represents the bows that shoot the arrows of the Male Shooting Chant. The protagonists of this story are the Sacred Twins, Monster Slayer and Born-for-Water. Náhookǫs bikạ'ii represents the bow of Monster Slayer, always the more dominant, more aggressive Twin; Náhookǫs ba'áadii symbolizes the bow of Born-for-Water, the more submissive, gentler Twin. Significantly, these qualities are representative of the male/female distinction, and the pairing of constellations reflects this: the male constellation represents the bow of the more aggressive Twin while the female constellation represents the bow of the gentler Twin.

Chanter E's interpretation was related to Chanter B's. He, too, interpreted

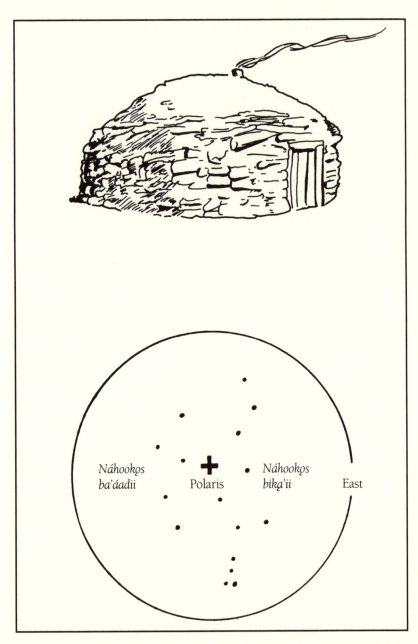

Fig. 6.5. Navajo hogan (top) and the two Náhookǫs (the Big Dipper and Cassiopeia) revolving around Polaris, which represents the central fire in the hogan. These constellations are taken from a drawing by Chanter A rather than directly from their appearance in the sky.

Náhookǫs bikạ'ii as an extended bowstring. Figure 6.6 shows his diagram of this constellation with a comparison of the Enemyway rattle stick design representing the symbol of the bow associated with Monster Slayer. Chanter E referred to the Enemyway rather than the Shootingway in his interpretation. The Enemyway is the only chant to use a rattle stick, which Haile (1938b:59) described at length in his monograph on this ceremonial. The extended bow symbol (*'ałtị'ya'o zt'i'*) represents the weapons in general that Monster Slayer used to slay the monsters (an event recounted in the Shootingway story). These weapons were obtained from his father, the Sun. The bow symbol was drawn on the body of Monster Slayer, and he is represented in the sandpaintings of other ceremonials with this symbol (specifically, in sandpaintings of the Shootingway). The same symbol appears on the prayer stick offered to Black God as a gift. The rattle stick was revealed to the people

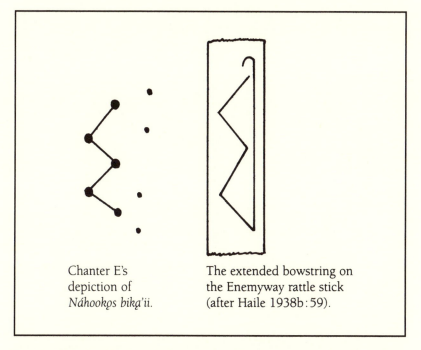

Chanter E's depiction of *Náhookǫs bikạ'ii.*	The extended bowstring on the Enemyway rattle stick (after Haile 1938b:59).

Fig. 6.6. Náhookǫs bikạ'ii as the bowstring on the Enemyway rattle stick. Chanter E's depiction of Náhookǫs bikạ'ii (left) actually resembles Cassiopeia more than the Big Dipper, which it represents. The extended bowstring on the Enemyway rattle stick (right) is adapted from a drawing by Haile (1938b:59).

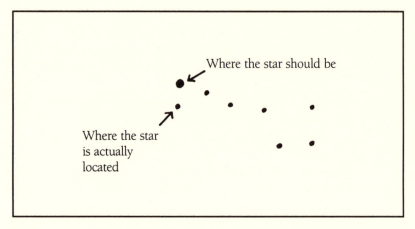

Fig. 6.7. Chanter D's diagram of the broken leg of Náhookǫs bikạ'ii (the Big Dipper).

by the Sun; on its east side this stick showed the bow (associated with Monster Slayer), while on its west side was the wide hair queue (symbolic of the other Twin, Born-for-Water).[4] These symbols are used in the Enemyway because of these three events: the drawing of the bow and the queue on the bodies of Monster Slayer and Born-for-Water, the use of these symbols on the prayer stick offering, and their presence on the Sun's rattle stick. A distinctive feature of the Enemyway is Monster Slayer's use of the extended bow as his weapon and symbol (Haile 1938b:37).

Chanter D provided an explanation for the position of the stars in Náhookǫs bikạ'ii. When the stars were being made, the wife of this *diyin dine'é* became angry with him and broke his leg. This is why the stars that represent his body are out of place. According to Chanter D, stars represent the joints of the body. He drew the diagram in figure 6.7 to show where the leg should be and where it actually is in its broken state.

Chanter D gave a general interpretation of Náhookǫs bikạ'ii as First Man and Náhookǫs ba'áadii as First Woman, associations that all consultants and ethnohistoric sources agreed upon.

DILYÉHÉ

Chanter A interpreted Dilyéhé (the Pleiades) as the portrayal of two sequential events. First, this constellation represents seven old men playing a dice game with dice which are white on one side, black on the other. The man who lost this game disagreed with the outcome and threw down the dice in a fit of anger. Figure 6.8 depicts Chanter A's drawing of the seven men and the dice thrown angrily by the loser. Second, Dilyéhé represents events after the outcome of the game. The man who lost said, "Let's go home." The stars within the constellation represent the man in front leading his wife and children home.

Chanter D's interpretation was quite different. He is a Nightway chanter, and Dilyéhé is the constellation of Black God, who is associated with the Nightway. Chanter D's interpretation, discussed below, centered on Black God.

Only one of the published sources (Brewer 1950) and none of the other consultants had a translation for *Dilyéhé*. Haile (1947c:28) said, "This name . . . is clouded in obscurity . . . the name *Dilyéhé* suggests no plausible interpretation." This is the only one of the eight constellations whose name lacks an agreed-upon translation. Max Littlesalt translated this term for Brewer (1950:135) as "Sparkling Figure," which is not dissimilar to Chanter D's translation of "Pin-like Sparkles." Chanter D said that this constellation

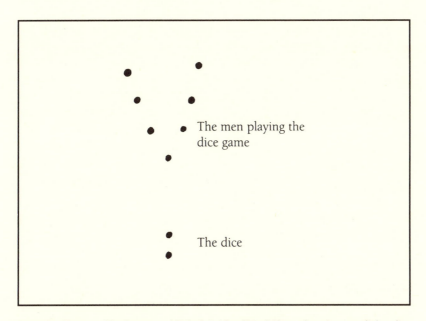

Fig. 6.8. Chanter A's diagram of Dilyéhé (the Pleiades) as the players of the dice game and the dice. This is the usual Navajo depiction of the Pleiades, which actually bears a greater resemblance to the star cluster called the Hyades, as the Hyades appear in the sky.

represents "very fine sparkling particles [which were] neat and pretty [when] laid [upon] the ground, then [they were] placed in the sky by First Man and First Woman. They were created [as] very fine particles."

Chanter Slim Curley (in Haile 1947c:33) said that the "black dancers" of Enemyway are identified with the seven Hard Flint Boys, who appeared to Monster Slayer in Pleiades formation:

> "The seventh star always follows the six important stars of this constellation" so that the seventh star always indicates the direction in which the configuration travels. Black God also mentions them in song as milky way and rainbow boys, in reference to their use of these as traveling means . . . the black dancers "pile out through the smokehole of the hogan, because they live in the sky."

As previously noted, Chanter D explained that Black God's face represents the whole universe, the whole sky; because Dilyéhé is so minute in comparison to the entire sky, this constellation is often not visible on Black God's mask. Night is associated with Black God, and Black God chose Dilyéhé to represent all the constellations (at the time of Creation) on the left temple of his mask because Dilyéhé is so neat and fine.

It is reasonable that the Pleiades would be chosen to represent all the constellations not only because it is such a compact open cluster of stars lending itself to depiction in a small space, but also because it is the most highly ordered of all the Navajo constellations, epitomizing the Navajo emphasis on order and balance. This distinctive cluster is probably the most easily recognizable of the Navajo constellations; its form permits the instant visual recognition required of an effective symbol. Thus, Dilyéhé is the perfect constellation for Black God's mask with its microcosmic representation of the Navajo heavens.

Because Haashch'ééshzhiní, or Black God, is the supernatural most closely associated with the constellations (no other Navajo supernatural wears a constellation on his mask), it will be helpful to discuss this *diyin dine'é* at this point. Black God is also known as Fire God; although not all accounts credit him with stellar creation, all accounts do attribute to him the fire and the light found in stars (Haile 1947c:2). As recounted previously, according to Beadway Singer who worked with Haile (1947c:1–2), the creator group turned the sky over to Black God when he moved Dilyéhé at will, thus demonstrating to the creator group that he had the power to beautify the "dark upper" (the sky) by placing stars in ordered patterns.

In *The Night Chant, a Navaho Ceremony* (1902:26), Washington Matthews explained that while there are several Black Gods, it is convenient to speak of this deity in the singular. Most of these supernaturals dwell in Tsé'nihoaílyíl (Rock-with-Dark-Place-in-Middle) near Tse'gíhi, north of the San Juan River.

Harry Walters described Black God as moody; because he lacks a sense of humor, he does not tolerate teasing. Black God travels around, passing himself off as poor so that people will give him things; he is greedy and he is a trickster (Walters, personal communication, 1989).

Matthews (1902:26) described Black God as "reserved and exclusive," a supernatural who does not associate freely with other supernaturals. Nor do other supernaturals visit him. He is the owner of all fire because he invented the tool for producing fire (i.e., the fire drill) and was the first to produce fire.

The Black God Impersonator dresses in black shirt, breechcloth, blanket, and moccasins with a foxskin collar. Traditionally, he wore white shell necklaces, but by the turn of the century when Matthews was writing, the Impersonator was wearing coral, turquoise, and other materials as well. Black God wears no kilt. His legs are painted black; each leg is marked in back with a line of white, which extends from the top of the heel to the top of the thigh. He carries a fire drill, wood and tinder, a faggot, and a bundle of corn cakes.

The Black God Impersonator is so unprepossessing that an untrained eye may not even recognize him as a supernatural. Mary Cabot Wheelwright (n.d.:36) described Black God at a Nightway that Tł'aii was conducting:

> There was a long pause and then at the end of the vista a strange little figure appeared. He had rough hair and was dressed in sackcloth, and as he approached he acted like a jester, hesitating, sitting down, scratching himself at intervals. In one hand he carried a little torch made of bound-up bark, in which form the Navaho carried fire when traveling. In the other hand he carried a string with four little doughnut-like cakes strung on it. The people laughed at him, but finally Tł'aii called to him to come and he ran up toward Tł'aii and the patient. To my amazement the patient thereupon dropped down on his face to the earth, while this strange little figure walked over him, and I realized that he was the Fire God [Black God] in strange guise.

When I myself saw a Black God Impersonator in December 1987, I was amazed by his disheveled look, which is so different from the well-dressed appearance of other Navajo Holy People. He wore a baglike mask with a shock of red yarn hair; his facial features were delineated only with wide white circles and curving lines. Surprisingly, Dilyéhé did *not* appear on his mask. He wore a fox-fur collar and his body was covered by a ragged dark gray blanket pinned together at the front. His shirt-sleeved arms protruded through holes cut into the blanket. He wore pants under his blanket and on his feet were old army boots. In his hands he carried the requisite torch and corn cakes.

Figure 4.9 illustrates Black God's mask. Haile (1947a:60) described the features of this mask as follows: to indicate that Black God is in charge of the months and seasons, the mouth on the mask is a full moon, while the forehead bears a crescent moon. Dilyéhé is on the left temple.

The Black God Impersonator does not appear at every performance of the Nightway. Matthews (1902:27) called the variety of the ceremonial in which he appears *to'nastsihégo hatál*. When the Impersonator is to appear, a sand-painting of Black God, such as the one in figure 6.9, is produced on the ninth day. This large painting has a figure of Monster Slayer in the center and the figure of a Black God with his torch and bundle of corn-cakes on each of the four stars. This painting remains on the floor of the hogan until the Black God Impersonator arrives in the evening.

The Black God Impersonator comes to the hogan early in the morning of the ninth day of the ceremonial, which takes place in its full form only in winter. He then proceeds to a point some distance east of the hogan. At sunrise he begins his slow day-long journey back to the hogan; this journey takes so long because he walks a few paces, lights his faggot with his fire drill, then lies down with his back to the fire—a favorite position of his, according to the sacred stories—and pretends to sleep and make camp. He rises a moment later to extinguish his fire and husband his faggot, which must last until he can deposit it as a sacrifice in the hogan in the evening.

The Black God Impersonator is not seen very often in Nightway performances. Harry Walters has seen this branch[5] once in fourteen years. Chanter D has not performed the Black God branch of the Nightway in four years. Chanter C, also a respected Nightway chanter who knows the Black God branch, said that chanters in the western part of the reservation cannot perform it because they have never learned the songs, procedures, and sand-paintings associated with Black God. He said that only once every four years could Black God appear as an Impersonator.

Chanter C characterized Black God as "the center of life and energy," associated with lightning, rainbow, and stars. Black God is "the most honored of all the gods"; he can do things that Talking God, Harvest God, and Water Sprinkler cannot do.

In October 1990 I attended a Nightway performed by Chanter D. The

Fig. 6.9. "Black God on Stars with Monster Slayer," Nightway. (Adapted from a painting collected by Newcomb; singer, Hastiin Tł'aii, date unknown. Courtesy Wheelwright Museum, P11#8.)

seventh day of the ceremonial was remarkably warm and sunny for this time of year on the reservation. However, on the eighth day the weather began to change as a fierce wind buffeted the ceremonial hogan; the fluorescent light by which the chanter and his helpers were working went off when the high winds stopped the electrical current. We were reluctant to go outside, to face the sweeping, howling wind that filled our mouths with grit and blinded our eyes with sand. The next day the wind had subsided, replaced by torrential rains that turned the reservation roads to oozing mud. When I later discussed this abrupt change of weather with the patient, who was learning about the Nightway from the chanter who had sung over him, he laughed as though he had expected the weather. "Didn't you know that Black God can call the wind? He also brought the rain."

Why would Black God appear? One reason would be a violation of ceremonial procedures while impersonating Black God (Chanter C). Because of Black God's association with fire, dreams about fire that become manifest as illnesses of the eyes, throat, and mouth (that is, smoke-related illnesses) are another reason for his appearance (Harry Walters, personal communication, 1989). Chanter D said that he performs the Black God version for a baby if its mother saw a Black God sandpainting while pregnant with this child.

Black God's association with Dilyéhé is further marked by the actual appearance of Dilyéhé in the night sky. All sources agreed on the seasonal significance of Dilyéhé. The season during which Nightway may be performed in its full form begins with the appearance of Dilyéhé at twilight at the end of October and ends when this constellation is no longer visible, at the end of April.

Sources also agree on the use of Dilyéhé as a nightly clock. All the chanters interviewed agreed that they use the position of Dilyéhé in the sky to determine the time of night when they are conducting a ceremonial. In this manner, they know whether to add or delete songs so that the closing or dawn song will correspond to the break of day. Figure 6.10 illustrates the relative position of this constellation in the night sky and the accompanying linguistic label. We will discuss the association of Dilyéhé and the agricultural season in connection with the constellation 'Átsé'ets'ózí.

Dilyéhę' and Sǫ'tsoh are the only two constellations whose shapes are still made in string today (plate 7). At one time all the constellations, as well as many nonastronomical figures, were produced in string games that had allegorical stories associated with them. A Navajo father who made these forms in string for his children explained for folklorist Barre Toelken the importance of representing the stars and other forms in string:

> These are all matters we need to know. It's too easy to become sick, because there are always things happening to confuse our minds. We need to have ways of thinking, of keeping things stable, healthy, beautiful. We try for a long life, but lots of things can happen to us. So we keep our thinking in order by these figures and we keep our lives in order with the stories. We have to relate our lives to the stars and the sun, the animals, and to all of nature or else we will go crazy, or get sick (Toelken 1979:96).

This passage tells us a great deal not only about the cultural significance of the string games but also about the significance of the constellations and

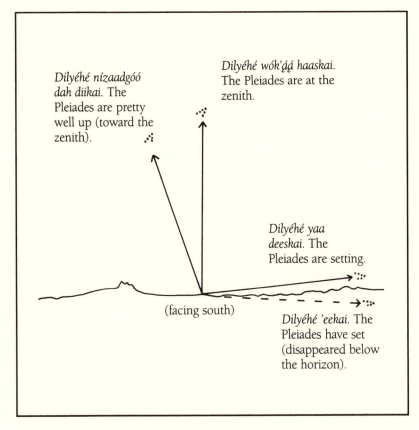

Fig. 6.10. Linguistic labels for the position of Dilyéhé (the Pleiades) at various times of night. (Navajo from Young and Morgan [1980:319].)

of all nature for the Earth Surface People. Once more, we see an example of the Navajos' spiritual comprehension of the universe: only by remembering their relationship to other living beings—and by practicing "right thinking"—can people live lives characterized by balance and order, sanity and health. Although Navajo versions may differ on the details of specific constellations, all accounts agree on the profound spiritual significance of the stars and constellations.

'ÁTSÉ'ETS'ÓZÍ

The name *'Átsé'ets'ózí* (Orion) is translated by all consultants as "First Slim One." Chanter A said that Coyote named both 'Átsé'ets'ózí and 'Átsé'etsoh (the front part of Scorpius, a name translated as "First Big One"). These two constellations could be conceptualized as another complementary pair because they are located at opposite ends of the sky and thus appear at opposite times of year. Because Coyote named 'Átsé'ets'ózí first, this constellation takes the diminutive form—ózí—of 'Átsé'etsoh.[6] Chanter A referred to 'Átsé'ets'ózí as "keeper of the months." He explained that while the other constellations are "more or less busy with their own internal lives," this one "keeps them in line," making sure that they appear in the night sky at the proper times during the year.

'Átsé'ets'ózí seems to be primarily associated with agriculture. Wetherill (in Wyman [1952:47, 50]) described three star groupings that are drawn side by side in a Big Starway sandpainting created by Yellow Singer (Sam Chief) between 1910 and 1918 (fig. 5.13): "south of center, circular patch with small red and green stars ('the seed basket'); east of it, 'the staff of the old man who carries the seed basket'; south of the latter, Orion."

As previously noted, Chanters A and B questioned whether this was an actual sandpainting because of its unusual content and composition. They did recognize the staff and agreed that there is a curved line of stars to the right of 'Átsé'ets'ózí that represents a digging stick; however, this stick is not a part of the constellation. Chanter A added that when 'Átsé'ets'ózí sets at twilight in late April or early May, the Navajos begin to plant crops, emphasizing the agricultural association with this constellation.

The aberrant nature of this sandpainting, as well as the other sandpainting (figure 5.7, also drawn by Sam Chief) in which the seed basket constellation appears, makes the identification of this constellation problematic. It is important not to read too much into constellation depictions in sandpainting reproductions. Wyman (1952: 10–11), who probably compared more sandpaintings than anyone else, found this series of sandpaintings to be so different from most that he prefaced the book in which this sandpainting appears with the comment: "Whether it [the Wetherill collection of sandpaintings] may be taken as representative of the [Kayenta] region, or merely idiosyncratic of Mrs. Wetherill's informant or informants, or perhaps modified by them for precautionary reasons, is questionable since the persons both Navaho and 'white' who were directly concerned in assembling the collection are now deceased, so further checking is impossible."

As mentioned previously, Dilyéhé is also associated with agriculture. Figure 6.11 summarizes information from Chanters A, B, and C regarding the key calendrical marker, Dilyéhé, and the agricultural role played by

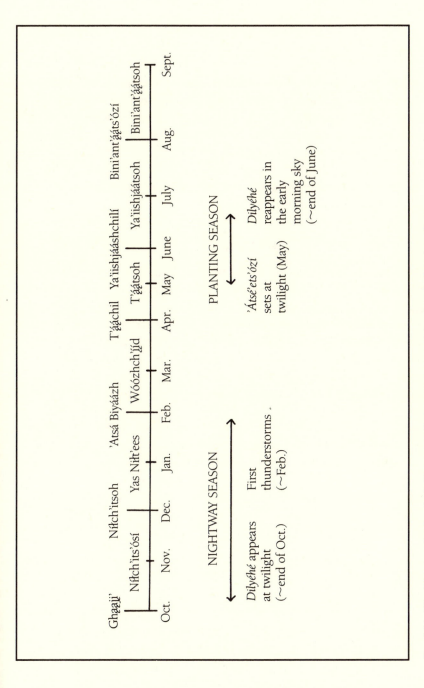

Fig. 6.11. The Navajo calendar, including constellations as ceremonial and agricultural markers.

'Átsé'ets'ózí. The Nightway season begins with the appearance of Dilyéhé at the end of October at twilight and ends with the coming of the first thunderstorms that signal spring. (This is also the season during which it is proper to discuss the stars.)

Planting begins when 'Átsé'ets'ózí sets at twilight in early May. Dilyéhé first reappears near the summer solstice (June 21) in the early morning sky to the northeast. This marks the end of planting season because it is now too late to plant any longer and still be able to harvest before the first frost. This is why Chanter C said, "Dilyéhé must not see you plant."

HASTIIN SIK'AI'Í

The name *Hastiin Sik'ai'í* (Corvus) is translated by all accounts as "Man with Legs Ajar." Chanters A and B attributed qualities of concentration, searching, and wisdom to this constellation. Chanter A said that this constellation is the one most closely associated with stargazing because Hastiin Sik'ai'í is always searching for something with great concentration. During two interviews—one in October 1985 and one thirteen months later—Chanter A felt moved to get up and demonstrate the position this constellation takes in the sky with his feet planted wide apart, knees slightly bent, right hand to his eyes as he scans the horizon intently from left to right. It is significant that this was the only constellation this chanter chose actually to imitate. He described this constellation as follows: "It's like when someone leaves the hogan. You wonder where he is so you go outside and look."

As Consultant P explained, "Hastiin Sik'ai'í stands above the earth with his legs wide apart and looks down on the earth so he knows everything, sees everything that goes on down on the earth. He looks down and can tell stargazers the answers they want to know."

'ÁTSÉ'ETSOH

'Átsé'etsoh (the front part of Scorpius and, according to Chanter A, part of Sagittarius; translated as "First Big One") is a constellation that contains the figure of a cane. The cane is needed because, as Chanter A said, "His limbs are weak and without it he might fall over. He is an old man." Other chanters had little to say about this constellation, beyond acknowledging it as one of the eight major constellations recognized by the Navajo today. Haile (1947c:7) said that "the big first one is also human in form, which suggests its application to first-man . . . the author of witchcraft. . . . Some pronounce it 'ace ecoh 'like a big tail (feather)'."

An interesting contrast can be drawn between Chanter A's identification of body parts within 'Átsé'etsoh and those identified by Haile's (1947c:7) informant, Son-of-the-Late-Cane. Figure 6.12 illustrates the contrast between these two depictions. Both chanters agreed that this constellation does have a cane, feathers, body, and legs (or parts of legs), even though they labeled these parts differently. Not only do we see more stars in the version drawn by Son-of-the-Late-Cane, but we also see greater elaboration of the body, including such internal organs as the heart, intestines, and bladder, and a greater elaboration of the legs, with the hip, knees, and feet marked. Unfortunately, it is impossible to say whether this is an idiosyncratic version or if this information, recorded by Haile in 1909, has simply been lost with the passage of time.

Oswald Werner (Pinxten 1979:51) decided to compile a Navajo encyclopedia of ethnomedical terms because "medicine and the preoccupations with health and disease seem to be the most important aspects of Navajo culture." In his research he discovered (Oswald Werner, personal communication, 1986) that the Navajos stress greater anatomical accuracy (as demonstrated by linguistic elaboration) than do Pueblo groups such as the Hopi, whose

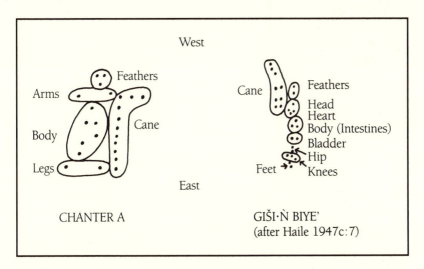

Fig. 6.12. A comparison of two versions of the constellation, 'Átsé'etsoh (the front of Scorpius).

preoccupation and focus of culture is fertility. This same difference in cultural foci is illustrated by the fact that no Hopi constellations are named after an individual human figure (Emory Sekaquaptewa, personal communication, 1987), while only one of the fourteen Zuni constellations represents a human figure (Harrington [1929] quoted in Young and Williamson [1981]), while five of the eight major Navajo constellations depict single human figures, with the component stars representing body parts.

Another, related reason that the Navajos divide constellations in terms of body parts is identification, a crucial means by which healing proceeds. After a kin relationship has been established through prayers (as described in chapter 3), the patient becomes identified with the Holy Person. Reichard (1950:112) described how the chanter accomplishes his final goal, which is the identification of

> the patient with the supernaturals being invoked . . . [through the] application of parts of deity to corresponding parts of the patient—foot to foot, knees to knees, hands to hands, head to head. . . . The chanter applies the bundle items to the body parts of the gods, then touches parts of the patient's body with his own—foot to foot, hand to hand, shoulder to shoulder in the ceremonial order—and finally with the bundle equipment; this is an elaborate rite of identification.

Constellations are not used in this manner in ceremonies. Nevertheless, by labeling the component stars of each constellation in terms of the basic parts of the human body, and by viewing the constellations themselves as supernaturals that have human form, the Navajos make the constellations more human, more lifelike, more reachable. They become forms with which the Earth Surface People can identify, reminding people once again of their kin relationship to these celestial bodies, as well as to all other living beings.

GAH HEET'E'II

All accounts agreed that Gah heet'e'ii (the tail of Scorpius, a name commonly translated as "Rabbit Tracks" [Haile 1947c:7]) represents the tracks of a rabbit. While 'Átsé'ets'ózí and Dilyéhé are associated with agriculture, Gah heet'e'ii symbolizes hunting. This constellation was placed in the sky to honor the rabbit, a very important food source before agriculture (Chanter A).

The famous chanter Tł'aii referred to the stars in this constellation as "the hunter's guide." Newcomb (1980:197) recorded Tł'aii's observations about

Gah heet'e'ii (with which Chanter A agreed): "When this constellation is in one position, the hunters lay aside their bows and arrows and remain at home. But when it tips to the east, the young of the deer and the antelope are no longer dependent on their mothers, and the hunting season begins."

Tł'aii expressed reverence for the lives of the animals that traditionally provided sustenance for the Navajo as well as an understanding of the interconnectedness between humans and these animals. The rabbit, by synecdoche, represents all animals killed by the Navajos for food. Inherent in honoring these animals with the placement of a rabbit constellation in the sky is the recognition that the act of hunting is the ultimate gift of life force from one being to another.

YIKÁÍSDÁHÍ

The name *Yikáísdáhí* (the Milky Way) means "Awaits-the-Dawn" (Chanters A, B, D, and E), a reference to the manner in which this Navajo constellation is said to appear to glow more brightly just before the break of day. Dawn is one of the four cardinal light phenomena, a vital life-giving source (these phenomena were discussed at greater length in chapter 4).

Consultant P explained that there is a also a cane in the sky for Yikáísdáhí and its associated star (planet), Sǫ'tsoh (Venus), because they are associated with the dawn. "Yikáísdáhí tells you that the new day, the dawn, is coming, and the cane belongs to an old man who leans on the cane while he waits for the sun to come up so that he can say prayers and make a pollen blessing."

Chanter A recounted a story about this constellation. Coyote stole a piece of ash bread (made of corn and baked in an outdoor oven or in the ashes, *łees'áán*) from First Man and First Woman. The ashes were then strewn across the sky to form the Milky Way.

OTHER NAVAJO CONSTELLATIONS

In addition to the eight major constellations recognized by the Navajo today (which are the only constellations placed on the body of Father Sky in sacred sandpaintings), a number of minor constellations are mentioned in other sources. The Coyote Star is called *sǫ'dondizidi* (monthless star) or *mą'ii bizǫ'* (Coyote's star), while *sǫ'hots'ihi*, the Pinching or Doubtful Stars, are probably the stars of the Hyades constellation (Haile 1947c:8–9). Chanter D showed

Fig. 6.13. Łeitsoh, the Horned Rattler constellation. (Adapted from a drawing by Begay 1990:15.)

me his Nightway rattles on which *Bisolyehe,* the ram constellation (which does not correspond to any Western constellation), was depicted; as introduced in chapter 2, the Humpback, a key Nightway figure, wears ram's horns and is the protector of the mountain sheep.

Three additional Navajo constellations are mentioned in the Upward Reachingway ceremonial: *łeitsoh,* the Horned Rattler (fig. 6.13); *shash,* the Bear (fig. 6.14); and *'ii'ni',* Thunder (fig. 6.15) (Begay 1990:15). In addition to the constellations described so far, Haile's classic monograph, *Starlore Among the Navaho* (1947c:7–10), mentioned these constellations: the Butterfly, the Fire God (Black God), the Porcupine, the Corn Beetle, Flash Light-

Fig. 6.14. Shash, the Bear constellation. (Adapted from a drawing by Begay 1990:15.)

ning, and the Red Heavens. He also discussed thirteen independent stars, sky colors associated with the cardinal directions and times of day, and trails of the sun along the horizon.

It is clear that Navajo constellations symbolize many forms of life, both natural and supernatural, reminding human beings of their interconnectedness with one another in the intricate web of creation. Through the moral stories they index, the stars and constellations serve as reminders of the right way to live one's life. The rules for appropriate behavior are based upon acting with great respect for one another, whether that "other" is human, divine, animal, or plant. These laws are reciprocal: not only do they govern people's actions but they also provide useful information that enriches human lives. By heeding the message of these stories, people grow in self-knowledge and self-respect, secure in their place in the universe. If human beings treat the other beings of the natural and supernatural worlds with the respect they would afford their own relatives, these beings in turn will take care of them. Following these rules calls forth a personal sense of relatedness and responsibility regarding other forms of life with which humanity shares the universe.

The constellations speak to human beings. The two Náhookǫs remind people how to relate to others by carrying out kinship responsibilities. Dilyéhé symbolizes a lesson in equanimity as well as standing for the beauty and majesty of the entire universe. 'Átsé'ets'ózí and Dilyéhé tell people when to begin and to stop planting, respectively, teaching them how to connect with the earth. Hastiin Sik'ai'í embodies qualities of wisdom and concentra-

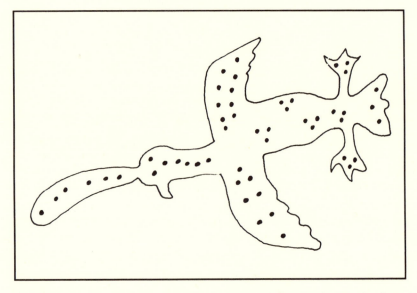

Fig. 6.15. 'Ii'ni, the Thunder constellation. (Adapted from a drawing by Begay 1990:15.)

tion, reminding humans that spiritual guidance is always present; they have but to seek it. 'Átsé'etsoh, in its representation of the human form, reminds people that they are related to the stars and are made of the same substance. Gah heet'e'ii teaches people how to relate to the animals they hunt, by honoring them as they give up their lives for human benefit. When human beings behave appropriately, treating other living beings as kindred, they are rewarded by a profound sense of connectedness and wholeness. The stars operate in the same manner as allegorical string games to "keep our thinking in order" and thus to keep lives in order, reminding people how to relate to others with respect and reverence. Only through the constant awareness that each individual is a harmonic and necessary component of the whole can people's minds stay sane, their spirits balanced, and their bodies healthy.

ASTRONOMICAL KNOWLEDGE

Clearly, astronomical knowledge is of a highly specialized nature, lying outside the main body of chantway myths. Given this lack of centrality to the ritual system, it is not surprising that each chanter's unique experience patterns his selective use of consensual knowledge. What one chanter considers to be central to the story that he was taught may be peripheral to another chanter's version. Thus, a Male Shootingway chanter (Chanter B) interpreted the two Náhookǫs in terms of the key symbols for his chant specialty—the bows of Monster Slayer and Born-for-Water. Chanter E, an Enemyway singer, interpreted Náhookǫs biką'ii in an Enemyway context: for him this constellation represents the extended bowstring associated with Monster Slayer as it is depicted on the Enemyway rattle stick. Chanter A, who knew the Blessingway, gave a Blessingway interpretation that relates the two Náhookǫs to a hogan, a key symbol of Blessingway.

Because the constellations are not key symbols themselves but rather vehicles for their expression, these interpretations are not in conflict. The underlying structure—a highly specialized and extremely complex ritual system—remains intact. What appears to be ambiguity and conflict is only a problem if we insist upon viewing it from a Western perspective: if we demand a single version of truth in a cultural inventory. Rather than being disruptive, variation at this level encourages greater complexity and richness because each chanter does not have to know the entire system. Through ceremonial specialization, greater symbolic elaboration becomes possible, and the same set of phenomena serves as a vehicle for many meanings, depending upon the specialization of the chanter. Each chanter's story contributes a new dimension, a greater depth and richness toward the understanding of the whole of Creation.

Mother Earth,
Father Sky

As the sandpainting is created, the image grows across the floor of the hogan, spreading outward with increasing complexity from the central image. The sandpainting is one part of a complex ceremonial made up of several ritual components. Only when the sandpainting and its ritual are synthesized into an entire, moving whole can one begin to sense the power and life of a Navajo sacred sandpainting. This book, like a sandpainting, began with the various components of Navajo ritual which, by themselves, may seem like unrelated, even mechanical, facts. At this point, I have created the forms in the sandpainting without conveying its living, affecting quality; what remains to be done is to animate these forms with power and substance in order to make it understandable how a particular sandpainting becomes a sacred, living entity.

I have chosen to focus on the "Mother Earth, Father Sky" sandpainting from the Male Shootingway partly because it presents the most detailed depiction of the Navajo heavens of the sandpaintings used today. In addition, since this sandpainting can only be used on the final day of the ceremonial, it embodies the Navajo concept of increase through accumulation.

Chanters consider this painting to be a particularly powerful one. Chanter A, who learned this painting nearly seventy years ago, said that he has performed it only four times in his life, each time at the request of the patient rather than by his own choice. Chanter B considers this to be the most sacred sandpainting he knows, so sacred that he limits its use to once a year. In the story of the Male Shootingway, only after Holy Girl has been restored by the Sacred Twins through sacred procedures is she "strong enough to hear the description of the Earth and Sky painting" (Newcomb and Reichard 1975:36). Franc Newcomb (in Wyman [1970b:33]) explains that this painting "represents a consummation of perfection, power, and benefaction."

In this chapter, I will describe the creation and use of the "Mother Earth, Father Sky" painting; explain how cosmological order and mythological meaning are woven into its creation, giving significance to each form; explore how this particular sandpainting operates as an affecting presence; and, finally, discuss the existence of this painting as a living entity, with particular attention to the concept of the Pollen Path.

Western society tends to value product over process, but the power of the Navajo sacred sandpainting derives from the activity of its making and ritual use; its meaning and cultural significance are inextricably woven into the process of creation. The efficacy of the sandpainting—its ability to reestablish order in the spiritual and physical world of the patient—is profoundly affected by and dependent upon the process through which the sandpainting is created. The Navajo emphasis on active process rather than static product is ultimately reflected in the final act of sandpainting ritual: the destruction of the painting itself.

In 1989 I was honored by being allowed to photograph the creation of the "Mother Earth, Father Sky" painting, which helped me to understand the steps of sandpainting creation as well as how the painting becomes a living entity. As I promised the chanter, because of the sacred nature of sandpaintings, only the chanter and I have copies of these photographs of the creative process. For this reason, no illustrations accompany the following description.

July 1989

Keith, my husband, and I turn off the highway two miles before the nearest town at the western part of the reservation. It has been months since rain has reached this part of the world, and the junipers look dry, parched, and withered. Dust rises in a plume behind our Honda Civic, and I can taste the fine-grained grit in my mouth.

Soon I spot our friends' extended family camp: the familiar blue-roofed hogan occupies the center of the clearing; between a cement-block house and a food preparation and sleeping ramada stand camper shells and a red tractor; sheep and goat corrals and an outhouse are at some distance on the other side of the hogan. Much farther away sits the hogan of a daughter and her husband. We turn off the main dirt road, carefully avoiding the sandy wash. The afternoon sun bathes everything in its blinding glare, but our friends are working tirelessly in the heat to prepare for tonight's beginning of the two-night Male Shootingway ceremonial. Already the accouterments of everyday life—two cots, a table, a Singer treadle sewing machine, and the stove with its black metal stovepipe—have been removed from the hogan. Our friends are carrying in fresh dirt by the shovelful; they pour water on the dirt and stamp on it, packing it firmly to create a level surface on the hogan floor for the sandpainting.

That night, around 10 p.m., the hogan is transformed from an everyday dwelling into a *hooghan bii' nahaghái* (hogan in which a ceremony is conducted) through the opening ritual of the ceremonial. The *hooghan da'iishdlish* ("hogan consecration," with reference to the rubbing of cornmeal) begins with singing to the constant beat of rattles. The wife of the chanter spreads pinches of sacred cornmeal on the rafters of the hogan to the east, west, south, and north, strewing the rest of the cornmeal over all those present as she walks sunwise around the inside of the hogan.

Various ceremonial procedures focus on the patient as the verses of song continue. The chanter goes outside in the darkness four times; each time we hear the characteristic whirring of the bull roarer[1] in a different direction as, according to the story of the Male Shootingway, he drives off any evil influences in the surroundings of the hogan (Haile, n.d.).

I sit back against the hogan wall, between two of the chanter's adult children who are like a sister and brother to me. The chanter's grandchild, a little girl named after me, is fast asleep in her mother's arms beside me. I let the comforting warmth of the hogan and my love for the family within it wash over me. I feel such a sense of well-being just from being within its walls once more, sitting on blankets on the earthen floor, surrounded by those who are close to me. The chanting voices and the steady rhythm of the rattles are soothing as they perform song after song, pausing slightly between verses until the chanter begins a new one and everyone follows his lead. This is where I am meant to be, and I feel a sense of joy and peace deep in my heart. The songs continue until the ritual is complete, and it is time to retire. The hogan and those within its walls have been blessed.

At dawn the next morning, the chanter erects a set-out mound outside the hogan; he has erected a waist-high, rectangular tentlike shelter to protect it from domestic animals. This collection of feathered prayer sticks and other ritual objects signifies that the hogan has been transformed from a family dwelling into a ceremonial hogan through the proper consecration ceremony. The space within the hogan, as well as the outside area bordered by the set-out mound is *hodiyiin,* sacred space, or more properly (to paraphrase Consultant A), "space that—at this moment in time—is blessed."

The morning's activities begin with a short Blessingway ritual for the patient, who washes with yucca suds in a ceremonial basket inside the hogan. After a short break, work begins on the "Mother Earth, Father Sky" sandpainting when a helper brings a load of clean, tan sand into the hogan and spreads it evenly in the center of the floor in an area that measures about seven feet by seven feet. For more than three hours, various family members and friends work diligently on the sandpainting.

The first step in the creation of this painting, as in all sandpaintings, is the proper orientation of forms to the four directions. The heads of Mother Earth and Father Sky must lie to the east, toward the hogan door, with the encircling guardian open to the east.

As I watch the construction of the "Mother Earth, Father Sky" painting, I am amazed once more at the care and precision lavished on sandpainting forms. Two helpers, positioned at the head (to the east) and feet (to the west) of the area where Father Sky will be located, stretch a length of string between them, while another person holds a string attached to the middle of the first string, pulling it outward to create one side of a diamond. When they are satisfied with the angular shape of Father Sky's right side, the first side is snapped into the sand, leaving behind a faint depression which will serve as a pattern to be filled in with black sand. Father Sky's left side is drawn in similar fashion. To ensure the symmetry of the two figures, another helper holds a metal tape measure over the projected area for each of the two deities before the string is snapped to delineate the projected body of Mother Earth. This symmetry is crucial for, as Chanter Bitter Water explained to Newcomb, "Mother Earth and Father Sky must be identical in shape and size, since they are the two halves of a whole creation laid side by side, like the two halves of an evenly cut melon" (in Wyman [1970b:34]).

Inherent in this carefully measured symmetry is the Navajo emphasis on complementary pairing, with both being necessary for the desired state of wholeness, and thus holiness. As the sandpainting unfolds, the perfect symmetry with which places and supernatural entities are rendered brings them, and the universe they represent, under control. The very process of creating a sandpainting is healing because the act of drawing such symmetrical, orderly images focuses everyone's thoughts on the principles of balance and order. Thus, from its inception, the painting begins to work its healing power. As order is established in the sandpainted forms, so too order is reestablished in the spiritual world, and thus in the physical world, of the patient.

After the outlines of the two deities have been delineated, work proceeds simultaneously on both Mother Earth and Father Sky. In the center of the diamond that is to be Mother Earth, one helper hollows out a small circular depression in which he places a small bowl buried to its rim; he fills the bowl with water and herbs that darken the surface of the water. Around the bowl, he draws a series of concentric rings to symbolize a circular rainbow for blessing. The waterfilled bowl is the lake that filled the Emergence Place after the people had emerged from the previous worlds; from this lake will grow the four sacred plants. The Emergence Place itself, and therefore also the lake that filled it, is usually represented as dark "since it is believed that the struggle of the Navajo to come out to this world was a struggle out of darkness" (Reichard 1977:38).

As the original act of Creation is repeated, the Emergence and the events following it are actually recreated, projected from the past into the present. The act of drawing the visual image often calls forth a recitation of the story that it illustrates or symbolizes, according to Consultant A; thus, the image operates as what M. Jane Young (1988:122) called a "metonym of narrative."

On this particular day, much of the conversation centers upon the correct execution of the sandpainting forms as well as upon an explanation of specific forms because two of the helpers—one of the chanter's sons who has come for a visit from Oklahoma and one of the chanter's nephews—are making this sandpainting for the first time. With the exception of a woman who is a clan sister to the chanter's wife, everyone who is working on the sandpainting belongs to the chanter's immediate or extended family.[2]

On the other side of the sandpainting from Mother Earth, the chanter's son from Oklahoma begins the long process of outlining and filling in the black body of Father Sky with a mixture of charcoal and sand. As he begins, visitors arrive, seeking an appointment for a future Male Shootingway; the chanter, his wife, and the wife's clan sister leave the hogan to visit and to discuss the plans for the ceremonial. When the chanter returns he is surprised to discover that mistakes have been made: his son has filled in the area where the figure painting of Father Sky should have been. He rubs out the mistakes with a weaving batten and places fresh tan sand over the area that must be redone.

It is crucial that the order in which the sand is laid down should reflect the three-dimensional figure of Mother Earth and Father Sky: the figure painting on their backs must be done first, on tan sand, before the blue-gray of Mother Earth or the black of Father Sky is laid down. This first layer of blue-gray or black sand is meticulously placed above, between, and below the lines of the figure painting. When none of the tan background sand is visible, another layer of blue-gray (or black) sand is laid down that completely covers the figure painting; this represents the front side of Mother Earth (or Father Sky). On top of this layer, sand is trickled to form the narrow lines of the body painting on the front of the figures.

It is the chanter himself who draws the figure painting across the chest of Father Sky: two white zigzagged lines of (male) rain streaks (or lightning, according to Consultant D, which is associated with the Male Shootingway) extend from a central blue solar disk (which also represents the pollen ball ingested by the patient).[3] The figure painting on the figures of Father Sky and Mother Earth, which will be drawn across their chests, arms, and legs, is the same as that which will be done on the body of the patient.

For practical reasons, the painting is begun in the center and is enlarged by working outward. This means that the inner (and more centrally located) side of a figure is outlined before the other side. The inner side of Father Sky is outlined with the white of morning light before his right, outer side. The blue-gray sand that fills in the body of Mother Earth symbolizes the turquoise dress of summer sky; she will be outlined with the yellow of evening twilight.

An assistant painstakingly finishes filling in black sand around the fine white lines of the figure painting. Above his painted chest, Father Sky's neck and head have been drawn in black sand to represent the back of his head and neck; again, the three-dimensional nature of the figure is represented. The black sand is then covered with blue-gray sand in the neck area, and a choker-style necklace is drawn in orange sand. Father Sky's black head is covered with brown sand to represent his face (according to Consultant D) or a mask (Harry Walters, personal communication, 1989).

In the longer form of the Male Shootingway, the Sun's house screen (fig. 5.20) would be erected at the west side of the hogan before work on the painting began, and Father Sky's face in the sandpainting would be covered with the Sun's house stripes: the yellow of evening twilight in a band across the chin, the blue of the midday sky above the mouth, the black of night's darkness across the eyes, and the white of dawn across the forehead. These same stripes would then be painted on the face of the patient to evoke the light-giving, healing power of the Sun. The Sun's house screen, another example of a vitally important visual "text" that operates as a metonym of narrative, evokes the part of the Male Shootingway myth when the Sacred Twins first see the house of their father, the Sun. The Twins have already overcome many supernatural obstacles when they finally see the house of the Sun above the horizon; this house, built like a Pueblo dwelling, has white at the east, blue at the south, yellow at the west, and black at the north (Reichard 1950:472, 1977:39).

While the chanter outlines the circular brown face of Father Sky with white, black, and red-orange, another one of his sons gently places a large empty can in two places just above and below the widest part of the diamond-shaped body of Father Sky to create the circular patterns for the Sun and Moon disks. He then covers the black sand inside the circular area with blue sand for the Sun disk, which is below (to the west of) the white Moon disk. The Sun and Moon disks are shown proceeding in a westward direction—that is, with the top of the disk oriented toward the west—according to their paths across the sky. After the circles have been filled in, horns of power are extended from the sides of each orb, and the solar and lunar disks are painted with eyes and mouth and outlined in red. Inside the outline, the Sun also is decorated with a white line, representing dawn, across the upper portion of the disk and a yellow line, symbolizing evening twilight, across the lower portion.

On both the Sun and Moon disks, feathers are drawn at the top of the disks to symbolize the powers of clear thought and good judgment (Harry Walters, personal communication, 1990). These feathers also symbolize the ability to float in the air, according to Consultant D, a visual reference to their spatial placement in the sky. Earrings hang at the base of each horn to symbolize the ability to learn—not only to hear but also to remember knowledge, according to Consultant D. Lines of rain extend from each orb to rainbow bars; for the (male) Sun, these rain streaks take the form of zigzagged, "male" lines, while the rain streaks for the (female) Moon take a straight, "female" form. The rainbow bars are sundogs, or parhelia; because they indicate moisture in the sky, their visual depiction has the power to summon rain, a desirable by-product of Navajo ceremonials, whose primary purpose is healing or blessing.

At the same time as this work has been progressing on Father Sky, the chanter's wife and her clan sister have been filling in the blue-gray of Mother Earth's body. In each of the four directions radiating from the lake, three white lines radiate outward (upward from the earth); these lines, which converge at the lake, represent the three roots of each plant. It is important that all four sets of roots should be drawn before work begins on any of the plants. (I will later examine the profound role that this metaphor—of rootedness and of connectedness to all that is—plays in Navajo thought and thus in the restoration of the patient to a state of harmony and health.)

The plants themselves are drawn just as they would grow, from the earth upward: as one assistant delineates the five stalks of the bean plant rising up to the south, another is at work to the east, drawing the cornstalk toward the head of Mother Earth. Corn has been described as being "more than human, it is divine . . . and was connected to the highest ethical ideals" (Reichard 1950:540). When Talking God gave corn to the lonely sisters of the Eagle Chant legend, he explained that "there is no better thing in the world, for it is the gift of life" (Reichard 1950:540).

A black squash plant, with yellow squash, zigzags towards the west, and the five blue stems of a tobacco plant topped with five flowers emerge to the north. The smoking of tobacco is a test of powers (Reichard 1950:265); in the story of the Male Shootingway, Big Snake succumbs to the effects of tobacco.

It is significant that only female assistants are drawing these plants to complete Mother Earth. "Mother Earth should be done by women, if possible, to symbolize [the] regeneration and renewal [of Changing Woman, the embodiment of the Earth]" (Harry Walters, personal communication, 1990).

While work on the plants has been progressing, the arms of the two main figures have been drawn so that the left arm of Father Sky overlaps the right arm of Mother Earth because the sky is over the earth. The legs are drawn in similar fashion, and all four limbs are decorated with figure painting appropriate to the gender of the entity: crooked (male) rain streaks for the arms and legs of Father Sky and straight (female) rain streaks for Mother Earth. All figure painting includes the four sacred colors symbolic of the four cardinal light phenomena and the Sun's house stripes. The hands and feet of Father Sky and Mother Earth are painted with yellow pollen to indicate fertility.

The clouds of black and blue mist upon which Mother Earth and Father Sky sit, respectively, are drawn, and each cloud is held together with a rainbow outline. After these clouds have been painted, the chanter begins filling in the spaces between the two figures with wavy black lines. Eventually, these lines will fill all spaces of the tan background. The wavy lines, which are not shown in sandpainting reproductions because they detract from the visual effect, are an essential part of every sandpainting because they add power and efficacy to the painting. The sandpainting is becoming more powerful.

Finally, it is time for the chanter to draw the constellations. It is essential that the constellations be properly placed with respect to their symbolic locations in the night sky. The act of placing the constellations on the body of Father Sky operates not only as a metonym of narrative but also as ritual synecdoche: this act evokes a verbal recitation of the accompanying myth—the well-known story of stellar creation—which is an interplay between the forces of order and disorder, symbolic of the entire ceremonial process.

In the story of stellar creation, Coyote, the "patron of disorder" in the words of Consultant G, intervenes in the orderly creative process by wilfully flinging the remaining, unplaced stars into the heavens. It is highly significant that the chanter draws only the constellations the supernaturals had carefully placed in ordered patterns before Coyote's intervention. Thus, the proper placement of the constellations in the sandpainting stands for the proper placement of all sandpainting forms; in turn, the correct, orderly placement of the sandpainting forms symbolizes the order the chanter seeks to restore in the "disordered" spiritual and physical world of the patient.

First, the chanter draws Yikáísdáhí, the Milky Way, which is associated with the dawn and thus with the east; this celestial feature is drawn at the eastern end of Father Sky, high on his chest. The next figures to be placed are Venus and the cane of Yikáísdáhí, who is thought to be an old man who needs to lean on a cane while he scans the eastern horizon for the Sun, waiting for the approach of dawn. The two constellations that compose Scorpius, Gah heet'e'ii and 'Átsé'etsoh, are also associated with the east and therefore lie just under the criss-crossed pattern of the Milky Way. To the north, at Father Sky's right side, are the two Náhookǫs, the Big Dipper and Cassiopeia, gọt they revolve around the North Star, Polaris. Hastiin Sik'ai'í, Corvus, is placed on the opposite (south) side of Father Sky. And in the northwest and southwest, respectively, lie Dilyéhé (the Pleiades) and 'Átsé'ets'ózí (Orion).

After the constellations have been placed, the Sun's tobacco pouch is placed just above Father Sky's right hand. Bat will go above Mother Earth's left hand; these guardians protect the eastern opening of the painting. Before Bat is drawn, however, I am told to take my final photographs. I carefully make my way between the edge of the sandpainting and the people who have worked so hard on its creation and who now rest as they contemplate the product of their labor. I stand at the west side of the hogan, at the feet of Father Sky, facing the entrance, and photograph the majestic forms at my feet.

At this point, before the *k'eet'áán,* or prayer sticks, have been placed, one of the chanter's sons tells me it is time for me to leave the hogan and return with the patient. It is time for me to change from observer to participant. The ceremony is being held for protection: to ensure the continued good health of the primary patient, who was cured in a previous five-night Male Shootingway, and to protect me in my work with the sandpaintings.[4]

We wait expectantly inside the house, dressed in our finest tiered skirts, velveteen blouses, moccasins, and turquoise. Finally, word comes from the sacred hogan, and we rise from our chairs, wrapping our vividly colored Pendleton blankets around us. As we walk across the yard, we talk about how nervous and excited we are; we are both glad to have someone with whom to share the experience.

We can hear the singing as we approach the hogan. Finally, we enter the doorway. The casual atmosphere has given way to an air of greater formality: family and friends now sit with their backs to the walls of the hogan; the tins of sand and other articles used in sandpainting preparation have been removed; the completed sandpainting lies isolated in the center of the floor. The painting appears to have grown in size, power, and beauty while I was gone; its surface is now covered with a light dusting of fine white corn pollen. Pollen balls have been placed in the mouths of Mother Earth and Father Sky and a line of pollen stretches between the two pollen balls, joining the two deities. Some of the plumed prayer sticks stand upright in the sand around the image, while others lie in piles beside Mother Earth and Father Sky; at the western side of the painting stand the four wide boards. The painting is clearly a powerful presence, alive and sacred.

The chanter directs us in strewing sacred pollen across the magnificent sandpainting that lies on the hogan floor before us. From the basket held in his left hand, with his other hand he takes a pinch of pollen, which he flings upward and outward. His expansive gesture scatters the powdery substance high above the painting. The pollen drifts onto the painting like a light flurry of snow. We futilely try to imitate the grace of his gesture.

We then take our places at the north side of the hogan and the blessing of our bodies begins as the chanter sprinkles pollen in our moccasins and touches our legs and arms with herbal water. We tremble with the solemnity of the experience. The sandpainting ceremony has begun.

THE WIDE BOARDS

The four wide boards, which will be pressed against the patient's body while she sits upon the sandpainting to transfer blessings and healing power,[5] also reflect cosmological motifs. The first wide board depicts a scene from the myth of the Male Shootingway in which Holy Young Man is being carried through the skyhole into the sky by one of the Thunder People against a curtain of white dawn. The second wide board depicts the Sun on one side and Father Sky, with the Sun's house stripes across his face, on the reverse side. The Moon and Mother Earth are on the two sides of the third wide board. Finally, one side of the fourth wide board depicts the black of Darkness on its left (south) side and the white of Dawn on its right (north) side; these two light phenomena are separated by lightning. The other side of this board depicts Horizontal Blue Sky on the right (north) side and Yellow Evening Twilight on its left (south) side (Wyman 1972b:135).

In addition to having a cosmological referent, the symbolism depicted on the wide boards reiterates the Navajo emphasis on balance and directionality as well as on pairing: the "male" entities (those embodying the stronger, more aggressive principle) of Sky and Sun are on the second wide board and the "female" entities (those representing the weaker, more submissive principle) of Earth and Moon are on the third wide board; Black Darkness is paired with White Dawn and Horizontal Blue Sky with Yellow Evening Twilight on the fourth board.

THE MALE SHOOTINGWAY MYTH

To better understand the symbolism of the four wide boards as well as of the sandpainting itself, it is important to know something more about the myth that the Male Shootingway ceremonial recreates[6] and about the relationship between the sandpainting and the myth. As previously explained, very few sandpaintings depict specific events in the plot of the accompanying chantway myth; rather, they holistically present an overview, or composite picture, of the protagonists, settings, and etiological factors (the causes of the illness which the particular ceremonial seeks to cure) associated with the chantway.

Chanter A explained the relationship between the "Mother Earth, Father Sky" painting and the story of the Male Shootingway. Holy Young Man, a major character in the Male Shootingway story, is the one who is actually responsible for using the "Mother Earth, Father Sky" painting as a part of this ceremonial. Chanter A explained,

> He [Holy Young Man] is the one that said, "This [sandpainting] will be made in this order because the Earth, the vegetation, the Emergence, the Sky, there is a holiness here." He said, "There is power here. We should utilize that for the good of the Earth Surface People," and therefore he is the one who is responsible for making this [the various components of the sandpainting] in this order. And in the Blessingway, they also talk about this sandpainting, "Mother Earth and Father Sky." And then in the Navajo Windway, there's also "Father Sky." So anything that pertains to Holy Young Man and the Earth and the Sky will have those paintings.

Thus, the relationship between the Male Shootingway myth and the "Mother Earth, Father Sky" sandpainting is complex. As is true of most sandpaintings, the "Mother Earth, Father Sky" painting is clearly much more than simply an illustration of an event in the accompanying myth. With this understanding, Katherine Spencer's (1957:116–17) summary of the myth follows:

> The story of the Male Shooting Way tells of the travels and adventures of twin brothers and their acquisition of ceremonial powers by contacts with supernaturals. The two principal versions (Newcomb and Reichard 1975, Reichard 1977:37–73) begin with familiar portions of the war god story from the general origin myth, but the sequence of incidents following upon this varies somewhat in the two versions. One story (Newcomb and Reichard 1975) first recounts visits to Changing Woman, two adventures of Monster Slayer (involving bullroarers and rattlesnake), a visit to Sun for ritual knowledge, and encounters with whirling-tail-feather, arrow people, and water ox; at several points these events are connected with previous material of the general origin myth. The other (Reichard 1977:37–73) tells of pulling down the sun and moon and of the hero's adventures with snake people. The central portions of both versions are more similar than these opening events; in both cases they include a hunting transgression, swallowed by fish, and encounter with buffalo people. Again the concluding events show variation: the Newcomb and Reichard account adds encounters with translucent rock people, dogs and bears, porcupine, and weasel; the Reichard version ends with a journey with ant people and the teaching of the ceremony for earth people. The hunting transgression and swallowed by fish are repeated in the third fragmentary version (Reichard 1934:194–95). After these adventures have been completed, the ceremonial knowledge thus gained is taught to earth people and the participants depart to live with the supernaturals (Reichard 1977).
>
> This story as a whole deals with the adventures of twin heroes provoked by

their inadvertent or intentional venturing into strange circumstances or forbidden territory and with the usual acquisition of ritual power consequent upon such encounters. Throughout the complicated and often confusing array of detail runs the theme of their courageous or foolhardy courting of danger. The heroes repeatedly undertake, wittingly or unwittingly, forbidden or dangerous adventures. From the resulting catastrophes they are protected or restored by supernatural aid, and gradually, as a sort of immunity is gained through the resulting accumulation of sacred power, they are better able to withstand and combat these dangers by their own efforts.

Courting of danger may take the form of venturing into forbidden territory, as when the older twin overcomes rattler, approaches the whirling-tail-feather, hunts in forbidden territory, or out of curiosity visits snake people despite his host's warnings. In each case he meets with some difficulty or danger but eventually emerges safe and wiser with ceremonial knowledge. As stated in one version (Newcomb and Reichard 1975) the hero takes pride in venturing into forbidden spots, "for he reasoned that he always came back restored and richer in lore for Earth People." His precarious situation may result from transgression of a taboo, as when the older twin ventures forth without his talking prayerstick or uses arrow feathers from the sacred grebe without permission. Accident may befall without the hero's knowledge of transgression, as when the younger brother reaches for a feathered cornstalk and falls into the water to be swallowed by fish. Or the hero may be attacked without apparent offense on his part, as when the older brother is torn up by dogs and bears or when he is shot by weasel. The rescue or restoration from these mishaps is usually by intervention and ritual treatment by supernaturals, in the course of which the hero gains ceremonial knowledge.

Two of the hero's adventures involve his marriage, first to a snake wife and later to buffalo women. In his snake marriage there is intimation of his father-in-law's trickery, and ultimately Coyote takes the hero's form and transforms him into a coyote in hopes of stealing his snake wife. From this accident he is, however, restored. Likewise, when the hero marries two buffalo women, he again meets difficulties, this time an attack by the offended buffalo husband. With his own power he is able not only to withstand this attack successfully but after the slaughter to restore the buffalo people for his wives.[7]

"MOTHER EARTH, FATHER SKY" AS AN AFFECTING PRESENCE

Because this painting depicts such a powerful image as the entirety of the universe, standing as a visual embodiment of our relationship to all that is, its evocative power is much greater than that of other images. Furthermore, in the long form of the Male Shootingway, this painting represents the culmination of nine days and nights of ceremonial activity—"some ninety hours of music, prayer, graphic arts, dramatic staging, movement, and costume" (McAllester 1980:199).

Earlier, I discussed the sandpainting as an affecting presence that derives its power and energy from its state of completeness and from its ability to compress time and space. Such temporal layering means that in the specific case of the "Mother Earth, Father Sky" sandpainting, several layers of mythic time coexist with the present moment of the actual ceremony: the moment when the Twins learned this painting at Dawn Mountain; the first time the ceremonial was given on earth by the Holy People; the moment when the Sacred Twins saw the earth and sky from the home of their father, the Sun. In addition, the painting recalls origin events that lie outside the body of the Male Shootingway myth; the depiction of the Place of Emergence on the body of Mother Earth recalls the Emergence of the Earth Surface People, and the depiction of each constellation on the body of Father Sky evokes its particular story. The orderly placement of all the constellations evokes the well-known story of stellar creation, which, because of its order-disorder theme, synecdochically stands for the orderly placement of all sandpainting forms. In turn, the order and symmetry of the sandpainted images symbolize the state of order and harmony that the ceremony seeks to reestablish in the life of the patient.

In addition to the compression of time in this painting, space is also collapsed: space expands both horizontally and vertically from an apparently flat surface. What appears to Anglos as a two-dimensional depiction is, for Navajos, three-dimensional.[8] As we have seen in the description of the making of the "Mother Earth, Father Sky" painting, directional orientation is a fundamental principle in the creation of the painting: the powers of the four directions and the light phenomena associated with them are evoked and are drawn into the painting. After the painting has been finished, the chanter animates it by performing the blessing, which expands the painting in a vertical direction. In addition to the placement of the prayer sticks and the invocation of prayers, he strews corn pollen with an expansive upward and outward ritual motion. The sandpainting then extends upward in space, through the chanter and his sweeping ritual actions. The painting is alive, and it is sacred.[9]

Although the image itself appears two-dimensional (with the exception of the bowl of water symbolizing the lake that filled in the Place of Emergence), the space represented is clearly three-dimensional. The depiction of the Place of Emergence evokes the movement upward through previous worlds that lie below the present world, while the depiction of the night sky represents the heavens, which are located above the earth's surface. The three-dimensional nature of Mother Earth and Father Sky is represented in the layers of sand used to depict them: first, the figure painting on their backs, then their fronts, and finally the figure painting across their chests. Thus, in the sacred sandpainting, "Mother Earth, Father Sky" not only does the past coexist with the present but also space expands outward and upward from an apparently two-dimensional image, resulting in an intensification of experience.

From the Navajo viewpoint, the power of the sandpainting is derived from its state of wholeness and completeness (Harry Walters, personal communication, 1990). Nothing is lacking when the painting is whole and thus holy. In chapter 4, I discussed the concept of interrelated totality that is fundamental to Navajo thought, citing the annual cycle and its component seasons as an embodiment of this principle. To reiterate, this concept is based on the understanding that each part of a whole is necessary and equally important, and that the whole is much greater than merely the sum of its parts.

This is why the completed sandpainting is much more—much more powerful—than the sum of its parts. The Navajo phrase that expresses this emphasis on wholeness, *sạ'a naghái bik'e hózhǫ́,* has been the subject of countless reinterpretations through the years.[10] *Sạ'a naghái bik'e hózhǫ́,* as defined in the Navajo Community College General Catalog (1987:7), "is the wholistic and ordered essence of life that encompasses the universe. It is the life force which is the reason for being and becoming; the pathway for continual learning and the renewal of aspiration."

Sạ'a naghái bik'e hózhǫ́ also relates directly to the earth and sky: Tl'aii (Klah 1942:63) considered *sạ'a naghái* to be the earth's inner form while *bik'e hózhǫ́* is sky's inner form. Slim Curley (in Haile 1947c:23–24) and Frank Mitchell (in Wyman 1970a:347), both well-known Blessingway chanters, had a somewhat different interpretation: the inner form of the earth, *sạ'a naghái* (the one who is long life), is paired with *bik'e hózhǫ́* (directs pleasant conditions), which includes vegetation, health, and prosperity. Thus, the earth's inner form directs beneficial conditions on its surface.

One of the most crucial aspects of the idea conveyed by this term is that the state of wholeness, or holiness, accompanies completion. Conversely, the state of incompleteness is dangerous. Farella (1984:164–76) presents evidence from chantway prayers that use this phrase to illustrate how dangerous this state of incompleteness or imbalance is considered to be. The first prayers describe the identification of the patient with the particular *diyin dine'é* (Holy People) who fight off the beings causing his illness; the prayers go on to describe the patient's protection from further contact with these and other dangerous supernaturals. The patient is described as having been transformed from a state of illness or incompleteness into a state of completeness or *sa'a naghái bik'e hózhǫ́*.

Farella (1984:166–67) cites one of the Enemyway songs as evidence that the patient is dangerous or feared because he is in a state of incompleteness: he is *sa'a naghái* without being *bik'e hózhǫ́*; that is, he is in a state of maleness unmediated by femaleness. Thus, while the Navajos divide nearly all natural phenomena into male and female complementary pairs, the idealized reality is the balance, or, as Toelken (personal communication, 1986) calls it, the "still point" between these two extremes.

According to Chanter A, it is because this state of incompleteness is so undesirable and even dangerous that some chanters do not draw Father Sky without Mother Earth in Holyway sandpaintings (compare Wyman [1970b:33]). This is also, he says, why all eight of the major Navajo constellations must appear on the body of Father Sky even if they are not mentioned in the accompanying songs or myth.

Harry Walters, director of the Ned Hatathli Museum at Navajo Community College, Tsaile, related an analogous situation to explain how important completeness is in a ceremonial context, such as the creation of a sandpainting. If a chanter went to a ceremonial with an incomplete *jish,* or medicine bundle, which included only those items he needed for the particular branch of the ceremonial that he was about to perform, he should still return to get the missing items. All the components of a *jish* are necessary—even the items that are not directly used in the context of the particular branch of the ceremonial being performed—because without the missing items, a *jish* is incomplete and ineffective. Thus, the chanter who attempts to heal a patient with an incomplete *jish* is only "cheating the patient and kidding himself about his ability to heal the patient." This example illustrates not only how vital completeness and order are in a ceremonial context, but also how the parts function to make the system whole and thus ceremonially effective.

The sandpainting depictions of constellations function in the same manner: were any of the eight constellations to be deleted from the night sky background, the sandpainting would be incomplete, ineffective, and even dangerous. Each constellation, the Sun, and the Moon are necessary to the interrelated totality of the heavens.

Another indication of how important the concept of completeness is to Navajo thought is the use of the same word, *hadaalt'é,* to mean both "it is complete" and "it is perfect" (Young and Morgan 1980:378). Thus, at a basic level, the "Mother Earth, Father Sky" painting derives its power from the fact that it represents female and male, the most fundamental of all binary pairs: the female Mother Earth (*są'a naghái*) and the male Father Sky (*bik'e hózhǫ́*), who together represent the entirety of the universe.

THE "MOTHER EARTH, FATHER SKY" SANDPAINTING AS A SACRED, LIVING ENTITY

Although sandpainting images seldom directly illustrate specific episodes in the myth associated with the ceremonial, these images are iconic: that is, they represent entities that are associated with the myth and place them in the appropriate space and time. Through the depicted images as well as through ritual procedures and prayers, the patient becomes identified with the supernaturals and with their world of mythic reality. Toelken (1977:80) eloquently described this process: "the patient is taken from his own context, the interior of his own hogan usually, and is described [in prayers] as standing on patterns, ledges, floating through the air with jewels, and other kinds of suggestive actions which bring the person simultaneously into two dimensions; this world and the 'other world' interpenetrate and reciprocate at the point of the ritual."

Thus, the depiction of certain images *evokes* the events of the myth time, causing these events to be created again in the present; simultaneously, these depictions *invoke* the sacred power carried by these deities.[11] Thus, the symbols depicted in the painting serve not only to link the mythic past with the here and now but also to summon the powers of the Holy People. These ritual symbols help the patient and all those present to focus inwardly, to participate with a "good heart," in a frame of mind characterized by *hózhǫ́ ntséskees* (thinking in beauty).

Pollen is one of the most important ritual symbols that serve as a bridge between belief and action in the sandpainting ceremony. As previously described, the strewing of pollen is the final ritual act that blesses the sandpainting; the expansiveness of this gesture as well as the pollen itself animate the sandpainting with life.

Reichard (1950:250) equated pollen with light by saying, "Light is an essential of life and protection, whose most outstanding symbol is pollen." Matthews (1902:42) explained the meaning of pollen: "Pollen is the emblem of peace, of happiness, of prosperity, and it is supposed to bring these blessings. When, in the Origin Legend, one of the war gods bids his enemy to put his feet down in pollen he constrains him to peace. When in prayer the devotee says, 'May the trail be in pollen,' he pleads for a happy and peaceful life."

Harry Walters explained that corn is a metaphor for human life because both go through the same stages of life. Both corn and humans reach a stage of fruition when they blossom: the corn bursts forth with pollen while humans also achieve a peak of development associated with *sạ'a naghái bik'e hózhǫ́*. Harry Walters (personal communication, 1990) described this state of being: "Everytime he talks, thinks, or acts, he does so in radiance, in a state of wisdom and perfect harmony." Just as the corn disseminates its pollen for the continuation of corn plants, so too humans have been entrusted with the sacred responsibility to disseminate their knowledge for the benefit and continuation of future generations. Because both corn and humans need nurturance from the four directions (four cardinal light phenomena) in order to reach old age, both possess knowledge from the four directions; it is this knowledge that they take into their beings and then have a responsibility to return to those that come after them.

Wyman (1970a:30–31) explained the significance of pollen as follows:

The pure, immaculate product of the corn tassel is food eaten by gods and man. Pollen, the beautiful, is a fit gift for the gods, [whose] paths should be strewn with it. When put in the mouth it really is a gift to the person [inner form] within the petitioner who should accompany his action with a prayer to that person. It enables the user to go on in life, to say kind and pleasant things. Pollen guards against abuse! "If I say so with it . . . that will be my guide in life" (Wyman 1970a:30).

As discussed in chapter 3, *bii'gistíín*, the inner form, is related to the concept of *nílch'i*, the Holy Wind, the powerful life force that animates and connects all living things in the universe. The act of putting pollen in one's mouth, while saying a prayer, is an offering to one's inner form and serves to identify the petitioner with the Holy People and with their wisdom and guidance (Wyman 1970a:30).

Whether the patient sits on the sandpainting or walks on pollen footprints, she absorbs the powers and guidance of the Holy People so that order and balance are restored in the patient's life. "The Liberation Prayer Song" from the Nightway ceremonial affirms this process:

> Now pollen of sitting place print exactly on top of this with you now he reseated himself
> Now pollen of foot place print exactly on top of this with you now he reseated himself
> Now pollen of hand place print exactly on top of this with you now he reseated himself.
> (Haile, n.d.: Box 16, Nightway)

Again, the patient/petitioner identifies herself with the powers of the Holy Person—in this case, Talking God—so that the inner, spiritual strength of Talking God is transferred to the patient. The patient leaves the ceremonial having incorporated Talking God's powers of guidance into her own being; in the future, she will be guided along the harmonious Pollen Path, which is traveled by Talking God and other Holy People.

The Pollen Path, Tádidíín bee Kék'ehashchíín, thus stands as a metaphor for "traveling"—for moving along one's life trail, and for living on a daily basis, in a way that is guided by ideals of harmony and balance. When I asked Consultant A what lasting philosophy remained with her after the sandpainting's destruction and the ceremony's completion, she explained that it was guidance:

> When the prayers say "your feet [referring to those of the depicted Holy Person] will become my feet" the words don't refer to physical strength but rather to spiritual strength. None of the prayers refer to *dooh,* physical strength. They never say, "your muscles become my muscles." Instead, the prayers use words like *'áni'*—mind—and *tsiis*—spiritual strength. The prayers say, "your spirit becomes my spirit." When they say, "Your feet become my feet," they mean that I [the patient] will walk in the right way from now on, on the path that the Holy People walk.

The patient and, indeed, all those present are reminded of their connectedness to the forces of the present world as well. When I asked Chanter B why he considers the "Mother Earth, Father Sky" painting to be the most sacred sandpainting, he replied, "[It is because] we walk everyday on our Mother the Earth, under our Father the Sky." He meant that this particular painting is a visual embodiment of humanity's place within the cosmos, an expression of oneness with all that is. Rather than existing apart from nature, humans have their existence within nature, as part of the intricate and infinite web of creation.

Human beings carry upon their body visual reminders of their connectedness to the earth and sky. The Navajo believe that people are connected to these entities, and to all the features and beings that live on the earth and in the sky, by the whorls on toes and fingertips, which are an expression of the Holy Wind that suffuses all living things. As a Navajo consultant told James McNeley (1981:35), "these (Winds sticking out of the) whorls at the tips of our toes hold us to the Earth. Those at our fingertips hold us to the Sky. Because of these, we do not fall when we move about."

Furthermore, as discussed in chapter 3, the act of breathing connects human beings to all living things. It is important to remember that *nílch'i,* Holy Wind, can also be translated as "air," and is "an omnipresent entity in which [all] living beings participate" (McNeley 1981:52). In the act of breathing, air is constantly being exchanged and boundaries being altered: "On inhaling, the powerful ones [the Holy People] enter one's lungs and are both a part of the breather as well as his being a part of and linked to all other beings" (Farella 1984:67). Thus, by breathing, one has direct access to the thought and speech of the Holy People (McNeley 1981:54). This is why the patient rises from the sandpainting and leaves the hogan to breathe in the power of the Sun. Through this ritual act the patient inhales the life-giving, healing power of the Sun into his being.

In the "Mother Earth, Father Sky" sandpainting the four sacred plants are a visual metaphor for connectedness and rootedness: as described above, all four sets of three roots each are drawn before work begins on the plants (these roots are visible in plates 2, 3, and 4, and in figs. 4.12 and 5.5). It is highly significant that when Miguelito explained the symbolism of the "Mother Earth, Father Sky" painting to Gladys Reichard (1975:55–56), he began his account of each of the four sacred plants with a description of its three roots: "a cornstalk whose three roots run into the water," "a squash with three roots running into the water," "three bean roots extend into the water," and finally, "three tobacco roots extend into the water." The sandpainting with "Sky-Reaching Rock" (plate 5) clearly demonstrates the significance of roots, and thus the metaphor of rootedness: the roots of the corn plant are as long as the plant itself. Many Navajos feel that the four cardinal light phenomena not only extend up into the sky but also have roots that stretch deep into the earth (see plate 2 and fig. 4.12).

The Anglo metaphor that equates people's beginnings with their "roots" also exists in Navajo: the correct way to begin in Navajo culture is with one's roots, whether it is working from the feet upward for ceremonial procedures,[12] or stating one's mother's clan and one's father's clan as a means of introducing oneself. It is only by establishing a deeply rooted foundation that people have strength and stability; if their roots are too shallow they fall over in the wind like a corn plant without sufficient root structure (here we see another aspect of the metaphor that equates the corn plant with human life). People's roots must go back into an established family structure and deep into the earth, connecting each individual to all other living beings and to the earth itself.

Farella found the concept of connectedness to be a key theme in Navajo philosophy, a theme so important that a Navajo elder, Grey Mustache, told a story to illustrate this concept only after two years of discussion. Farella (1984:177–78) explained that Grey Mustache "presented it as something very important . . . as the story that would put things together for me." The story tells of the role that First Man played in Creation, including how "he placed the responsibility for generational increase into his children *sǫ'a naghái* and *bik'e hózhǫ́*." Grey Mustache concluded his story, "And along these lines these things will be asked about from child to father to grandfather. And the questions about these things and all else will ultimately be questions about kinship, how we are related to the beginnings." Farella correctly concluded that "the unifying principle in everything"—or, as Grey Mustache said, the only type of question to ask about important matters—is the question of kinship, or relatedness.

This, I believe, is the principle, the source of the power, behind the sacred sandpainting. Not only is the patient reconnected in time and space through the forced realization of her profound relationship to sacred forces of the past and present, but also she is reminded of her connectedness to the humans who are present in either physical or spiritual reality. Consultant A explained, "What I feel when I sit on a sandpainting is a sense of connectedness to the people surrounding me there in the hogan, to the people in the myth that goes with the ceremony, and to all the people in the past who have been healed by this ceremony."

Chanter A described how it feels to sit on the "Mother Earth, Father Sky" sandpainting:

> When you sit on it [the "Mother Earth, Father Sky" sandpainting], think about yourself. If you have a prayer, if you know how to pray, you say a silent prayer. If you don't, you listen to the medicine man pray because this is for you and your faith and all of that together [the universe], with Mother Earth and Father

Sky because you are a child of both of them and you think about from here on to the future and that you will have a good life, *hózhǫ́*, a state of beauty and happiness. *Sǫ'a naghái bik'e hózhǫ́*; you think in terms of that. From here on everytime the Earth is mentioned you will think of Her as your mother and everytime the Sky is mentioned you will think of Him as your father; this is how you will have respect for Them. This is what you think when you sit on the sandpainting. . . . And if you have the body painting . . . the token is tied to your necklace. . . . Father Sky [and] everything—the Sun, the Moon, the stars, the Milky Way—all of these things in the heavens will recognize you by that. And the same way for everything on the Earth—the different plants, the animals, the mountains—all of these will recognize you [as their child].

Chanter A was explaining how the ritual symbols of earth and sky help the patient to focus inward upon the most basic of Navajo principles—reciprocity based upon the interrelated totality that is the universe. He was saying that the painting should remind all those who are present how profoundly their thoughts and actions affect the balance of the world around them. People must act responsibly, treating the creatures of the earth and the entities of the sky with the same respect they would accord their own parents, and in turn the beings of the earth and sky will respond by blessing people with all the good things of life, as parents would provide for their beloved children. He was also saying that human beings must remember the creative power of human thought: people are responsible for their thoughts and actions, and the ceremonial is an opportunity to refocus on the right ways of thinking and acting so that people are reconnected with this desired state of *hózhǫ́*. I believe that it is in reestablishing this powerful sense of connectedness, of oneness with all that is, that we find the true meaning and greatest gift of the sandpainting, wherein its ultimate healing power resides.

✤ 8 ✤
Conclusion

To what extent do Navajos still draw sustenance from their traditional spiritual practices and beliefs? Like other Native Americans, they are caught in the conflicting tide between the old and new. As one drives across the reservation, it is not unusual to see a satellite dish behind a house while a hogan stands nearby; many Navajos have videocassette recorders, and chanters themselves sometimes have family members tape songs and even portions of ceremonials.

As was discussed earlier, the Navajos have always been known for their cultural resilience and their pronounced ability to borrow items from other cultures which they "remake" into distinctly Navajo items. It has long been assumed that the Navajos borrowed sandpaintings, as well as other aspects of their ceremonialism, from the Pueblos. However, rather than copying the fairly simple designs that are just one part of Pueblo altar complexes, the Navajo made the paintings the focus, the altar itself, as they elaborated the sandpainting concept into a vast complex of intricate designs.

To illustrate further the characteristic Navajo ability to blend the old and new, I will resume the account of the Nightway ceremonial I attended in January 1986, with which I began this book. The ninth and concluding night of this ceremonial provided a perfect example of the ease with which Navajos move between the world of Western technology and their traditional world.

The night was penetratingly cold, and we stood beside one of the four evenly placed fires built for the audience, in a futile effort to stay warm. Everyone shivered as we anxiously awaited the next team of Yeibichai dancers. As we conversed with one of the more outgoing bystanders, Zonnie emerged from the darkness. "Come inside where it's warmer. We'll come back later to see the dancers." We followed her to her brother's cement-block house where the family, stretched out on sofas, were watching Bob Hope's parody of the Super Bowl. This apparent clash between the old and new, so characteristic of Navajo life today, does not create confusion for the Navajo who have developed an ability to integrate the two cultures. Half an hour later, the family had no difficulty in leaving the warm house with its television and VCR and reentering the world of mythic reality outside, which was represented by the teams of chanting Yeibichai dancers.

As Farella (1984:189) pointed out, adaptation from the Navajo perspective is quite different than it is from the Western viewpoint. While Westerners generally seek technological solutions—ones that alter the world—as their adaptive, or problem-solving, strategy, Navajos tend to take an epistemological approach, which emphasizes an alteration of perception, a change in the way one perceives the world. As this book has shown, the purpose of Navajo ritual is to bring about just this kind of gestalt shift, or change in inner consciousness, which in turn results in outer, "objective" change.

One of the ways in which this shift is accomplished is through the sandpainting and its perceived ability to summon the powers of the past and present. By realigning oneself spiritually, mentally, and emotionally with the powers of the universe, outer health then naturally manifests itself.

The sandpainting clearly is an affecting presence, a sacred, living entity that draws its power from its completeness and its ability to enable the one-sung-over to transform his mental and physical state by focusing upon powerful mythic symbols. These symbols recreate the chantway odyssey of the story's protagonist, causing those events to live again in the present. The images in the sandpainting *invoke* the presence of the Holy People while simultaneously *evoking* a powerful mythic reality. The past informs the events of the present as the myth coexists with the here and now. This fusion of past and present reminds the one-sung-over, as well as everyone else, that the Holy People are present and that they are directly involved in the life of the patient, caring about him as they would their own beloved child. Healing of mind and spirit, and thus of body, is indeed possible.

George Blueeyes, a Navajo elder, wrote a poem that expresses the Navajo reverence for the earth and sky with great lyricism and dignity:

> We say *Nahasdzáán Shimá:*
> Earth, My Mother.
> We are made from her.
> Even though she takes us daily,
> We will become part of her again.
> For we ARE her.

The Earth is Our Mother.
The Sky is Our Father.
Just as a man gives his wife beautiful things to wear,
So Our Father Sky does the same.
He sends rain down on Mother Earth,
And because of the rain the plants grow,
And flowers appear of many different colors.
She in turn provides food for him.

He dresses her as a man would dress his woman.
He moves clouds and male rain.
He moves dark mists and female rain.
Dark mists cloak the ground,
And plants grow with many colored blossoms.

The plants with colored blossoms are her dress.
It wears out. Yes, the earth's cover wears out.
The plants ripen and fade away in the fall.
Then in the spring when the rains come again,
Mother Earth once again puts on her finery.
The plants are restored again in beauty.
This is what the stories of the Elders say.

(in *Between Sacred Mountains* [1982:18–19])

This spiritual perspective is inseparable from everyday reality, so that the rigid distinction that exists in most Western minds between the daily round of work and play, on the one hand, and religion, on the other, is nonexistent for the Navajos. On a daily basis, the order and continual regeneration inherent in the cosmos—the changing seasons (personified by Changing Woman), night and day, life and death—serves as a constant reminder of how to live one's life in balance, in a state of *hózhǫ*. The traditional Navajo awakens with the dawn and scatters pollen to the east outside the hogan, as Coyote taught in Blessingway. By beginning the day with prayers of protection and blessing, he or she summons not only the powers of the present but also those of the past. At night, the constellations, through the moral stories they index as well as through their repetitive, cyclical movements, serve as constant reminders of the right way to live one's life.

Just as the traditional Navajo weaver turns for inspiration to the spiritual forces of the natural world that constantly surround her, "modern" Navajos, those who have adopted a Western lifestyle, also have access to these same sources of guidance and strength. As a Navajo friend, a professor at a major university in the Southwest, confided, "When I am lonely, the Mountains call me." The Mountains, alive with power and presence, are an ever-present source of spiritual strength. By realigning oneself with the powers of the universe, one becomes reconnected with that which is timeless and eternal. The Mountains are calling to all of us if only we will listen.

Appendix: Field Procedures
and Documentation

As described in chapter 1, my initial involvement with the Navajos began in the summer of 1970 when I lived in the hogan of a traditional Navajo family near Many Farms, Arizona, as an informally adopted daughter. Through living with this family for various periods of time between 1970 and 1972 and participating in many daily activities—herding sheep, chopping firewood, cooking meals, and many other tasks and experiences—I began to understand Navajo culture.

In the summer of 1983 I began photographing the sandpainting collections at the Wheelwright Museum of the American Indian in Santa Fe, New Mexico, and at the Museum of Northern Arizona in Flagstaff. I included all aspects of the sky: sun, moon, stars, thunder, rainbow, rain, and wind, out of concern that there might not be sufficient data on the constellations alone and that because of Reichard's (1950:470) characterization of stars as "uncontrollable" and "feared by the Navaho," Navajos might be unwilling to share information about the constellations. Both concerns later proved to be unfounded.

In 1985 I visited the Museum of Northern Arizona to photograph sandpainting reproductions and to check the completeness of my data with the Wyman sandpainting file. I then made a final trip to Santa Fe to finish photographing sandpainting reproductions with celestial features.

In the spring of 1984 I went to Navajo Community College in Tsaile, Arizona, to meet with Consultant G, a Navajo specialist in astronomy. This preliminary trip helped me to focus on the nature of Navajo astronomical knowledge.

I completed the collection of the corpus of visual material—500 photographs of sandpainting reproductions—in the summer of 1985, checking the completeness of my data once more with the Wyman sandpainting file at the Museum of Northern Arizona, which contains over 1,000 entries.

I then analyzed these photographs for similarities and differences in the depiction of constellations, supplementing this information with a search of the ethnohistoric literature. I found that while anthropologists had recorded some data about Navajo constellations, their limited knowledge of astronomy had curtailed their ability to relate Navajo constellations to those identified by the Western scientific astronomical tradition.

Field work was conducted for short periods of time between April 1985 and November 1990 in the central part of the reservation as well as in Tucson with Consultants A and P. During this time I conducted interviews and attended ceremonials. The format of my interviews evolved from a very structured question-by-question format that had a series of specific questions for each sandpainting photograph to a much more open-ended interview in which I used no questionnaires.

In my astronomical research, I asked consultants to name and to identify the constellations they knew rather than only to identify constellations that had appeared in the literature (such as Chamberlain [1983]). As a means of further checking these data, after the consultants had named and identified those constellations with which they were familiar, I then asked about constellations that had appeared in other sources (see table 4.3), but which they had not mentioned. None of the consultants was familiar with any of these.

The astronomical focus of this book is a study of the constellations *as they appear in the sandpaintings*. For this reason I used photographs of sandpainting reproductions as foci for interviews rather than the night sky itself. Furthermore, it soon became clear that the eight major Navajo constellations, which are clearly identifiable with their Western counterparts, were the only ones with which the consultants were familiar, making interviews under the night sky unnecessary.

Initial questions led deeper into selected topics. Astronomy led into cosmology, in discussions about the Navajo universe as an embodiment of order and harmony. As my understanding grew, I synthesized what I knew and then returned to ask the consultants about the accuracy of my synthesis.

I have chosen to refer to the twelve Navajos with whom I worked as "consultants" rather than informants because they are all respected specialists in the area of Navajo ceremonialism. All possess great knowledge gathered over the course of many years. It is through their respect for this knowledge and their generosity that they patiently shared this knowledge with me.

The Navajo specialists with whom I worked were six chanters (Chanters A–F), a diagnostician (Stargazer A), and six consultants (Consultants A, D, G, H, and P, and Harry Walters, director of the Ned Hatathli Museum at

Navajo Community College, Tsaile, Arizona). The five consultants have worked closely with chanters in their families and communities and possess a great deal of astronomical/ceremonial knowledge because of their involvement with ceremonial activity.

Chanter A was born in 1906 and died in 1991. He knew the Blessingway, Mountainway, Male Shootingway, Red Antway, Navajo Windway, Apache Windway, Nightway, Enemyway, Evilway, Big Starway, Hand Tremblingway, stargazing, and short prayers involving offerings. Chanter B, who is in his sixties, knows the Male Shootingway, Enemyway, Blessingway, and Evilway. Chanter C, also in his sixties, is primarily known as a Nightway chanter but also knows the Coyoteway. Chanter D, who is thirty-eight years old, specializes in the Nightway and Blessingway but also knows the Chiricahua Windway (also known as the Apache Windway) and Enemyway. The fifth chanter, Chanter E, a man in his sixties, knows the Male Shootingway, Nightway, Enemyway, Windway, Suckingway, Hand Tremblingway, and stargazing, and is a herbalist. The final chanter, Chanter F, also in his sixties, declined to tell me what chants he knew. Stargazer A, a man from Lukachukai, is forty-six years old.

Notes

PREFACE

1. I use the term *sandpainting* because of its common usage. However, *drypainting* is the technically correct term because sand is not the only pigment used in the construction of these sacred images.

2. As will be seen in this book, there are many versions of stories and myths. Like people of other cultures, Navajos share a distinctive culture but differ in the interpretation of specific cultural symbols. As Peter Stromberg (1986:13) has demonstrated, cultural symbols blend with personal experience to create interpretations of the same symbols. Variation is evident in the way in which chanters draw the constellations and in how they project key symbols from their chant specializations onto the constellations. Rather than being disruptive of the system, variation at this level encourages greater symbolic elaboration because each chanter does not have to know the entire system. Through ceremonial specialization, greater symbolic elaboration becomes possible, and the same set of phenomena serves as a vehicle for many meanings (Griffin-Pierce 1987:248). Culture is dynamic, at both the individual and collective levels.

CHAPTER I: INTRODUCTION

1. I use the anglicized, though technically incorrect, spelling of the Navajo word *hooghan* because *hogan* has made its way into the English dictionary and thus into general usage.

2. I have used the terms *Western* and *Anglo* to designate those who are Euro-Americans. Although *Anglo* is not a technically accurate term, it is the term used by Navajos to refer to non-Indians; I have therefore adopted that usage.

3. The growing awareness that no account is without cultural bias and that quantitative studies of cultural behavior describe only a small segment of the entire cultural spectrum has led to the emergence of interpretive anthropology, an approach whose dominant interest is how interpretations are constructed by the anthropologist. Interpretive ethnography and reflexive anthropology seek to portray other worlds from the inside as richly as possible, giving priority to the "messier," less quantifiable side of social action.

4. As I am sure Joseph Campbell would agree, the Bible itself does not condemn nature. Although many religions interpret the phrase, "dominion over nature," which

appears in the Book of Genesis, to mean stewardship, unfortunately this phrase has been interpreted as a mandate to exploit nature by too many non-Native Americans.

5. Duane Elgin, in his book, *Voluntary Simplicity*, draws an excellent contrast between Western and Eastern (which includes that of Native Americans) views of reality and how an integration of these two views could be synthesized, both by individuals and by societies.

CHAPTER 2: THE ROOTS OF NAVAJO CULTURE

1. See chapter 6 for a discussion of these symbols on the Enemyway rattle stick and for an interpretation of the Big Dipper as Monster Slayer's bow (illustrated in figure 6.6).

2. Washington Matthews (1902:307), who wrote the most detailed account of the Nightway, places the canyons that are the home of the Yé'ii mentioned in this myth north of the San Juan River, in Colorado and Utah.

3. In 1887 Congress passed the Dawes Severalty Act, or "Allotment Act," which divided up communal Indian land among individuals. After the land had been allotted to Native American families and individuals, whatever was left over was sold to Anglo settlers.

4. Louise Lamphere (1977:4–5) discussed reasons for the contradictions in the analyses of Navajo social organization. Aberle (1963) and Shepardson and Hammond (1970) have shown that the extended family is not always matrilocal and that the only function of the dispersed matrilineal clan is the regulation of marriage. Alternatives to the disputed term *outfit* are "cooperating group" (Collier 1966), "matrilineage" (Shepardson and Hammond 1970), "resident lineage" (Adams 1963), and "Local Clan Element" (Aberle 1961). Lamphere (1977) prefers the concepts of "set," defined as "those adults within one or two genealogical links of any particular ego" (p. 127), and "network," defined as the "unbounded system of relationships between pairs of people making up a field of activity" (p. 94).

5. Hastiin Tł'aii was the famous Navajo chanter around whose ceremonial knowledge and equipment Mary Cabot Wheelwright founded what is now the Wheelwright Museum of the American Indian in Santa Fe, New Mexico. His name is also spelled Tł'aáh or Klah, depending upon the source.

CHAPTER 3: THE NAVAJO SPIRITUAL WORLD

1. Mike Mitchell's words have been paraphrased by Suzanne Page. I know Mike Mitchell personally, and I believe that Page conveys his thoughts accurately.

2. The phrase, "sa'a naghái bik'e hózhǫ́," often glossed as "long life and happiness," is explained in chapter 7.

3. Louise Lamphere (1977) documents cooperative behavior among the Navajo in terms of a generalized conception of "help" or "aid," which is expressed by using a form of the verb stem *-ghoł* (to run), which is used in phrases like "bíká adeeshghoł" ("I'll help him" or "I'll run after him").

4. I refer to the chanter as "he" because, although some chanters are women, there are many more male chanters. Women are much more common as diagnosticians rather than as chanters.

5. The performance of a sandpainting on the final day of a nine-night Nightway depends upon the participation of a Black God Impersonator: if this Impersonator participates, then one of the Black God sandpaintings is performed; conversely, if a Black God sandpainting is to be made, then a Black God Impersonator must appear.

6. See chapter 7 for a detailed description of this kind of layering in the creation of the "Mother Earth, Father Sky" sandpainting.

7. The Place-of-Emergence is represented as dark to symbolize the Navajos' struggle out of the darkness of the previous worlds (Reichard 1977:38).

8. The extent of the accuracy of museum reproductions of sacred sandpaintings is problematic. The primary purpose of the sandpainting is to attract the Holy People to assist in healing; when healing is not intended, as in these reproductions, slight changes have often been made so as *not* to attract their presence. Furthermore, because photography and drawing in the consecrated hogan are usually not permitted, the ethnographers who recorded these sacred images had to memorize the paintings as they sat through the ceremonies, which could be quite long. They later made sketches on butcher paper, recording what they remembered of the features and colors. The ethnographer then redrew the painting in more elaborate form and consulted with the chanter until both were satisfied. In some cases, the chanter purposely included minor but significant changes from the sacred version for protection because the Navajo Holy People had prohibited the preservation of these images in permanent form. Parezo (1983:75–99) explored the process of rationalization among Navajo chanters and weavers that allowed them to break the prohibition against recording sacred designs in permanent form. See Faris (1990:109–12) for a discussion of the accuracy of museum sandpainting reproductions.

9. The noun *jish* can be singular or plural; this is may be why the grammatically incorrect *phenomena* rather than *phenomenon* was used to describe the *jish* in this quotation.

10. By referring to the activity of making the sandpainting as a creative endeavor, I mean that the individuals involved are bringing something into visual existence which existed previously only on a spiritual, supernatural, unseen level. The sandpainting forms are prescribed; they do *not* involve creative manipulation or imaginative play. They clarify a spiritual reality by putting it into tangible form; by bringing the unseen into palpable reality, they are creative endeavors.

CHAPTER 4: COSMOLOGICAL ORDER AS A MODEL FOR NAVAJO PHILOSOPHY AND LIFE

1. The myths of the Male Shootingway and "When the Two Came to Their Father" tell of the Sacred Twins and the trials they undergo to prove their relationship to their father, the Sun.

2. This difference may be due to the nomadic heritage, which the Navajos brought

with them into the Southwest, and to their emphasis on movement, ideas that were explored in chapter 2. In contrast, the sedentary and more agricultural Pueblos focus more on the life-giving power of a single entity, the sun. Furthermore, the permanent, localized nature of Pueblo villages makes the precise measurement of the sun's annual position possible through the use of a horizon calendar. For example, when the sun sets in a specific place on the horizon, the Hopi know that the winter solstice will occur about eleven days later (Williamson 1984:77–84). I do not mean to imply, however, that Pueblo groups, such as the Zuni, were not interested in the stars (see Young and Williamson [1981:183–91] for a discussion of Zuni astronomy).

3. The work of Father Berard Haile (1947c), as well as other research, indicates that once many other Navajo constellations were known than simply the eight major constellations recognized today.

4. M. Jane Young (1988:106–7) refers to the Zuni "aesthetic of accumulation," which she defines as "an elaborate redundancy in Zuni sacred and secular environments."

5. As previously discussed, maleness and femaleness refer to the basic Navajo distinction between that which is coarser and more aggressive, called male (*biką'*), and that which is finer and gentler, called female (*ba'ááá*). These differences are not sexual (thus Born-for-Water can be referred to as female) but instead represent a complementary pair with both halves necessary for completion and wholeness.

6. Von Del Chamberlain (personal communication, 1991) pointed out the inferred relationship in this passage of text between femaleness, the lunar cycle, and birth.

7. I have chosen to use Haile's "Father Sky" rather than Chanter A's because this figure is sacred knowledge. Even though Chanter A did not object to my using his "Father Sky" in this book, I believe that it is not appropriate to publish it because other chanters who learned from the same teacher use a similar "Father Sky" in their sandpaintings today. Instead, I have isolated individual constellations from Chanter A's "Father Sky," which I have redrawn in figures 4.5 through 4.8. These same constellations appear in the post-Emergence universe (fig. 4.12).

8. Astronomically, this is called an open cluster of faint stars and actually consists of several hundred stars. This constellation is distinctive because it forms a compact unit in relative isolation.

9. Orion exemplifies Arnheim's (1971:55) type of constellation whose component stars fit into an order and display a definite shape. The three closely spaced stars of Orion's belt are distinctive for their uniformity in brightness and spacing. The brightness and distinctive red color of the star Betelgeuse in Orion is another landmark for the human eye (Krupp 1983:9). The brightness of the other component stars results in a striking grouping that is seen as a human figure in both the Navajo and Western traditions.

10. Haile (1947c:7) claims that this constellation contains ten stars. One reason that Corvus, a constellation generally unnoticed by anyone but astronomers, is recognized by the Navajo is the empty space around it: while the stars that compose Corvus are not particularly bright, they do form a quadrilateral figure surrounded by only a few fainter stars and set in a comparatively dark part of the sky.

11. Antares, the red star of first magnitude in the heart of the Scorpion, also helps to identify this constellation.

12. M. Jane Young suggested to me (as Dell Hymes had suggested to her) that *personator* better conveys what happens in those ceremonies in which a God Impersonator appears. Although I use the phrase *God Impersonator* in this book as a matter of convention, I agree that this fails to convey the transference of supernatural power that occurs when the appropriate person puts on the mask of a supernatural being, whom the person then becomes for the duration of the ceremonial.

13. The classification of this painting as a Blessingway drypainting is questionable. I agree with the chanters with whom I worked, who thought that this reproduction might belong to the Male Shootingway because of the Sun's House stripes on the face of Father Sky. The Wheelwright Museum, where this reproduction is housed, catalogued it as Blessingway, although it was previously classified under Upward Reachingway. This painting is reproduced in Newcomb, Fishler, and Wheelwright (1956:14) but is not identified by chant. Leland Wyman (1970a:66–67), who put together the only all-inclusive index of Navajo sandpainting reproductions (at the Museum of Northern Arizona, Flagstaff) said that he had been uncertain about the attribution of this painting and a similar Father Sky painting (depicted in Wyman [1952:76, fig. 33]). He explained that he had recently decided that "they could very well have been taken from Blessingway." His phrasing still expressed an element of doubt; for this reason and because of the Sun's House stripes—a Male Shootingway attribute—I have put a question mark beside "Blessingway" on the caption to this painting.

14. Accounts differ on the identity of the four Sacred Mountains.

CHAPTER 5: THE NAVAJO HEAVENS IN VISUAL IMAGE AND VERBAL NARRATIVE

1. Many Navajos object to the use of the terms *myth* and *mythology,* because of their connotation of "imaginary, fictional." I do not use these terms in a pejorative sense to imply that the Navajo worldview is of a lesser order of knowledge than that of the Western world, which values science, simply because Navajo stories speak of an intangible world. Instead, I use the terms for two reasons: first, because they express the epic quality of stories comparable to those of the Greeks or to that which is recounted in the Christian Bible, and second, because these terms are used to differentiate the origin stories of ceremonials from other narratives, such as Coyote tales, which do not form the basis for ceremonials.

2. Navajos vary in the level of meaning they attribute to the myths, just as Christians vary in the degree to which they accept the Bible as fact or as allegory. Farella (1984:9) claimed that "we have treated Navajo philosophy as if its adherents were all fundamentalists. Much of what is offered is less concrete and more in the realm of metaphor." I agree with this statement in part, but I feel that it treats the Navajo as too homogeneous a culture. I have found that some Navajos interpret the myths literally, while others see them as allegorical stories intended to teach us how to live a human life.

3. The eight major Navajo constellations recognized today are: *Náhookǫs biką'ii* (the Big Dipper), *Náhookǫs ba'áadii* (Cassiopeia), *Dilyéhé* (the Pleiades), *'Átsé'ets'ózí* (Orion), *Hastiin Sik'ai'í* (Corvus), *'Átsé'etsoh* (the front part of Scorpius), *Gah heet'e'ii* (the tail of Scorpius), and *Yikáísdáhí* (the Milky Way).

4. Von Del Chamberlain (personal communication, 1991) commented on the similarity between the Navajo concept of "the props that hold up the heavens" and the four world-quarter stars of the Skidi Pawnee, which "became the pillars of heaven, with their feet touching the ground and their hands holding up the sky" (Chamberlain 1982:96).

5. Although chantway myths vary in length, when recorded by anthropologists, these epic narratives are quite lengthy. For example, Slim Curley's version of Blessingway (in Wyman 1970a) spans over 200 pages. Primarily because of space limitations, but also because, in general, individual episodes are not related in this coherent and unified fashion, I have included only those portions of the myths that specifically describe the heavens and the beings who inhabit the heavens.

6. This version of the myth was told to Mary C. Wheelwright by Yuinth-nezi of the Tachini clan, who got the story from a chanter, Hasteen-baazhon, formerly called Dinneh-kloth.

7. Because the plots and settings of various myths overlap, as explained earlier in this chapter, settings that are described in the narrative of one myth may be depicted in greater visual (but less verbal) detail in the sandpaintings of another myth. Therefore, I have integrated sandpaintings from various chants with the myths from the Big Star Chant and the Male Shootingway.

8. Perhaps because this painting (collected by Louisa Wetherill) belongs to Beadway rather than to the Great Star Chant, Wetherill identified these homes as belonging to the Eagle People rather than to other birds of prey as well.

9. Sundogs, or parhelia, are rainbow-colored spots located 22 degrees to the left and right of the sun; they are caused by hexagonal ice crystals generally located in high cirrus clouds.

10. Stars are depicted in several visual formats: in pictures of the night sky, as in the Beadway painting in figure 5.7, stars are represented by dots or crosses. When they are big stars and serve as the primary or secondary subject of the painting (what Wyman [1983a:62] calls the main theme or subsidiary symbol), they may be four- or eight-pointed stars. Big stars shown in this format occur in paintings from the Big Star chant and the Hand Tremblingway.

11. Diamond-shaped big stars also appear in paintings from the Nightway and Plumeway ceremonials.

12. The modern astrophysical view confirms this statement: human beings are indeed made from the same elements as the stars.

13. The translator has probably confused this constellation with Cassiopeia. If recognized at all, the Little Dipper is not one of the major Navajo constellations. The Navajo name for the Big Dipper and Cassiopeia, the two Náhookǫs, often misleads translators, who seldom know much about astronomy, into the assumption that the Navajo name refers to the two Dippers, which it does not. Rather, it refers to the

Male and Female Revolving Ones, the Big Dipper and Cassiopeia, which are paired because of their balanced location and repetitive revolving movement around Polaris.

14. Louisa Wetherill (in Wyman [1952:110–12]), from whom this account is taken, labeled this story, "Beauty Chant Story." It is not part of the generalized myth of the Beauty Way, (that is, the Beauty Way myth as recognized by chanters), but I have included it because it is one of the few chantway accounts that deals specifically with the placing of the constellations. Wyman (1952:112) believes that the painting (fig. 5.7) labeled by Wetherill as "Beauty chant, second picture, emergence," actually belongs to Beadway because it so closely illustrates the homes of the Eagle People in the Land-beyond-the-Sky, a key setting in the Beadway myth.

15. This account of the Male Shootingway is taken from Newcomb and Reichard (1975) who got the myth from Blue Eyes of Luckachukai. McAllester's (1980:201–3) version of this myth, which was given by chanter Ray Winnie, makes an interesting comparison with Newcomb and Reichard's version, which was told by Ray Winnie's teacher, Blue Eyes.

16. Changing Woman's house itself is depicted in a drypainting from Blessingway, in whose myth she plays a central role.

17. This particular painting is from the second day of the Rain ceremony, which is related to the Waterway. Unfortunately, the bulk of Waterway material comes from the 1930s; after that decade neither the sandpaintings nor the myth were recorded for this ceremonial. Luckert (in Haile [1979:136]) attributes this more to a decline in interest in religious and mythic subject matter among scientific anthropologists than to the demise of an already weakened Waterway tradition (when established Waterway and Rainway chanters died without leaving behind fully trained successors).

18. The Male Shootingway is one of the most thoroughly documented chantways of all those in the Navajo ceremonial system as well as one of the most popular ceremonials performed today.

19. Thanks to two popular books on Navajo sandpainting, those by Newcomb and Reichard (1975) and Reichard (1977), these two paintings are among the most familiar of Navajo sandpaintings. Newcomb and Reichard (1975:55) claimed that the "Mother Earth, Father Sky" painting can be used in a number of chants beside the Male Shootingway. Wyman (1970b:33), as well as the chanters and consultants with whom I spoke, said that the "Mother Earth, Father Sky" painting belongs to the Male Shootingway only. Earthway, which is considered to be extinct, is the only other chant for which I have found a sandpainting reproduction of Earth and Sky together; sandpaintings from other chants depict these two entities separately.

20. Reichard (1977:42) says that the four wide stripes represent the four times of day, while McAllester (1980:206–7) says they represent the four deities.

CHAPTER 6: THE CONSTELLATIONS AS A CULTURAL TEXT

1. See figure 1.1 for a map and plate 5 for a representation of Sky-Reaching Rock in a sandpainting.

2. Morgan uses the term *shaman* to refer to the chanter, who is technically a priest rather than a shaman.

3. As we have seen, some Plumeway sandpaintings contain big stars; however, stars cannot be considered a principal element, or "main theme," in the entire corpus of Plumeway paintings. See Wyman (1983a:144–51) for a description of the symbols and designs found in the paintings of the Blessingway rites and the chantways.

4. See Figure 2.2 for an illustration of these symbols in Navajo rock art.

5. I use the term *Black God branch* to designate those performances of the Nightway in which the Black God Impersonator appears and in which his sandpainting is made. As Faris (1990:39–40) points out, contemporary Nightway chanters acknowledge three branch labels associated with the three sites at which the hero of the Nightway was instructed in this ceremonial so that he might teach it to the Earth Surface People for their benefit. These are the Mid Rock branch, named for the Nightway held at Canyon de Chelly; the To the Trees branch, named for the ceremonial held near Chama; and the Across the Waters branch, named for the Nightway that took place north of San Juan. Confusion occurs because the branch designation can also be used to refer to features of ceremonial practice, such as sandpaintings. Because the branches and the sandpaintings often overlap (the same sandpainting can be used for different branches but is not necessarily required), and because the chanters with whom I worked used this term, I have used *Black God* branch as a designation.

6. This kind of linguistic pairing (*-ózí/-tsoh*) is seen in the names of two pairs of months: *bini'ant'ą́ą́ts'ózí* (August) with *bini'ant'ą́ą́tsoh* (September) and *níích'its'ósí* (November) with *níích'itsoh* (December). In these examples, the one named first has the diminutive form because this is the natural order of growth, from small to large.

CHAPTER 7: MOTHER EARTH, FATHER SKY

1. The bull roarer, made from a tree struck by lightning, measures roughly 6 1/2 inches by 1 1/2 inches by 1/4 inch and is suspended from a long buckskin thong and is whirled around one's head at the end of the thong.

2. The assistants do not necessarily belong to either the chanter's family or to the patient's family.

3. Reichard (1950:628–29, 645–48) differentiates between body painting, which is done to facilitate the impersonation of supernaturals, and figure painting, which depicts the symbols of the chant to which it belongs on the body of the patient.

4. Because of the sacred nature of the ceremony, I believe it would be inappropriate for me to describe the ceremonial procedures in detail. Kluckhohn and Wyman (1940) provide an account of Navajo chant practices.

5. The chanter must use some kind of sacred paraphernalia to transfer blessing and healing power. He serves as an intermediary between the Holy People and the Earth Surface People but he cannot transfer the power of the Holy People without an instrument, such as medicine, feathered prayer sticks, or wide boards.

6. A portion of this myth was recounted in chapter 5.

7. Spencer (1957:117) notes that "Reichard has summarized two versions of the legend, one informant giving the form according-to-holiness [Holyway chant] (New-

comb and Reichard 1975), the other, a pupil of the former, giving the story that combines both holiness and evil-chasing [Evilway chant] elements (Reichard 1977). She characterizes these stories as not differing in essentials, the latter being 'in almost all respects supplementary and complementary to' the former. Her third version (Reichard 1934) is a fragmentary summary."

8. The Anglo perception of the sandpainting as a two-dimensional depiction probably results from a cultural emphasis on the printed page and the television screen; it is through a two-dimensional format that Anglos transmit and receive most of the information in their culture.

9. Opinions vary as to when the sandpainting becomes sacred: some chanters believe the sand is sacred the moment it is brought into the hogan; other say that the sandpainting is not sacred until it has been sprinkled with corn pollen and blessed with a prayer.

10. Many scholars agree with Witherspoon's explication, which holds that *są'ah naagháí* (Witherspoon's spelling) and *bik'e hózhǫ́*, sometimes equated as Young Man and Young Woman, are personifications of thought and speech. Together, they are the source of animation and life for the inner forms of all beings. *Są'ah,* according to Witherspoon (1977:21, 23), "expresses the Navajo concern for and emphasis upon life, and their attitude toward death of old age as a goal of life," while *naagháí* refers to "the continual reoccurrence of the life cycle." Farella (1984) gave the most far-reaching analysis of these key concepts by explaining that *są'a nagháí* and *bik'e hózhǫ́* have far more levels of metaphoric and symbolic meaning than many previous interpretations had revealed. He showed that they form the basis of the Navajo perception of existence, which expresses a conception of wholeness and process in life and nature. In my dissertation (Griffin-Pierce 1987:304–34) I discussed how the constellations embody the concept of *są'a nagháí bik'e hózhǫ́*.

11. I am indebted to M. Jane Young (1988:159) for an understanding of this process in Zuni rock art.

12. See Matthews (1902:6, 57–58) for his essay on "the law of butts and tips," which explains that in ceremonial procedures the root end of an object is touched or treated before the tip end of an object.

Bibliography

Aberle, David F. 1961. "The Navajo." In *Matrilineal Kinship,* ed. D. Schneider and K. Gough. University of California Press, Berkeley and Los Angeles.
———. 1963. "Some Sources of Flexibility in Navajo Social Organization." *Southwestern Journal of Anthropology* 19:1–8.
———. 1966. *The Peyote Religion among the Navaho.* Aldine Press, Chicago.
———. 1967. "The Navajo Singer's Fee: Payment or Presentation." In *Studies in Southwestern Ethnolinguistics,* ed. D. H. Hymes and W. E. Bittle, pp. 15–32. Mouton, The Hague.
———. 1982. "The Future of Navajo Religion." In *Navajo Religion and Culture Selected Views: Papers in Honor of Leland C. Wyman,* ed. D. M. Brugge and C. J. Frisbie, pp. 219–31. Museum of New Mexico Press, Santa Fe.
Adair, John. 1944. *The Navajo and Pueblo Silversmiths.* University of Oklahoma Press, Norman.
———. 1972. *Through Navajo Eyes: An Exploration in Film Communication and Anthropology.* Indiana University Press, Bloomington.
Adams, William T. 1963. *Shonto: A Study of the Role of the Trader in a Modern Navaho Community.* Bureau of American Ethnology Bulletin 188. U. S. Government Printing Office, Washington, D.C.
Albert, Ethel M. 1956. "The Classification of Values: A Method and Illustration." *American Anthropologist* 58:221–48.
American Indian and Alaska Native Areas: 1990. Prepared by Edna Paisano, Joan Greendeer-Lee, June Cowles, and Debbie Carroll. Racial Statistics Branch, Population Division, Bureau of the Census, Washington, D.C. June 1991.
Amsden, Charles A. 1934. *Navaho Weaving: Its Technic and History.* The Fine Arts Press, Santa Ana.
Armer, Laura. 1931. "Navaho Sand-paintings." *American Anthropologist* 33:657.
Armstrong, Robert Plant. 1971. *The Affecting Presence: An Essay in Humanistic Anthropology.* University of Illinois Press, Urbana.
———. 1975. *Wellspring: On the Myth and Source of Culture.* University of California Press, Berkeley.
———. 1981. *The Powers of Presence: Consciousness, Myth and Affecting Presence.* University of Pennsylvania Press, Philadelphia.

Arnheim, Rudolf. 1971. *Visual Thinking.* University of California Press, Berkeley.

Bailey, Garrick, and Roberta Bailey. 1986. *A History of the Navajos: The Reservation Years.* School of American Research Press, Santa Fe.

Baity, Elizabeth. 1973. "Archaeoastronomy and Ethnoastronomy So Far." *Current Anthropology* 14:389–449.

Basso, Ellen B. 1985. *A Musical View of the Universe: Kalapalo Myth and Ritual Performance.* University of Pennsylvania Press, Philadelphia.

Basso, Keith H. 1976. "'Wise Words' of the Western Apache: Metaphor and Semantic Theory." In *Meaning in Anthropology,* ed. K. Basso and H. Selby, pp. 93–121. School of American Research and University of New Mexico Press, Albuquerque.

———. 1984. "'Stalking with Stories': Names, Places, and Moral Narratives among the Western Apache." In *Text, Play, and Story: The Construction and Reconstruction of Self and Society,* ed. E. Bruner, pp. 19–55. The American Ethnological Society, Washington, D.C.

Bateson, Gregory. 1936. *Naven: A Study of the Problems Suggested by a Composite Picture of the Culture of a New Guinea Tribe Drawn from Three Points of View.* University of Cambridge Press, Cambridge.

Beck, Peggy V., and Anna L. Walters. 1977. *The Sacred: Ways of Knowledge, Sources of Life.* Navajo Community College Press, Tsaile, Arizona.

Begay, Wallace. 1990. "Navajo Constellations: From the Legend of the Upward Reaching Way Ceremony." *Navaho* 2(3):14–17.

Berman, Morris. 1981. *The Reenchantment of the World.* Cornell University Press, Ithaca.

Between Sacred Mountains: Navajo Stories and Lessons from the Land. 1982. Sun Tracks and the University of Arizona Press, Tucson.

Biebuyck, Daniel P. 1969. "Introduction." In *Tradition and Creativity in Tribal Art,* ed. D. P. Biebuyck, pp. 1–23. University of California Press, Berkeley.

Boas, Franz. 1955. *Primitive Art.* Dover, New York.

Brewer, Sallie Pierce. 1950. "Notes on Navaho Astronomy." In *For the Dean: Essays in Anthropology in Honor of Byron Cummings,* pp. 133–36. The Hohokam Museums Association and the Southwestern Monuments Association, Tucson and Santa Fe.

Britt, Claude, Jr. 1975. "Early Navaho Astronomical Pictographs in Canyon de Chelly, Northeastern Arizona, U.S.A." In *Archaeoastronomy in Pre-Columbian America,* ed. A. Aveni, pp. 89–107. University of Texas Press, Austin.

Brody, J.J. 1976. "The Creative Consumer: Survival, Revival and Invention in Southwest Indian Arts." In *Ethnic and Tourist Arts: Cultural Expressions from the Fourth World,* ed. N. Graburn, pp. 70–84. University of California Press, Berkeley and Los Angeles.

Brown, Joseph Epes. 1982. *The Spiritual Legacy of the American Indian.* Crossroads, New York.

Bunzel, Ruth. 1932. "Introduction to Zuni Ceremonialism." In *Forty-seventh Annual Report of the BAE*, pp. 467–544. Government Printing Office, Washington, D.C.

————. 1972. "The Pueblo Potter: A Study of Creative Imagination in Primitive Art." *Columbia University Contributions to Anthropology* 8. Dover, New York.

Campbell, Joseph. 1988. *The Power of Myth.* Doubleday, New York.

Chamberlain, Von Del. 1974. "American Indian Interest in the Sky as Indicated in Legend, Rock Art, Ceremonial and Modern Art." *The Planetarian* 3:89–106, 123.

————. 1977. "Sky Symbol Rock Art." In *American Indian Rock Art Volume IV: Papers Presented at the Fourth Annual ARARA Symposium.* American Rock Art Research Association, El Toro, Calif.

————. 1982. *When Stars Came Down to Earth: Cosmology of the Skidi Pawnee Indians of North America.* Ballena Press and The Center for Archaeoastronomy, Los Altos, Calif.; College Park, Md.

————. 1983. "Navajo Constellations in Literature, Art, Artifact, and a New Mexico Rock Art Site." *Archaeoastronomy* 5:48–58.

Clifford, James, and George Marcus. 1986. *Writing Culture: The Poetics and Politics of Ethnography.* University of California Press, Berkeley.

Colby, Benjamin, James Fernandez, and David Kronenfeld. 1981. "Toward a Convergence of Cognitive and Symbolic Anthropology." *American Ethnologist* 8:422–50.

Collier, Malcolm C. 1966. *Local Organization among the Navaho.* Human Relations Area File (Flex Book, NT 13-001).

Colton, Harold S. 1959. *Hopi Kachina Dolls, with a Key to Their Identification.* University of New Mexico Press, Albuquerque.

Coolidge, Dane C., and Mary Roberts Coolidge. 1930. *The Navajo Indians.* Houghton Mifflin, Boston.

Deharport, David L. 1953. "An Archaeological Survey of the Canyon de Chelly: Preliminary Report for the 1951 Season." *El Palacio* 60:20–25.

Dockstader, Frederick. 1954. "The Kachina and the White Man: A Study of the Influences of White Culture on the Hopi Kachina Cult." Cranbrook Institute of Science Bulletin 35. Bloomfield Hills, Mich.

Dougherty, Janet W.D., and James Fernandez. 1981. "Introduction." *American Ethnologist* 8:413–21.

————. 1982. "Afterword." *American Ethnologist* 9:820–32.

Durkheim, Emile, and Marcel Mauss. 1969. *Primitive Classification.* University of Chicago Press, Chicago.

Dutton, Bertha P. 1941. "The Navaho Wind Way Ceremonial." *El Palacio* 48:78–82.

Elgin, Duane. 1981. *Voluntary Simplicity: Toward a Way of Life that Is Outwardly Simple, Inwardly Rich.* William Morrow, New York.

Fanshel, Suzanne. 1987. "A Weave of Time: The Story of a Navajo Family

1938–1986." A film based on the work of John Adair. Direct Cinema, Los Angeles.

Farella, John. 1984. *The Main Stalk.* University of Arizona Press, Tucson.

Faris, James C. 1990. *The Nightway: A History and a History of Documentation of a Navajo Ceremonial.* University of New Mexico Press, Albuquerque.

Farrer, Claire. 1980. "Singing for Life: The Mescalero Apache Girls' Puberty Ceremony." In *Southwestern Indian Ritual Drama,* ed. C. J. Frisbie, pp. 125–60. School of American Research, University of New Mexico Press, Albuquerque.

Farrer, Claire, and Bernard Second. 1981. "Living the Sky: Aspects of Mescalero Apache Ethnoastronomy." In *Archaeoastronomy in the Americas,* ed. R. A. Williamson, pp. 137–50. Ballena Press, Los Altos, Calif.

Feld, Steven. 1982. *Sound and Sentiment: Birds, Weeping, Poetics, and Song in Kaluli Expression.* University of Pennsylvania Press, Philadelphia.

Fernandez, James. 1974. "The Mission of Metaphor in Expressive Culture." *Current Anthropology* 15:119–45.

Foster, Kenneth E. 1964. "The Art of Sandpainting Practised by the American Navajo Indians." *Illustrated London News* 244:608–11.

Franciscan Fathers. 1910. *An Ethnologic Dictionary of the Navajo Language.* St. Michael's Press, St. Michael's, Ariz.

Frisbie, Charlotte J. 1980. "Ritual Drama in the Navajo House Blessing Ceremony." In *Southwestern Indian Ritual Drama,* ed. C. J. Frisbie, pp. 161–98. School of American Research, University of New Mexico Press, Albuquerque.

———. 1987. *Navajo Medicine Bundles or Jish: Acquisition, Transmission, and Disposition in the Past and Present.* University of New Mexico Press, Albuquerque.

Geertz, Clifford. 1958. "Ethos, World-View and the Analysis of Sacred Symbols." *The Antioch Review* (1957–58):421–37.

———. 1964. "Ideology as a Cultural System." In *Ideology and Discontent,* ed. D. Apter, pp. 47–56. Macmillan, New York.

———. 1966. "Religion as a Cultural System." In *Anthropological Approaches to the Study of Religion,* ed. M. Banton, pp. 1–46. Association of Social Anthropologists Monograph 3. Frederick A. Praeger, New York.

———. 1973. "Thick Description: Toward an Interpretative Theory of Culture. In *The Interpretation of Cultures,* ed. C. Geertz, pp. 3–30. Basic Books, New York.

Gifford, Edward W. 1940. "Culture Element Distributions: XII—Apache-Pueblo." University of California Anthropological Records 4:1–208. Berkeley.

Gill, Sam. 1974. "A Theory of Navajo Prayer Acts: A Study in Ritual Symbolism." Ph.D. diss. University of Chicago Divinity School.

———. 1976. "The Shadow of a Vision Yonder." In *Seeing with a Native Eye: Essays on Native American Religion,* ed. W. H. Capps, pp. 44–57. Harper and Row, New York.

Gilpin, Laura. 1968. *The Enduring Navaho.* University of Texas Press, Austin.

Gladwin, Thomas. 1970. *East Is a Big Bird.* Harvard University Press, Cambridge.

Goddard, Pliny E. 1933. "Navajo Texts." *Anthropological Papers of the American Museum of Natural History* 34:127–79.

Goodman, James. 1982. *The Navajo Atlas: Environments, Resources, People, and History of the Diné Bikéyah.* University of Oklahoma Press, Norman.

Grant, Campbell. 1978. *Canyon de Chelly: Its People and Rock Art.* University of Arizona Press, Tucson.

Griffin-Pierce, Trudy. 1986. "Ethnoastronomy in Navajo Sandpaintings of the Heavens." *Archaeoastronomy* 9:62–69.

———. 1987. "Power Through Order: Ethnoastronomy in Navajo Sandpaintings of the Heavens." Ph.D. diss., University of Arizona, Department of Anthropology.

———. 1988. "Cosmological Order as a Model for Navajo Philosophy." *American Indian Culture and Research Journal* 12(4):1–15.

———. 1991a. "The Healing Power of Place in Navajo Sandpaintings and Myth." *The Messenger* (Wheelwright Museum of the American Indian) (Summer 1991):3–5.

———. 1991b. "Navajo Ceremonial Sandpaintings: Sacred, Living Entities." *American Indian Art,* winter, 1991:58-67, 88.

———. 1992. "The *Hooghan* and the Stars." In *Earth and Sky: Visions of the Cosmos in Native American Folklore,* ed. R. Williamson and C. Farrer. University of New Mexico Press, Albuquerque.

Haile, Father Berard. 1932. "Where People Moved Opposite." Unpublished manuscript. Museum of Northern Arizona Library, Flagstaff.

———. 1938a. "Navaho Chantways and Ceremonials." *American Anthropologist* 40:639–52.

———. 1938b. *Origin Legend of the Navaho Enemyway.* Yale Publications in Anthropology 17, New Haven, Conn.

———. 1943a. *Origin Legend of the Navaho Flintway.* University of Chicago Publications in Anthropology, Linguistic Series, Chicago.

———. 1943b. *Soul Concepts of the Navaho.* Annali Lateranesi 7, Città del Vaticano Tipografia Poliglotta Vaticana.

———. 1947a. *Head and Face Masks in Navaho Ceremonialism.* St. Michaels Press, St. Michaels, Ariz.

———. 1947b. *Prayerstick Cutting in a Five Night Navaho Ceremonial of the Male Branch of Shooting Way.* University of Chicago Press, Chicago.

———. 1947c. *Starlore among the Navaho.* Museum of Navajo Ceremonial Art, Santa Fe.

———. 1979. *Waterway,* ed. K. Luckert and I. Goossen. Museum of Northern Arizona, Flagstaff.

———. 1981a. *The Upward Moving Emergence Way.* University of Nebraska Press, Lincoln.

———. 1981b. *Women Versus Men: A Conflict of Navajo Emergence.* University of Nebraska Press, Lincoln.

———. n.d. Berard Haile Papers: Blessingway, Nightway, and Shootingway. Unpublished manuscripts. Special Collections, University of Arizona Library.

Haile, Father Berard, Maud Oakes, and Leland Wyman. 1957. *Beautyway: A Navaho Ceremonial.* Bollingen Series 53. Pantheon Books, New York.

Hatcher, Evelyn Payne. 1974. *Visual Metaphors: A Formal Analysis of Navajo Art.* American Ethnological Society Monograph 58. West Publishing Co., Boston.

Hester, James. 1962. *Early Navajo Migrations and Acculturation in the Southwest.* Navajo Project Studies 5. Museum of New Mexico, Santa Fe.

Hill, W.W. 1935. "The Hand Trembling Ceremony of the Navaho." *El Palacio.* 38:65-68.

Hoijer, Harry. 1964. "Cultural Implications of Some Navaho Linguistic Categories." In *Language in Culture and Society,* ed. D. Hymes, pp. 142–53. Harper and Row, New York.

Horton, Robin, and Ruth Finnegan. 1931. *Introduction to American Indian Art.* The Exposition of Indian Tribal Arts, Inc., New York.

———. 1973. *Modes of Thought: Essays on Thinking in Western and Non-Western Societies.* Faber and Faber, London.

Jett, Stephen, and Virginia Spencer. 1981. *Navajo Architecture: Forms, History, Distributions.* University of Arizona Press, Tucson.

Josephy, Alvin M., Jr. 1968. *The Indian Heritage of America.* Alfred A. Knopf, New York.

Klah (Tl'aii), Hasteen. 1942. *Navajo Creation Myth.* Recorded by Mary C. Wheelwright. Museum of Navajo Ceremonial Art, Santa Fe.

Kluckhohn, Clyde. 1941. "Notes on Eagle Way." *New Mexico Anthropologist* 5:6–14.

———. 1960. "Navaho Categories." In *Culture in History: Essays in Honor of Paul Radin,* ed. S. Diamond, pp. 65–98. Columbia University Press, New York.

———. 1968. "The Philosophy of the Navajo Indians." In *Readings in Anthropology, Vol. II,* ed. M. H. Fried, pp. 674–99. Thomas Y. Crowell, New York.

Kluckhohn, Clyde, and Dorothea Leighton. 1962. *The Navaho.* Anchor Books, Doubleday, Garden City, N.Y.

Kluckhohn, Clyde, and Leland C. Wyman. 1940. *An Introduction to Navaho Chant Practice, with an Account of the Behaviors Observed in Four Chants.* American Anthropological Association Memoir 53, Menasha, Wis.

Krupp, E. C. 1983. *Echoes of the Ancient Skies: The Astronomy of Lost Civilizations.* Harper and Row, New York.

Lamphere, Louise. 1969. "Symbolic Elements in Navajo Ritual." *Southwestern Journal of Anthropology* 25:279–305.

————. 1977. *To Run after Them: Cultural and Social Bases of Cooperation in a Navajo Community*. University of Arizona Press, Tucson.

Leach, Edmund R. 1966. "Ritualization in Man." *Philosophical Transactions of the Royal Society* ser. B, col. 251:403–8.

Lessa, William A., and Evon Z. Vogt, Eds. 1979. *Reader in Comparative Religion: An Anthropological Approach*. Harper and Row, New York.

Louis, Ray B. 1975. *Child of the Hogan*. Brigham Young University Press, Provo, Utah.

Luckert, Karl W. 1979. *Coyoteway, A Navajo Holyway Healing Ceremonial*. University of Arizona Press, Tucson.

————. 1981. *The Navajo Hunter Tradition*. University of Arizona Press, Tucson.

————. 1982. "Toward a Historical Perspective on Navajo Religion." In *Navajo Religion and Culture: Selected Views, Papers in Honor of Leland C. Wyman*, ed. D. Brugge and C. Frisbie, pp. 187-197. Museum of New Mexico Press, Santa Fe.

Maquet, Jacques. 1971. *Introduction to Aesthetic Anthropology*. Addison-Wesley, Reading, Mass.

————. 1986. *The Aesthetic Experience: An Anthropologist Looks at the Visual Arts*. Murray Printing, Westford, Mass.

Marcus, George E., and Michael M.J. Fischer. 1985. *Anthropology as Cultural Critique: An Experimental Moment in the Human Sciences*. University of Chicago Press, Chicago.

Matthews, Washington. 1883. "A Part of the Navajo's Mythology." *American Antiquarian* 5:207–24.

————. 1887. "The Mountain Chant: A Navaho Ceremony." In *The Fifth Annual Report of the Bureau of American Ethnology 1883–1884*, pp. 379–467. Government Printing Office, Washington, D.C.

————. 1897. *Navaho Legends*. American Folk-lore Society Memoirs 5, Boston.

————. 1902. *The Night Chant, A Navaho Ceremony*. Memoirs of the American Museum of Natural History 6. American Museum Press, New York.

McAllester, David P. 1980. "Shootingway, An Epic Drama of the Navajos." In *Southwestern Indian Ritual Drama*, ed. C. J. Frisbie, pp. 199–237. School of American Research, University of New Mexico Press, Albuquerque.

————. n.d. "The First Snake Song." Unpublished manuscript.

McNeley, James K. 1981. *Holy Wind in Navajo Philosophy*. University of Arizona Press, Tucson.

Mills, George T. 1959. *Navaho Art and Culture*. Taylor Museum, Colorado Springs.

Mindeleff, Cosmos. 1898. "Navaho Houses." In *Seventeenth Annual Report of the Bureau of American Ethnology for the Years 1895–1896, Pt. 2*, pp. 469–517. Government Printing Office, Washington, D.C.

Momaday, N. Scott. 1976. "Native American Attitudes to the Environment." In *Seeing with a Native Eye,* ed. W. H. Capps, pp. 79–85. Harper and Row, New York.

Morgan, William. 1931. "Navajo Treatment of Sickness: Diagnosticians." *American Anthropologist* 33:390–402.

Navajo Community College General Catalogue 1987–1988. Navajo Community College, Tsaile, Ariz.

Newcomb, Franc Johnson. 1940. *Navajo Omens and Taboos.* The Rydal Press, Santa Fe.

————. 1967. *Navaho Folk Tales.* Museum of Navaho Ceremonial Art, Santa Fe.

————. 1980 [1964]. *Hosteen Klah: Navaho Medicine Man and Sand Painter.* University of Oklahoma Press, Norman.

Newcomb, Franc Johnson, Stanley Fishler, and Mary C. Wheelwright. 1956. *A Study of Navajo Symbolism.* Papers of the Peabody Museum 32, No. 3. Harvard University, Cambridge.

Newcomb, Franc Johnson, and Gladys Reichard. 1975 [1937]. *Sandpaintings of the Navajo Shooting Chant.* Dover, New York.

Noel, Daniel, Ed. 1976. *Seeing Castaneda.* G. P. Putnam's Sons, New York.

Oakes, Maude, Joseph Campbell, and Jeff King. 1969 [1943]. *Where the Two Came to Their Father.* Bollingen Series 1. Princeton University Press, Princeton, N.J.

O'Bryan, Aileen. 1956. *The Diné: Origin Myths of the Navaho Indians.* Smithsonian Bureau of American Ethnology Bulletin 163. Government Printing Office, Washington, D.C.

Olin, Caroline Bower. 1972. "Navajo Indian Sandpainting: The Construction of Symbols." Ph.D. diss., University of Stockholm, Department of Art.

Opler, Morris E. 1965 [1941]. *An Apache Life-Way.* Cooper Square, New York.

————. 1969. *Apache Odyssey: A Journey Between Two Worlds.* Holt, Rinehart, and Winston, New York.

Ortner, Sherry. 1979. "On Key Symbols." In *Reader in Comparative Religion: An Anthropological Approach,* ed. W. A. Lessa and E. Z. Vogt, pp. 92–98. Harper and Row, New York.

Ortiz, Alphonso. 1972. "Ritual Drama and the Pueblo World View." In *New Perspectives on the Pueblos,* ed. A. Ortiz, pp. 135–61. School of American Research, University of New Mexico Press, Albuquerque.

Page, Suzanne. 1989. *A Celebration of Being: Photographs of the Hopi and Navajo.* Northland, Flagstaff.

Parezo, Nancy J. 1981. "Navajo Sandpaintings: From Religious Act to Commercial Art." Ph.D. diss., University of Arizona, Department of Anthropology.

————. 1983. *Navajo Sandpainting: From Religious Act to Commercial Art.* University of Arizona Press, Tucson.

Parsons, Elsie Clews. 1939. *Pueblo Indian Religion*, 2 volumes. University of Chicago Press, Chicago.

Pinxten, Rik. 1979. *On Going Beyond Kinship, Sex, and the Tribe: Interviews with Contemporary Anthropologists in the U.S.A.* Story, Ghent.

Pinxten, Rik, Ingrid Van Dooren, and Frank Harvey. 1983. *Anthropology of Space: Explorations into the Natural Philosophy and Semantics of the Navajo.* University of Pennsylvania Press, Philadelphia.

Reichard, Gladys A. 1934. *Spider Woman: A Story of Navajo Weavers and Chanters.* Macmillan, New York.

————. 1944a. *The Story of the Navajo Hail Chant.* Barnard College, Columbia University, New York.

————. 1944b. *Prayer: The Compulsive Word.* Monographs of the American Ethnological Society 7. J. J. Augustin, New York.

————. 1945. "Distinctive Features of Navaho Religion." *Southwestern Journal of Anthropology* 1:2:199–220.

————. 1948. "Navajo Classification of Natural Objects." *Plateau* 21:7–12.

————. 1950. *Navaho Religion: A Study of Symbolism.* Bollingen Series 18. Princeton University Press, Princeton, N.J.

————. 1977 [1939]. *Navajo Medicine Man Sandpaintings.* Dover, New York.

Remington, Judith A. 1982. "An Epistemological Study of Navajo Divination and European Science." Ph.D. diss., Northwestern University, Department of Anthropology.

Roessel, Ruth, Ed. 1973. *Navajo Stories of the Long Walk Period.* Navajo Community College Press, Tsaile, Ariz.

————. 1981. *Women in Navajo Society.* Rough Rock Demonstration School, Rough Rock, Ariz.

Sapir, Edward. 1935. "A Navajo Sandpainting Blanket." *American Anthropologist* 37:4:609–16.

Sapir, Edward, and Harry Hoijer. 1942. *Navaho Texts.* University of Iowa, Iowa City.

Schaafsma, Polly. 1966. *Early Navaho Rock Painting and Carvings.* Museum of Navajo Ceremonial Art, Santa Fe.

————. 1971. *Rock Art in the Navajo Reservation District.* Museum of New Mexico Papers in Anthropology 7. Museum of New Mexico Press, Santa Fe.

————. 1972. *Rock Art in New Mexico.* State Planning Office, Santa Fe.

Schevill, Margaret Erwin. 1947. *Beautiful on the Earth: A Study of Navajo Mythology.* Hazel Dreis Editions, Santa Fe.

Shepardson, Mary, and Blodwen Hammond. 1970. *The Navajo Mountain Community: Social Organization and Kinship Terminology.* University of California Press, Berkeley and Los Angeles.

Smith, Robert J. 1975. "The Art of the Festival." *University of Kansas Publications in Anthropology.* No. 6. University of Kansas Libraries, Lawrence.

Spencer, Katherine Halpern. 1957. *Mythology and Values: An Analysis of*

Navaho Chantway Myths. Memoirs of the American Folklore Society 48, Philadelphia.

Spencer, Robert F., Jesse D. Jennings, et al. 1977. *The Native Americans.* Harper and Row, New York.

Spicer, Edward H. 1961. "Types of Contact and Processes of Change." In *Perspectives in American Indian Culture Change,* ed. E. H. Spicer, pp. 517–44. University of Chicago Press, Chicago.

Stephen, Alexander M. 1930. "Navajo Origin Legend." *Journal of American Folk-Lore.* 43:88-104.

———. 1936. *Hopi Journal of Alexander M. Stephen,* ed. E. C. Parsons. Columbia University Contributions to Anthropology 23. Columbia University Press, New York.

Stevenson, James. 1891. "Ceremonial of Hasjelti Dailjis and Mythical Sandpainting of the Navajo Indians." In *Eighth Annual Report of the Bureau of American Ethnology 1886–1887,* pp. 229–85. Government Printing Office, Washington, D.C.

Stromberg, Peter. 1986. "Consensus and Variation in the Interpretation of Religious Symbolism: A Swedish Example." *American Ethnologist* 8:544–59.

Toelken, Barre. 1976a. "A Circular World: The Vision of Navajo Crafts." *Parabola* 1:30–37.

———. 1976b. "Seeing With a Native Eye: How Many Sheep Will It Hold?" In *Seeing with a Native Eye: Essays on Native American Religion,* ed. W. H. Capps, pp. 9–24. Harper and Row, New York.

———. 1977. "The Demands of Harmony: An Appreciation of Navajo Relations." *Parabola* 2:74–81.

———. 1979. *The Dynamics of Folklore.* Houghton Mifflin, Boston.

Tozzer, Alfred M. 1908. "A Note on Star-Lore among the Navajos." *The Journal of American Folk-Lore* 21:28–32.

———. 1909. "Notes on Religious Ceremonies of the Navaho." In *Putnam Anniversary Volume, Anthropological Essays Presented to Frederick Ward Putnam in Honor of His Seventieth Birthday, April 16, 1909.* G. E. Stechert, New York.

Trimble, Stephen, Ed. 1986. *Our Voices, Our Land.* Northland Press, Flagstaff.

Turner, Victor. 1967. *The Forest of Symbols.* Cornell University Press, Ithaca, N.Y.

———. 1974. *Dramas, Fields, and Metaphors: Symbolic Action in Human Society.* Cornell University Press, Ithaca, N.Y.

———. 1982. "Introduction." In *Celebration: Studies in Festivity and Ritual,* ed. V. Turner, pp. 11–30. Smithsonian Institution Press, Washington, D.C.

Underhill, Ruth. 1953. *Here Come the Navaho!* Haskell Indian Institute, Lawrence, Kans.

Urton, Gary. 1981. *At the Crossroads of the Earth and Sky.* University of Texas Press, Austin.

Van Valkenburgh, Richard. 1941. *Diné Bikéyah*. U.S. Dept. of the Interior, Office of Indian Affairs, Navajo Service, Window Rock.

Vogt, Evon Z. 1961. "Navaho." In *Perspectives in American Indian Culture Change*, ed. E. H. Spicer, pp. 278–336. University of Chicago Press, Chicago.

Walters, Anna Lee. 1989. *The Spirit of Native America: Beauty and Mysticism in American Indian Art*. Chronicle Books, San Francisco.

Werner, Oswald. 1969a. *Ethnoscience: Explorations in the Anthropology of Cultural Knowledge*. Northwestern University, Evanston.

———— 1969b. "The Basic Assumptions of Ethnoscience." *Semiotica* 1(3):329–38.

Werner, Oswald, Allen Manning, and Kenneth Yazzie Begishe. 1983. "A Taxonomic View of the Traditional Navajo Universe." In *The Handbook of North American Indians Vol. 10*, ed. W. C. Sturtevant, pp. 579–91. Smithsonian Institution Press, Washington, D.C.

Wheelwright, Mary C. 1942. *Navajo Creation Myth*. Rydal Press, Santa Fe.

————. 1946a. *Hail Chant and Water Chant*. Museum of Navajo Ceremonial Art, Santa Fe.

————. 1946b. *Wind Chant and Feather Chant*. Museum of Navaho Ceremonial Art Bulletin 4, Santa Fe.

————. 1949. *Emergence Myth*. Museum of Navaho Ceremonial Art, Santa Fe.

————. 1988. *The Myth and Prayers of the Great Star Chant and The Myth of the Coyote Chant*. Navajo Community College Press, Tsaile, Ariz.

————. n.d. *Journey Towards Understanding*. Unpublished manuscript. Wheelwright Museum of the American Indian, Santa Fe.

Wheelwright Museum Exhibition Brochure. 1985. *IĮ KÁÁH: The Paintings that Heal: From the Permanent Collection, February 24 through May 12, 1985*. Wheelwright Museum of the American Indian, Santa Fe.

Wheelwright Museum Sandpainting Reproduction Catlogue. n.d. Unpublished manuscript. Wheelwright Museum of the American Indian, Santa Fe.

Williamson, Ray A. 1983. "Sky Symbolism in a Navajo Rock Art Site, Chaco Canyon National Historical Park, New Mexico." *Archaeoastronomy* 6:59–65.

————. 1984. *Living the Sky*. Houghton Mifflin, Boston.

Williamson, Ray A., and Claire Farrer, Eds. 1992. *Earth and Sky: Visions of the Cosmos in North American Folklore*. University of New Mexico Press, Albuquerque.

Witherspoon, Gary J. 1971. "Navajo Categories of Objects at Rest." *American Anthropologist* 73:110–27.

————. 1974. "The Central Concepts of the Navajo World View (Part I)." *Linguistics: An International Review* 119:41–59.

————. 1975. "The Central Concepts of the Navajo World View (Part II)." *Linguistics: An International Review* 161:69–88.

———. 1977. *Language and Art in the Navajo Universe.* University of Michigan Press, Ann Arbor.

———. 1983. "Navajo Social Organization." In *Handbook of North American Indians, Vo. 10: Southwest,* ed. Alfonso Ortiz, pp. 524–535. Smithsonian Institution, Washington, D.C.

Worth, Sol and John Adair. 1972. *Through Navajo Eyes: An Exploration in Film Communication and Anthropology.* Indiana University Press, Bloomington.

Wyman, Leland C. 1936. "Navaho Diagnosticians." *American Anthropologist* 38:235–46.

———. 1940. "Hand Trembling Evil Way." In *An Introduction to Navaho Chant Practice, with an Account of Behaviors Observed in Four Chants,* by C. Kluckhohn and L. C. Wyman, pp. 169–83. American Anthropological Association Memoir 53, Menasha, Wis.

———. 1952. *The Sandpaintings of the Kayenta Navaho.* University of New Mexico Publications in Anthropology 7. University of New Mexico Press, Albuquerque.

———. 1957. *Beautyway: A Navaho Ceremonial* (with myths recorded by Father Berard Haile and Maud Oakes). Bollingen Series 53. Pantheon Books, New York.

———. 1959. *Navaho Indian Painting: Symbolism, Artistry, and Psychology.* Boston University Press, Boston.

———. 1962. *The Windways of the Navaho.* Taylor Museum, Colorado Springs.

———. 1970a. *Blessingway.* University of Arizona, Tucson.

———. 1970b. *Sandpaintings of the Navajo Shootingway and the Walcott Collection.* Smithsonian Contributions to Anthropology 13. Government Printing Office, Washington, D.C.

———. 1971. *Navajo Sandpaintings: The Huckel Collection.* Taylor Museum, Colorado Springs.

———. 1972a. "Navajo Ceremonial Equipment in the Museum of Northern Arizona." *Plateau* 45:17–30.

———. 1972b. "A Navajo Medicine Bundle for Shootingway." *Plateau* 44:131–49.

———. 1972c. "Ten Sandpaintings from Male Shootingway." *Plateau* 45:55–67.

———. 1973. *The Red Antway of the Navaho.* Museum of Navajo Ceremonial Art, Navajo Religion Series 5. Museum of Navajo Ceremonial Art, Santa Fe.

———. 1975. *The Mountainway of the Navaho.* University of Arizona Press, Tucson.

———. 1983a. *Southwest Indian Drypainting.* School of American Research Southwest Indian Arts Series, Santa Fe, and University of New Mexico Press, Albuquerque.

————. 1983b. "Navajo Ceremonial System." In *Handbook of North American Indians, Vol. 10: Southwest,* ed. Alfonso Ortiz, pp. 536–57. Smithsonian Institution, Washington, D.C.

Wyman, Leland C., and Clyde Kluckhohn. 1938. *Navaho Classification of Their Song Ceremonials.* Memoirs of the American Anthropological Association 50, Menasha, Wis.

Wyman, Leland C., and Franc J. Newcomb. 1962. "Sandpaintings of Beautyway." *Plateau* 35:37–52.

————. 1963. "Drypaintings Used in Divination by the Navajo." *Plateau* 36:18–24.

Yazzie, Ethelou. 1971. *Navajo History.* Navajo Community College Press, Many Farms, Ariz.

Young, M. Jane. 1988. *Signs from the Ancestors: Zuni Cultural Symbolism and Perceptions of Rock Art.* University of New Mexico Press, Albuquerque.

Young, M. Jane, and Ray A. Williamson. 1981. "Ethnoastronomy: The Zuni Case." In *Archaeoastronomy in the Americas,* ed. R. A. Williamson, pp. 183–91. Ballena Press, Los Altos, Calif.

Young, Robert W., and William Morgan. 1943. *The Navaho Language.* Educational Division, Bureau of Indian Affairs, Phoenix.

————. 1980. *The Navajo Language: A Grammar and Colloquial Dictionary.* University of New Mexico Press, Albuquerque.

Serigraphs are available for purchase. Please write to the author at P.O. Box 57014, Tucson, Arizona, 85732.

Index

p 92   hoo- place   -ghan home   hogan